Quaker faith & practice

Volume 1

Introduction – Chapter 13

The book of Christian discipline of the Yearly Meeting of the Religious Society of Friends (Quakers) in Britain

Quaker faith and practice: the book of Christian discipline of the Yearly Meeting of the Religious Society of Friends (Quakers) in Britain
was approved by Yearly Meeting 1994.

Fourth edition, with revisions approved 1995–2008
and corrections.

The full text is also available on the Yearly Meeting website www.quaker.org.uk/qfp. That text will be updated within a few weeks of any revision being approved by Yearly Meeting.

The typeface is *Frutiger Serif*, an evolution of *Meridien*, designed by Adrian Frutiger in 1957.

This three-volume set is the large-print edition of *Quaker faith and practice*

ISBN 978-1-907123-05-4 (set)
ISBN 978-1-907123-06-1 (Volume 1)
ISBN 978-1-907123-07-8 (Volume 2)
ISBN 978-1-907123-08-5 (Volume 3)

Quaker faith and practice is also available in a standard edition

ISBN 978-0-901689-95-5 (paperback)
ISBN 978-1-907123-01-6 (hardback)

Published by The Yearly Meeting of the
Religious Society of Friends (Quakers) in Britain
173 Euston Road, London NW1 2BJ
Registered charity number: 1127633

Printed by Digital Book Print

Contents

Introduction

This book of faith and practice constitutes the Christian discipline of the Yearly Meeting of the Religious Society of Friends (Quakers) in Britain. Discipline is not now a popular word. It has overtones of enforcement and correction but its roots lie in ideas of learning and discipleship. Discipline in our yearly meeting consists for the most part of advice and counsel, the encouragement of self-questioning, of hearing each other in humility and love.

Words must not become barriers between us, for no one of us can ever adequately understand or express the truth about God. Yet words are our tools and we must not be afraid to express the truth we know in the best words we can. It is this conviction which has prompted the selection of a wide variety of extracts for inclusion in this book, confirming our testimony that truth cannot be confined within a creed. We must trust that faith is robust, compassionate and 'not quick to take offence', and that the Spirit which gives the words is communicated through them.

Our book of discipline was first issued – in manuscript form – in 1738. There had been requests for a compilation to be made of the minutes of advice and counsel which had been sent out from time to time in earlier years to quarterly and monthly meetings. The first printed collection appeared in 1783 with many deletions and additions. Every generation has felt the need for revision; the present is the tenth edition. Pressure for revision has always come from the generality of Friends, but each revision has met with resistance from some who had lived with the old words and had found them entirely satisfying. Nevertheless, it has been the experience of Britain Yearly Meeting that necessary change has, despite occasions of great tension, been effected in love and unity.

From 1861, the book of discipline was divided into separate chapters – later, parts – *Christian doctrine, Christian practice*, and *Church government*. In 1921, *Christian doctrine* became *Christian life, faith and thought*, substantially a new work attempting, as was said in the preface, 'to state truth, not by formulating it, but by expressing it through the vital personal and corporate experience of Friends'. Thus began the use of extracts which has subsequently been developed as an acceptable method of expressing the breadth of our theology.

The 1959 revision brought together *Christian life, faith and thought* and *Christian practice* into one volume, *Christian faith and practice*, which, with the 1967 revision of *Church government* (including the 1964 revision of *Advices and queries*) comprised the book of discipline at the time of the present revision in 1994.

Again, in 1985, London Yearly Meeting responded to proposals for revision that had arisen 'not from the centre but from local meetings and individual Friends, as well as committees', and asked Meeting for Sufferings to appoint a revision committee. The previous thirty years had seen changes in language, in religious thought and social attitudes and in the nature of British society itself. Lives of ordinary people had been affected by advances in communication. Images of famine, war and disaster, wherever they occur in the world, are now brought into our own homes. The immediacy of our knowledge oppresses us with the feeling that the distress and violence of our time are greater than ever before. In Britain, however, it has been the good fortune of this generation to be free from war and conscription and, though poverty, homelessness and unemployment are widespread, many live with expectation of comfort, care and length of life.

There is no yardstick by which the experience of one generation can be judged against that of another, but we do know that, whatever the circumstances, we are called to rediscover the Quaker way and to find appropriate words to express it. We are not without consolation. Signals come to us from all over the world that there is in the human spirit a prompting towards a better way that is persistent and will not be put down. This enduring hope confirms the truth asserted in John's gospel that the light shines in darkness.

The arrangement of the text within this book is intended to show the interdependence of our faith and our practice. Therefore matters of church government no longer stand alone, but are integrated with other material in order to encourage deeper understanding of the nature of our organisation as an expression of community, of the right ordering of our affairs and of the religious foundations on which our structures are built. The revised advices and queries – which may prompt the ministry that enriches and deepens our meetings for worship – form the opening chapter of the book. They are an essential part of it but they are also printed separately.

Worship is at the heart of Quaker experience. For God is met in the gathered meeting and through the Spirit leads us into ways of life and understandings of truth which we recognise as Quaker. As we follow these leadings in our community and in the wider world we are enabled to reflect on their meaning, testing our vision within our discipline and tradition. This book follows this sequence. It begins with worship and the gathering and ordering of our worshipping community; then it shows the ways of life, both individual and corporate, which have sprung from our faith, and the testimonies into which we have been guided. The book includes accounts of the lives of individual Friends whose commitment is an example to us. Towards the close of the book come statements and descriptions of our faith that spring from our experience. These in turn lead on to the final chapter, which indicates some of the ways in which the Holy Spirit is still known among us and challenges us to create anew a Society in which human lives are changed.

Special attention has been given to the inclusion of a wider range of contributions from women, from earlier days as well as more recent times.

Friends are enjoined in *Advices and queries* to 'avoid hurtful criticism and provocative language', but sensitivity to gender-exclusive language and the hurt it causes has only now become recognised amongst us. Effort has been made to avoid such modes of expression, accepting that quotations from earlier times must remain in the language of their age, but exercising discretion when there has been a choice of extracts. The aim has been to be truthful to the testimony of the past as well as the present. Similarly, we recognise the likelihood that in other areas the language used now may in the future seem insensitive.

Britain Yearly Meeting is becoming increasingly aware that it is part of a world-wide Quaker family. It is privileged to be geographically where George Fox was called to undertake his mission and where Margaret Fell nourished the publishers of truth, but there are now over sixty yearly meetings together with other groupings of Friends in six continents. Friends World Committee for Consultation performs an essential role in supporting this international community and Britain Yearly Meeting is committed to this work.

Many other yearly meetings publish their own books of discipline and we are finding, increasingly, that we are learning from and valuing a shared understanding. Writings by Friends in other countries which reflect our shared experience find a place in our book.

The extension of Quakerism world-wide has added diversity of theological outlook, varieties of worship and forms of organisation. When three hundred Young Friends from thirty-four countries met in North Carolina in 1985, they were 'challenged, shaken up, at times even enraged by these differences in each other'. After much travail, they came through this experience and were able to say, in a final epistle:

> We have wondered whether there is anything Quakers today can say as one. After much struggle we have discovered that we can proclaim this: there is a living God at the centre of all, who is available to each of us as a present teacher at the very heart of our lives. We seek as people of God to be worthy vessels to deliver the Lord's transforming word, to be prophets of joy who know from experience and can testify to the world, as George Fox did, 'that the Lord is at work in this thick night'.

The final chapter to this book, *Leadings,* which looks for signs of how the Spirit is continuing to lead us, contains this epistle in full.

There is also diversity among us in Britain Yearly Meeting. It is reflected in part in the number of informal groups established in recent years. Some welcome this development as an indication of vigorous life, while others view it anxiously as a threat to the corporate commitment of Friends. However, we continue to know the experience of unity. Week by week, in Britain, more than four hundred meetings of Quakers assemble in expectant worship. They know the seventeenth-century experience of Robert Barclay: 'When I came into the silent assemblies of God's people, I felt a secret power among them, which touched my heart...'

Friends find unity in the depth of the silence, when the worshippers are truly gathered and deeply centred on the things of the spirit. We struggle with differences in our meetings for church affairs and here, too, as we consider what action we are called to take over issues that confront us, we know the experience of unity in conviction and purpose. It is a unity which is not to be found in optional attitudes but in discovering the place in which we can stand together.

It is hoped that readers of this book will pick up some responsive echoes from its pages, a resonance which touches their own lives, for, as London Yearly Meeting asserted in 1978:

> We have great riches to share in; riches from the words used by Friends down the last three centuries who have put their experience of God down on paper and have searched out new ways to describe the infinite variety of God... There are great riches too in other branches of the Christian Church and in other faiths, for each one who seeks the truth may see a different part of it.

We are seekers but we are also the holders of a precious heritage of discoveries. We, like every generation, must find the Light and Life again for ourselves. Only what we have valued and truly made our own, not by assertion but by lives of faithful commitment, can we hand on to the future. Even then, we must humbly acknowledge that our vision of the truth will, again and again, be amended.

In the Religious Society of Friends we commit ourselves not to words but to a way.

Chapter 1

Advices and queries

Introduction

1.01 As Friends we commit ourselves to a way of worship which allows God to teach and transform us. We have found corporately that the Spirit, if rightly followed, will lead us into truth, unity and love: all our testimonies grow from this leading.

Although the corporate use of advices and queries is governed by more flexible regulations (1.05–1.07) than in the past, they should continue to be a challenge and inspiration to Friends in their personal lives and in their life as a religious community which knows the guidance of the universal spirit of Christ, witnessed to in the life and teachings of Jesus of Nazareth.

Advices and queries are not a call to increased activity by each individual Friend but a reminder of the insights of the Society. Within the community there is a diversity of gifts. We are all therefore asked to consider how far the advices and queries affect us personally and where our own service lies. There will also be diversity of experience, of belief and of language. Friends maintain that expressions of faith must be related to personal experience. Some find traditional Christian language full of meaning; some do not. Our understanding of our own religious tradition may sometimes be enhanced by insights of other faiths. The deeper realities of our faith are beyond precise verbal formulation and our way of worship based on silent waiting testifies to this.

Our diversity invites us both to speak what we know to be true in our lives and to learn from others. Friends are encouraged to listen to each other in humility and understanding, trusting in the Spirit that goes beyond our human effort and comprehension. So it is for the comfort and discomfort of Friends that these advices and queries are offered, with the hope that we may all be more faithful and find deeper joy in God's service.

> Dearly beloved Friends, these things we do not lay upon you as a rule or form to walk by, but that all, with the measure of light which is pure and holy, may be guided; and so in the light walking and abiding, these may be fulfilled in the Spirit, not from the letter, for the letter killeth, but the Spirit giveth life.
>
> Postscript to an epistle to 'the brethren in the north' issued by a meeting of elders at Balby, 1656

Advices and queries

1.02

1. Take heed, dear Friends, to the promptings of love and truth in your hearts. Trust them as the leadings of God whose Light shows us our darkness and brings us to new life.

2. Bring the whole of your life under the ordering of the spirit of Christ. Are you open to the healing power of God's love? Cherish that of God within you, so that this love may grow in you and guide you. Let your worship and your daily life enrich each other. Treasure your experience of God, however it comes to you. Remember that Christianity is not a notion but a way.

3. Do you try to set aside times of quiet for openness to the Holy Spirit? All of us need to find a way into silence which allows us to deepen our awareness of the divine and to find the inward source of our strength. Seek to know an inward stillness, even amid the activities of daily life. Do you encourage in yourself and in others a habit of dependence on God's guidance for each day? Hold yourself and others in the Light, knowing that all are cherished by God.

1.02 4. The Religious Society of Friends is rooted in Christianity and has always found inspiration in the life and teachings of Jesus. How do you interpret your faith in the light of this heritage? How does Jesus speak to you today? Are you following Jesus' example of love in action? Are you learning from his life the reality and cost of obedience to God? How does his relationship with God challenge and inspire you?

5. Take time to learn about other people's experiences of the Light. Remember the importance of the Bible, the writings of Friends and all writings which reveal the ways of God. As you learn from others, can you in turn give freely from what you have gained? While respecting the experiences and opinions of others, do not be afraid to say what you have found and what you value. Appreciate that doubt and questioning can also lead to spiritual growth and to a greater awareness of the Light that is in us all.

6. Do you work gladly with other religious groups in the pursuit of common goals? While remaining faithful to Quaker insights, try to enter imaginatively into the life and witness of other communities of faith, creating together the bonds of friendship.

7. Be aware of the spirit of God at work in the ordinary activities and experience of your daily life. Spiritual learning continues throughout life, and often in unexpected ways. There is inspiration to be found all around us, in the natural world, in the sciences and arts, in our work and friendships, in our sorrows as well as in our joys. Are you open to new light, from whatever source it may come? Do you approach new ideas with discernment?

1.02

8. Worship is our response to an awareness of God. We can worship alone, but when we join with others in expectant waiting we may discover a deeper sense of God's presence. We seek a gathered stillness in our meetings for worship so that all may feel the power of God's love drawing us together and leading us.

9. In worship we enter with reverence into communion with God and respond to the promptings of the Holy Spirit. Come to meeting for worship with heart and mind prepared. Yield yourself and all your outward concerns to God's guidance so that you may find 'the evil weakening in you and the good raised up'.

10. Come regularly to meeting for worship even when you are angry, depressed, tired or spiritually cold. In the silence ask for and accept the prayerful support of others joined with you in worship. Try to find a spiritual wholeness which encompasses suffering as well as thankfulness and joy. Prayer, springing from a deep place in the heart, may bring healing and unity as nothing else can. Let meeting for worship nourish your whole life.

11. Be honest with yourself. What unpalatable truths might you be evading? When you recognise your shortcomings, do not let that discourage you. In worship together we can find the assurance of God's love and the strength to go on with renewed courage.

12. When you are preoccupied and distracted in meeting let wayward and disturbing thoughts give way quietly to your awareness of God's presence among us and in the world. Receive the vocal ministry of others in a tender and creative spirit. Reach for the meaning deep within it, recognising that even if it is not God's word for you, it may be so for others. Remember that we all share responsibility for the meeting for worship whether our ministry is in silence or through the spoken word.

1.02 13. Do not assume that vocal ministry is never to be your part. Faithfulness and sincerity in speaking, even very briefly, may open the way to fuller ministry from others. When prompted to speak, wait patiently to know that the leading and the time are right, but do not let a sense of your own unworthiness hold you back. Pray that your ministry may arise from deep experience, and trust that words will be given to you. Try to speak audibly and distinctly, and with sensitivity to the needs of others. Beware of speaking predictably or too often, and of making additions towards the end of a meeting when it was well left before.

14. Are your meetings for church affairs held in a spirit of worship and in dependence on the guidance of God? Remember that we do not seek a majority decision nor even consensus. As we wait patiently for divine guidance our experience is that the right way will open and we shall be led into unity.

15. Do you take part as often as you can in meetings for church affairs? Are you familiar enough with our church government to contribute to its disciplined processes? Do you consider difficult questions with an informed mind as well as a generous and loving spirit? Are you prepared to let your insights and personal wishes take their place alongside those of others or be set aside as the meeting seeks the right way forward? If you cannot attend, uphold the meeting prayerfully.

16. Do you welcome the diversity of culture, language and expressions of faith in our yearly meeting and in the world community of Friends? Seek to increase your understanding and to gain from this rich heritage and wide range of spiritual insights. Uphold your own and other yearly meetings in your prayers.

1.02 17. Do you respect that of God in everyone though it may be expressed in unfamiliar ways or be difficult to discern? Each of us has a particular experience of God and each must find the way to be true to it. When words are strange or disturbing to you, try to sense where they come from and what has nourished the lives of others. Listen patiently and seek the truth which other people's opinions may contain for you. Avoid hurtful criticism and provocative language. Do not allow the strength of your convictions to betray you into making statements or allegations that are unfair or untrue. Think it possible that you may be mistaken.

18. How can we make the meeting a community in which each person is accepted and nurtured, and strangers are welcome? Seek to know one another in the things which are eternal, bear the burden of each other's failings and pray for one another. As we enter with tender sympathy into the joys and sorrows of each other's lives, ready to give help and to receive it, our meeting can be a channel for God's love and forgiveness.

19. Rejoice in the presence of children and young people in your meeting and recognise the gifts they bring. Remember that the meeting as a whole shares a responsibility for every child in its care. Seek for them as for yourself a full development of God's gifts and the abundant life Jesus tells us can be ours. How do you share your deepest beliefs with them, while leaving them free to develop as the spirit of God may lead them? Do you invite them to share their insights with you? Are you ready both to learn from them and to accept your responsibilities towards them?

20. Do you give sufficient time to sharing with others in the meeting, both newcomers and long-time members, your understanding of worship, of service, and of commitment to the Society's witness? Do you give a right proportion of your money to support Quaker work?

1.02 21. Do you cherish your friendships, so that they grow in depth and understanding and mutual respect? In close relationships we may risk pain as well as finding joy. When experiencing great happiness or great hurt we may be more open to the working of the Spirit.

22. Respect the wide diversity among us in our lives and relationships. Refrain from making prejudiced judgments about the life journeys of others. Do you foster the spirit of mutual understanding and forgiveness which our discipleship asks of us? Remember that each one of us is unique, precious, a child of God.

23. Marriage has always been regarded by Friends as a religious commitment rather than a merely civil contract. Both partners should offer with God's help an intention to cherish one another for life. Remember that happiness depends on an understanding and steadfast love on both sides. In times of difficulty remind yourself of the value of prayer, of perseverance and of a sense of humour.

24. Children and young people need love and stability. Are we doing all we can to uphold and sustain parents and others who carry the responsibility for providing this care?

25. A long-term relationship brings tensions as well as fulfilment. If your relationship with your partner is under strain, seek help in understanding the other's point of view and in exploring your own feelings, which may be powerful and destructive. Consider the wishes and feelings of any children involved, and remember their enduring need for love and security. Seek God's guidance. If you undergo the distress of separation or divorce, try to maintain some compassionate communication so that arrangements can be made with the minimum of bitterness.

1.02 26. Do you recognise the needs and gifts of each member of your family and household, not forgetting your own? Try to make your home a place of loving friendship and enjoyment, where all who live or visit may find the peace and refreshment of God's presence.

27. Live adventurously. When choices arise, do you take the way that offers the fullest opportunity for the use of your gifts in the service of God and the community? Let your life speak. When decisions have to be made, are you ready to join with others in seeking clearness, asking for God's guidance and offering counsel to one another?

28. Every stage of our lives offers fresh opportunities. Responding to divine guidance, try to discern the right time to undertake or relinquish responsibilities without undue pride or guilt. Attend to what love requires of you, which may not be great busyness.

29. Approach old age with courage and hope. As far as possible, make arrangements for your care in good time, so that an undue burden does not fall on others. Although old age may bring increasing disability and loneliness, it can also bring serenity, detachment and wisdom. Pray that in your final years you may be enabled to find new ways of receiving and reflecting God's love.

30. Are you able to contemplate your death and the death of those closest to you? Accepting the fact of death, we are freed to live more fully. In bereavement, give yourself time to grieve. When others mourn, let your love embrace them.

1.02 31. We are called to live 'in the virtue of that life and power that takes away the occasion of all wars'. Do you faithfully maintain our testimony that war and the preparation for war are inconsistent with the spirit of Christ? Search out whatever in your own way of life may contain the seeds of war. Stand firm in our testimony, even when others commit or prepare to commit acts of violence, yet always remember that they too are children of God.

32. Bring into God's light those emotions, attitudes and prejudices in yourself which lie at the root of destructive conflict, acknowledging your need for forgiveness and grace. In what ways are you involved in the work of reconciliation between individuals, groups and nations?

33. Are you alert to practices here and throughout the world which discriminate against people on the basis of who or what they are or because of their beliefs? Bear witness to the humanity of all people, including those who break society's conventions or its laws. Try to discern new growing points in social and economic life. Seek to understand the causes of injustice, social unrest and fear. Are you working to bring about a just and compassionate society which allows everyone to develop their capacities and fosters the desire to serve?

34. Remember your responsibilities as a citizen for the conduct of local, national, and international affairs. Do not shrink from the time and effort your involvement may demand.

35. Respect the laws of the state but let your first loyalty be to God's purposes. If you feel impelled by strong conviction to break the law, search your conscience deeply. Ask your meeting for the prayerful support which will give you strength as a right way becomes clear.

1.02 36. Do you uphold those who are acting under concern, even if their way is not yours? Can you lay aside your own wishes and prejudices while seeking with others to find God's will for them?

37. Are you honest and truthful in all you say and do? Do you maintain strict integrity in business transactions and in your dealings with individuals and organisations? Do you use money and information entrusted to you with discretion and responsibility? Taking oaths implies a double standard of truth; in choosing to affirm instead, be aware of the claim to integrity that you are making.

38. If pressure is brought upon you to lower your standard of integrity, are you prepared to resist it? Our responsibilities to God and our neighbour may involve us in taking unpopular stands. Do not let the desire to be sociable, or the fear of seeming peculiar, determine your decisions.

39. Consider which of the ways to happiness offered by society are truly fulfilling and which are potentially corrupting and destructive. Be discriminating when choosing means of entertainment and information. Resist the desire to acquire possessions or income through unethical investment, speculation or games of chance.

40. In view of the harm done by the use of alcohol, tobacco and other habit-forming drugs, consider whether you should limit your use of them or refrain from using them altogether. Remember that any use of alcohol or drugs may impair judgment and put both the user and others in danger.

41. Try to live simply. A simple lifestyle freely chosen is a source of strength. Do not be persuaded into buying what you do not need or cannot afford. Do you keep yourself informed about the effects your style of living is having on the global economy and environment?

1.02 42. We do not own the world, and its riches are not ours to dispose of at will. Show a loving consideration for all creatures, and seek to maintain the beauty and variety of the world. Work to ensure that our increasing power over nature is used responsibly, with reverence for life. Rejoice in the splendour of God's continuing creation.

Be patterns, be examples in all countries, places, islands, nations, wherever you come, that your carriage and life may preach among all sorts of people, and to them; then you will come to walk cheerfully over the world, answering that of God in every one.

George Fox, 1656

Cynghorion a holiadau

1.03 1. Ystyriwch, Gyfeillion annwyl, gymhellion cariad a gwirionedd yn eich calonnau. Ymddiriedwch ynddynt fel arweiniad Duw, Goleuni yr hwn sy'n dangos i ni ein tywyllwch gan ein dwyn i fywyd newydd.

2. Dygwch eich holl fywyd dan reolaeth Ysbryd Crist. A ydych yn agored i allu iachusol cariad Duw? Coleddwch yr hyn sydd o Dduw ynoch, fel y bo i'r cariad hwn dyfu ynoch a'ch arwain. Boed i'ch addoliad a'ch bywyd beunyddiol gyfoethogi eu gilydd. Trysorwch eich profiad o Dduw, pa fodd bynnag y daw i'ch rhan. Cofiwch nad damcaniaeth yw Cristnogaeth, eithr ffordd.

3. A ydych yn ceisio neilltuo adegau o dawelwch i fod yn agored i'r Ysbryd Glân? Y mae ar bob un ohonom angen canfod ffordd i mewn i ddistawrwydd sy'n ein galluogi i ddyfnhau'n hymwybyddiaeth o'r dwyfol ac i ganfod tarddle mewnol ein nerth. Ceisiwch lonyddwch mewnol, hyd yn oed ynghanol gweithgareddau bywyd beunyddiol. A ydych yn meithrin ynoch eich hun ac mewn eraill yr arfer o ddibynnu ar arweiniad dyddiol Duw? Daliwch eich hunain ac eraill yn y Goleuni, gan wybod fod Duw yn coleddu pawb oll.

1.03 4. Gwreiddiwyd Cymdeithas Grefyddol y Cyfeillion mewn Cristnogaeth a chafodd ysbrydoliaeth yn wastad o fywyd a dysgeidiaeth Iesu. Pa fodd y dehonglwch eich ffydd yng ngoleuni'r dreftadaeth hon? Pa fodd y llefara Iesu wrthych heddiw? A ydych yn dilyn esiampl Iesu o gariad ar waith? A ydych yn dysgu o'i fywyd realiti a chost ufudd-dod i Dduw? Pa fodd y mae ei berthynas â Duw yn eich herio a'ch ysbrydoli?

5. Cymerwch amser i ddysgu am brofiadau pobl eraill o'r Goleuni. Cofiwch bwysigrwydd y Beibl, ysgrifeniadau Cyfeillion a phob llyfr sy'n datguddio ffyrdd Duw. A chwithau'n cael eich dysgu gan eraill, a fedrwch yn eich tro gyfrannu'n rhydd o'r hyn a dderbyniasoch? Tra'n parchu profiadau ac opiniynau pobl eraill, nac ofnwch fynegi yr hyn a gawsoch a'r hyn yr ydych yn ei gyfrif yn werthfawr. Cofiwch y gall amheuaeth a chwestiynu arwain hefyd at dwf ysbrydol ac at ymwybyddiaeth ehangach o'r Goleuni sydd ynom oll.

6. A ydych yn cydweithio'n llawen gyda grwpiau crefyddol eraill tuag at amcanion cyffredin? Gan fod yn ffyddlon i'r weledigaeth Grynwrol, ceisiwch gyda dychymyg ran ym mywyd a thystiolaeth aelwydydd eraill o ffydd, gan greu ynghyd rwymau cyfeillgarwch.

7. Ymglywch ag ysbryd Duw ar waith yng ngweithgareddau cyffredin a phrofiad eich byw beunyddiol. Pery addysg ysbrydol gydol bywyd, yn aml mewn ffyrdd annisgwyl. Ceir ysbrydoliaeth o'n hamgylch ym mhobman, ym myd natur, yn y gwyddorau a'r celfyddydau, yn ein gwaith a'n cyfeillgarwch, yn ein gofidiau fel yn ein llawenydd. A ydych yn agored i oleuni newydd, o ba ffynhonnell bynnag y dêl? A ydych yn ddetholgar wrth ystyried syniadau newydd?

1.03 8. Addoliad yw ein hymateb i ymglywed â Duw. Gallwn addoli ar ein pennau'n hunain, ond pan ymunwn ag eraill mewn aros disgwylgar, gallwn ddarganfod ymwybyddiaeth ddyfnach o bresenoldeb Duw. Yn ein cyrddau addoli ceisiwn ymgynnull mewn llonyddwch fel y cawn oll deimlo nerth cariad Duw yn ein tynnu ynghyd ac yn ein tywys.

9. Yn yr addoliad, fe awn gyda pharch i gymundeb â Duw, gan ymateb i anogaethau'r Ysbryd Glân. Deuwch i'r cyfarfod addoli wedi ymbaratoi yn eich calon a'ch meddwl. Ildiwch eich hunain a'ch holl ofalon allanol i arweiniad Duw, fel y caffoch 'y drwg yn gwanhau ynoch a'r da yn ymddyrchafu'.

10. Deuwch yn gyson i'r cwrdd addoli, hyd yn oed pan fyddoch ddig, neu'n isel-ysbryd, neu'n flinedig, neu'n oer yn ysbrydol. Yn y distawrwydd, ceisiwch a derbyniwch gefnogaeth weddigar eich cyd-addolwyr. Ceisiwch ganfod cyfanrwydd ysbrydol sy'n cwmpasu dioddefaint yn ogystal â diolchgarwch a llawenydd. Yn anad unpeth arall fe all gweddi sy'n tarddu o ddwfn y galon ddwyn gwellhad ac undod. Gadewch i'r cwrdd addoli faethu eich holl fywyd.

11. Byddwch onest â chwi'ch hunan. Pa wirioneddau diflas y dichon eich bod yn eu hosgoi? O adnabod eich ffaeleddau, na foed i hynny eich digalonni. Mewn cydaddoli, gallwn ganfod y sicrwydd o gariad Duw a chanfod o'r newydd y dewrder i ddal ati.

12. Pan fyddoch synfyfyriol neu ddryslyd yn y cwrdd addoli, gadewch i feddyliau cyndyn neu anesmwyth ymollwng yn dawel i'r ymwybod o bresenoldeb Duw yn ein mysg ac yn y byd. Derbyniwch weinidogaeth lafar eraill mewn ysbryd addfwyn a chreadigol. Estynnwch am yr ystyr sy'n ddwfn ymhlyg ynddo. Hyd yn oed os nad yw'n air Duw i chwi, gall fod felly i eraill. Cofier ein bod oll yn rhannu cyfrifoldeb am y cwrdd addoli, pa un bynnag ai mewn distawrwydd neu ynteu trwy'r gair llafar y bo'n gweinidogaeth.

1.03 13. Na thybiwch na fydd eich rhan chwi byth yn weinidogaeth lafar. Fe ddichon cywirdeb a didwylledd wrth siarad, hyd yn oed yn fyr, agor y ffordd i weinidogaeth lawnach gan eraill. Pan ysgogir chwi i lefaru, arhoswch yn amyneddgar i wybod fod yr arweiniad a'r adeg yn briodol, ond na foed ymdeimlo â'ch annheilyngdod eich hun yn rhwystr. Gweddïwch am i'ch gweinidogaeth godi o ddyfnder profiad, ac ymddiriedwch y rhoir geiriau i chwi. Ceisiwch siarad yn glywadwy a chroyw, gan feddwl am anghenion pobl eraill. Gochelwch rhag siarad yn ystrydebol neu'n rhy aml. Gochelwch rhag ymhelaethu tua diwedd cwrdd pan fyddid eisoes wedi'i iawn derfynu.

14. A gynhelir eich cyrddau ynglŷn â materion eglwysig mewn ysbryd addolgar gan ddibynnu ar gyfarwyddyd Duw? Cofiwch nad ydym yn ceisio penderfyniad trwy fwyafrif na hyd yn oed trwy gonsensws. Tra'n aros yn amyneddgar am arweiniad dwyfol, ein profiad yw y bydd y llwybr iawn yn ymagor ac y cawn ein tywys i undod.

15. A ydych yn cymryd rhan mor fynych ag y galloch mewn cyrddau ynglŷn â materion eglwysig? A ydych yn ddigon cyfarwydd â'n llywodraeth eglwysig i gyfrannu i'w phrosesau disgybledig? A ydych yn ystyried cwestiynau anodd gyda meddwl gwybodus yn ogystal ag mewn ysbryd haelfrydig a chariadus? A ydych yn fodlon i'ch dirnadaeth a'ch dymuniadau personol gymryd eu lle ochr yn ochr â'r eiddo eraill, neu gael eu gosod o'r neilltu, wrth i'r cwrdd chwilio am y llwybr cywir ymlaen? Oni ellwch fod yn bresennol, cynhaliwch y cwrdd yn weddigar.

16. A ydych yn croesawu'r amrywiaeth mewn diwylliant ac iaith a mynegiant ffydd sydd o fewn ein cyfarfod blynyddol ac yn y gymuned fyd-eang o Gyfeillion? Ceisiwch gynyddu eich amgyffred gan elwa o'r dreftadaeth gyfoethog hon a'r ystod eang o ddirnadaeth ysbrydol. Cynhaliwch yn eich gweddïau eich cyfarfod blynyddol a hefyd gyfarfodydd blynyddol eraill.

1.03 17. A ydych yn parchu'r hyn sydd o Dduw ym mhawb, er y gall fod wedi ei fynegi mewn ffyrdd anghyfarwydd neu ynteu'n anodd ei ddirnad? Y mae i bob un ohonom brofiad neilltuol o Dduw a rhaid i bob un ohonom ganfod sut i fod yn ffyddlon i'r profiad hwnnw. Pan fo geiriau'n ddieithr i chwi neu'n tarfu arnoch, ceisiwch synhwyro o ba le y daethant, gan ystyried yr hyn a fu'n maethu bywydau pobl eraill. Gwrandewch yn amyneddgar, a cheisiwch y gwirionedd fo i chwi yn naliadau pobl eraill. Gochelwch rhag beirniadaeth sy'n clwyfo ac iaith sy'n cythruddo. Peidiwch â gadael i gryfder eich argyhoeddiadau beri ichwi wneud gosodiadau neu honiadau annheg neu anwir. Ystyriwch y gellwch fod yn camsynied.

18. Pa fodd y gallwn wneud y cwrdd yn gymuned lle caiff pob person ei dderbyn a'i faethu, a lle caiff dieithriaid groeso? Ceisiwch adnabod eich gilydd yn y pethau tragwyddol; dygwch faich methiannau'ch gilydd a gweddïwch bawb dros eich gilydd. Wrth i ni gyfranogi mewn tynerwch o lawenydd a thrallod bywyd beunyddiol ein gilydd, yn barod i roddi help ac i'w dderbyn, gall ein cwrdd fod yn gyfrwng i gariad a maddeuant Duw.

19. Llawenhewch ym mhresenoldeb plant a phobl ifanc yn eich cwrdd, gan gydnabod y doniau sydd ganddynt. Cofiwch fod y cwrdd oll yn rhannu cyfrifoldeb am bob plentyn yn ei ofal. Ceisiwch iddynt hwy, fel i chwi'ch hunain, ddatblygiad llawn o ddoniau Duw a'r bywyd helaeth y dywedodd Iesu y gallem ei feddiannu. Pa fodd yr ydych yn cydrannu'ch daliadau dyfnaf â hwy, gan adael rhyddid iddynt ddatblygu yn y modd yr arweinio ysbryd Duw hwynt? A ydych yn eu gwahodd i rannu gyda chwi eu dirnadaeth? A ydych yn barod i ddysgu ganddynt ac, ar yr un pryd, i dderbyn eich cyfrifoldebau tuag atynt?

1.03

20. A roddwch ddigon o amser i rannu gydag eraill, yn newydd-ddyfodiaid ac yn rhai a fu'n aelodau ers tro, eich dealltwriaeth o addoli ac o wasanaeth ac o ymrwymiad i dystiolaeth y Gymdeithas? A roddwch gyfran briodol o'ch arian i gynnal gwaith Crynwrol?

21. A ydych yn anwylo pob cyfeillgarwch, fel y byddont yn dyfnhau ac yn cynyddu mewn dealltwriaeth a pharch o'r ddeutu? Ym mhob perthynas glòs efallai y bydd raid mentro poen yn ogystal â chanfod llawenydd. Wrth brofi hapusrwydd mawr neu loes fawr, efallai ein bod yn fwy agored i waith yr Ysbryd.

22. Perchwch yr amrywiaeth eang sydd yn ein mysg yn ein bywydau a'n cysylltiadau. Gochelwch rhag ffurfio barn ragfarnllyd am deithiau bywyd pobl eraill. A ydych yn meithrin yr ysbryd o gyd-ddyheu ac o faddeuant a fynnir gennym, a ninnau'n ddisgyblion? Cofiwch fod pob un ohonom yn unigryw, yn werthfawr, yn blentyn i Dduw.

23. Ystyriodd Cyfeillion erioed fod priodas yn ymrwymiad crefyddol yn hytrach na chytundeb sifil yn unig. Dylai'r ddeuddyn gynnig gyda chymorth Duw fwriad i goledd y naill a'r llall gydol eu hoes. Cofiwch fod hapusrwydd yn dibynnu ar ddealltwriaeth a serch diysgog o'r ddeutu. Pan ddaw amseroedd anodd, cofiwch werth gweddi a dyfalbarhad a synnwyr digrifwch.

24. Y mae ar blant a phobl ifanc angen cariad a sefydlogrwydd. A ydym yn gwneud a allom i gynnal rhieni ac eraill sy'n dwyn y cyfrifoldeb o ddarparu'r gofal hwn?

1.03

25. Y mae perthynas tymor-hir yn dwyn tyndra yn ogystal â boddhad. Os yw eich perthynas â'ch partner dan straen, ceisiwch gymorth i ddeall safbwynt y llall ac i archwilio'ch teimladau eich hunan, teimladau a all fod yn bŵerus a dinistriol. Ystyriwch ddymuniadau a theimladau unrhyw blant sydd ynghlwm wrthych, gan gofio eu hangen parhaol am gariad a sicrwydd. Ceisiwch arweiniad Duw. Os wynebwch y trallod o ymwahanu neu o ysgaru, ceisiwch gadw rhyw gyswllt tosturiol fel y galloch wneud trefniadau heb fwy o chwerwder nag sydd raid.

26. A ydych yn adnabod anghenion a doniau pob aelod o'ch tŷ a'ch tylwyth, heb anghofio'r eiddoch chwi'ch hunan? Ceisiwch wneud eich cartref yn drigfa cyfeillgarwch cariadus a mwynhad, lle y gall pawb sy'n byw neu'n ymweld ddod o hyd i dangnefedd ac adfywiad presenoldeb Duw.

27. Byddwch fyw yn anturus. Pan fo modd dewis, a ddewiswch y llwybr a rydd ichwi fwyaf o gyfle i ddefnyddio'ch doniau yng ngwasanaeth Duw a'r gymuned? Boed i'ch bywyd lefaru. Pan fo'n rhaid penderfynu, a ydych yn barod i ymuno ag eraill wrth chwilio am lwybr eglur, gan ofyn am arweiniad Duw a chan gynnig cyngor y naill i'r llall?

28. Ym mhob gris yn ein bywyd y mae cyfleusterau newydd o hyd. Gan ymateb i arweiniad dwyfol, ceisiwch ymglywed â'r adeg briodol i ysgwyddo neu i drosglwyddo cyfrifoldebau heb falchder nac euogrwydd amhriodol. Gofalwch am yr hyn a ofyn cariad oddi arnoch; efallai nad prysurdeb mawr mo hynny.

29. Wynebwch henaint yn ddewr a gobeithiol. Hyd y gellir, gwnewch mewn da bryd drefniadau am eich gofal, fel na bo baich afresymol yn disgyn ar bobl eraill. Er y dichon henaint ddwyn anabledd ac unigrwydd cynyddol, gall hefyd ddod â llonyddwch ac arwahanrwydd a doethineb. Gweddïwch am gael eich galluogi yn eich blynyddoedd olaf i ganfod ffyrdd newydd o dderbyn ac adlewyrchu cariad Duw.

1.03 30. A ydych yn abl i ystyried eich marwolaeth a marwolaeth eich anwyliaid? O dderbyn marwolaeth fel ffaith, fe'n rhyddheir i fyw yn llawnach. Mewn profedigaeth, caniatewch i chwi'ch hunan amser i alaru. Pan fo eraill yn galaru, gadewch i'ch cariad eu cofleidio.

---

31. Gelwir arnom i fyw 'yn rhinwedd y bywyd a'r gallu sy'n symud achos rhyfeloedd'. A ydych yn cynnal yn ffyddlon ein tystiolaeth fod rhyfel, a pharatoi am ryfel, yn anghyson ag ysbryd Crist? Chwiliwch yn eich ffordd o fyw am unrhyw arwydd o hadau rhyfel. Sefwch yn gadarn yn ein tystiolaeth, hyd yn oed pan fo eraill yn cyflawni neu'n paratoi i gyflawni gweithredoedd o drais; ond cofiwch eu bod hwythau hefyd yn blant i Dduw.

32. Dygwch i oleuni Duw yr emosiynau, yr agweddau, y rhagfarnau hynny ynoch eich hunan sydd wrth wraidd gwrthdaro dinistriol, gan gydnabod fod arnoch angen maddeuant a gras. Ym mha ffyrdd yr ydych yn llafurio i gymodi rhwng unigolion a grwpiau a chenhedloedd?

33. A ydych yn effro i arferion, yma a thrwy'r byd, sy'n gwahaniaethu yn erbyn pobl ar sail pwy neu beth ydynt neu oherwydd yr hyn a gredant? Dygwch dystiolaeth i ddynoliaeth pob un, gan gynnwys y rhai sy'n tramgwyddo confensiynau neu ddeddfau cymdeithas. Ceisiwch ddirnad y mannau lle ceir tyfiant newydd mewn bywyd cymdeithasol ac economaidd. Ceisiwch ddeall yr achosion am anghyfiawnder ac aflonyddwch cymdeithasol ac ofn. A ydych yn gweithio i greu cymdeithas gyfiawn a thosturiol a rydd gyfle i bawb ddatblygu eu galluoedd ac a feithrin eu hawydd i wasanaethu?

34. Cofiwch eich cyfrifoldeb fel dinesydd am reolaeth materion lleol, cenedlaethol a rhyng-genedlaethol. Peidiwch ag arbed yr amser a'r ymdrech y gall eich ymrwymiad ei hawlio.

1.03

35. Perchwch ddeddfau'r wladwriaeth ond boed eich teyrngarwch pennaf i fwriadau Duw. Os cymhellir chwi gan argyhoeddiad cryf i dorri'r ddeddf, chwiliwch eich cydwybod i'w ddyfnderau. Gofynnwch i'ch cwrdd am y gefnogaeth weddigar a'ch nertha wrth i'r llwybr cywir agor o'ch blaen.

36. A ydych yn cynnal y rhai hynny sydd yn gweithredu dan gonsyrn, hyd yn oed os nad yw eu ffordd yr un â'r eiddoch chwi? Tra'n chwilio gydag eraill am ewyllys Duw ar eu cyfer, a ellwch osod o'r neilltu eich dymuniadau a'ch rhagfarnau eich hunan?

37. A ydych yn onest a didwyll ym mhob peth a ddywedwch ac a wnewch? A ydych yn gwbl onest mewn trafodion masnachol ac yn eich ymwneud ag unigolion a sefydliadau? A ydych yn trin arian a gwybodaeth a ymddiriedir i chwi mewn modd doeth a chyfrifol? Y mae tyngu llwon yn awgrymu safon ddeublyg o wirionedd: wrth ddewis yn hytrach gadarnhau, cofiwch eich bod yn haeru gonestrwydd.

38. Os pwysir arnoch i ostwng eich safon o gywirdeb, a ydych yn barod i wrthsefyll hynny? Gall ein cyfrifoldebau i Dduw ac i'n cymydog olygu gwneud safiad amhoblogaidd. Na foed i'r awydd am fod yn gymdeithasol, neu ofn ymddangos yn od, gyflyru eich penderfyniad.

39. Ystyriwch pa ffyrdd i hapusrwydd a gynigir gan gymdeithas sy'n rhoi gwir fodlonrwydd a pha rai sy'n dwyn hadau llygredd a dinistr. Byddwch yn ofalus wrth ddewis cyfryngau difyrrwch a gwybodaeth. Gwrthwynebwch yr awydd i ennill meddiannau neu incwm trwy fuddsoddi'n anfoesol, neu trwy fentro arian yn anfoesol, neu trwy hap-chwarae.

1.03 40. Yn wyneb y niwed a achosir trwy'r defnydd o alcohol a thybaco a chyffuriau eraill sy'n creu dibyniant, ystyriwch a ddylech gyfyngu eich defnydd ohonynt neu ymwrthod yn gyfan-gwbl â hwynt. Cofiwch y gall unrhyw ddefnydd o alcohol neu gyffuriau amharu ar eich gallu i farnu, gan roi'r defnyddiwr ac eraill mewn perygl.

41. Ceisiwch fyw yn syml. Y mae dewis dull syml o fyw yn ffynhonnell cryfder. Peidiwch â chael eich perswadio i brynu dim nad oes arnoch mo'i angen neu na ellwch ei fforddio. A ydych yn gofalu cael gwybod am effeithiau eich dull chwi o fyw ar yr economi a'r amgylchedd byd-eang?

42. Nid ni piau'r byd, ac nid eiddom ni mo'i oludoedd i'w gwaredu fel y mynnom. Dangoswch ofal cariadus am bob creadur, a cheisiwch warchod prydferthwch ac amrywiaeth y byd. Ymdrechwch i sicrhau fod ein goruchafiaeth gynyddol ar natur yn cael ei ddefnyddio'n gyfrifol, gyda pharch at fywyd. Llawenhewch yn ysblander creadigaeth barhaol Duw.

Byddwch yn batrymau, yn esiamplau yn y gwledydd, lleoedd, ynysoedd a'r cenhedloedd oll, i ba le bynnag y deloch; fel y byddo eich ymarweddiad a'ch bywyd yn bregeth ymhlith pobl o bob math, ac yn llefaru wrthynt. Felly y derfydd i chwi deithio drwy'r byd yn siriol, gan ymateb i'r hyn sydd o Dduw ym mhob dyn.

George Fox, 1656

History

1.04 When Yearly Meeting in 1682 decided to ask the representatives from each quarterly meeting to reply to three questions orally, Yearly Meeting itself had only been meeting consecutively for the previous few years and the systematic organisation of quarterly and monthly meetings had been recently completed. These questions were intended to produce factual information from Friends with local knowledge, so that the progress of the Society throughout the country could be seen and help given in the areas where it was most needed.

> What Friends in the ministry, in their respective counties, departed this life since the last yearly meeting?
>
> What Friends imprisoned for their testimony have died in prison since the last yearly meeting?
>
> How the Truth has prospered amongst them since the last yearly meeting, and how Friends are in peace and unity?

These three questions were expanded into six in 1694 and further amended in the early 1700s but their purpose was still mainly to elicit factual information. The practice of requiring oral replies to the questions soon became too cumbersome and was replaced, following Yearly Meeting decisions in 1700 and 1706, by written replies from the quarterly meetings. The system of replying to the questions took root in the Society and the term 'query' was increasingly used, in Yearly Meeting minutes from 1723 onwards, instead of 'question'.

As the practice of replying to the queries became more formal their purpose also began to change. In the early eighteenth century Friends generally ceased to believe that the whole nation would accept the truth that they had been preaching and became more concerned in preserving the Society as 'a precious remnant' devoted to the truth. The queries were increasingly used to ensure consistency of conduct among Friends and to obtain information as to the state of the Society. In 1721, for example, a query was added as to the receipt and payment of tithes, and in 1723 as to defrauding the king of his customs and excise, and many other subjects were included in additional queries.

The Society declined in numbers in the eighteenth century. Yearly Meeting in 1760, troubled that standards in the Society were falling, set up a committee 'for the promotion and revival of wholesome discipline', which visited meetings all over the country. One of its principal instruments was to insist on a more systematic reading and answering of the queries by monthly and quarterly meetings. The purpose of the queries after 1760 became principally disciplinary, and monthly and quarterly meetings and their elders and overseers regarded the queries as a touchstone on which they could rely in administering the discipline.

There were periodic revisions of the queries during the next hundred years, although the number of substantial changes was few. When the queries were revised in 1791 Yearly Meeting adopted the first 'general advices' for consideration by monthly and quarterly meetings. They were short, and mainly concerned with the domestic life of the Society and its members. They were regarded as being of subsidiary importance to the queries, and were treated as an additional aid to the discipline. During the early nineteenth century Friends were much influenced by the evangelical movement and this was illustrated in the revision of the general advices in 1833. They were completely re-written and much expanded. They became of much greater importance than before, and their purpose was no longer mainly disciplinary but instead they were used to emphasise the importance of evangelical principles and to encourage Friends to consider whether they should not adopt them personally.

As Friends in the early nineteenth century entered more into the public and social life of the times, many of them began to question traditional practices of the Society including the very large amount of time spent at business meetings in reading and drawing up answers to the queries, which were often formal in nature. The value of the queries for self-examination had been commended by Yearly Meeting from 1787 onwards; increasingly Friends came to regard this aspect as more important than their disciplinary use and this change in emphasis resulted in the revision of the queries in 1860 and 1875. The requirement of preparing written answers was virtually abolished, and while the regulations continued to provide for a corporate consideration of the queries by monthly and preparative meetings, this in turn became in many places a formality. The general advices were revised over the same period. They were lengthened and extended in scope, and provision was made for them to be read at the close of meeting for worship.

No major revision of the general advices and queries took place until 1928. By this time many Friends considered that they were too negative in approach, had become uneasy at the evangelical language then in use, and wished for greater emphasis on the social responsibilities of Quakerism. These views were reflected in the revised general advices and queries; the general advices were again increased in length, and divided for convenience into three parts, while the queries, covering much of the same ground as the general advices, were also increased in number. The requirement of corporate deliberation on the queries by Friends' business meetings remained but this became of much less significance. The use of the queries became increasingly devotional – 'a collection of exhortations on the right management of one's own affairs both inward and outward, and a collection of questions, or groups of questions, in pondering which a whole meeting can achieve a corporate examination of conscience'. The practice was established in many meetings of reading the queries in meetings for worship in addition to the general advices, which under the regulations adopted in 1931 were required to be read there.

In 1928 the advices on ministry were for the first time brought before members of the yearly meeting as a whole. Twenty years later, in response to a plea that they should be rewritten in modern language and should encourage those who had not yet taken part in vocal ministry, additional advice on ministry was adopted in 1949.

A revision of *Advices and queries*, adopted in 1964, contained a number of alterations to the previous edition and included references to social problems not apparent in 1928. The principal change was that the advices on ministry and additional advice were no longer separate documents, although much of the material in them was again included.

By 1984 some monthly meetings were expressing unease with the 1964 edition of *Advices and queries*. Hesitations had been aroused by the use of masculine nouns and pronouns no longer seen as justifiable, by some of the theological language used, by the difficulty of reading aloud some of the longer paragraphs and by the absence of reference to some more recently evolved concerns. In 1986 Meeting for Sufferings appointed a Book of Discipline Revision Committee, and among the earliest tasks which this committee took up was a revision of the advices and queries.

As part of a major programme of consultation with the yearly meeting, the committee drafted a provisional document with the title *Questions and counsel*. Meeting for Sufferings agreed to publish the draft in 1988 and invited meetings to use it for two or three years and to join in the process of revision by telling of their experience. In the light of these responses and after several more years of work on the revision of the whole book, the committee submitted a text to Yearly Meeting 1994, which, after making a number of changes and additions, approved a final text.

Duty of reading

1.05 The advices and queries are intended for use in our meetings, for private devotion and reflection, as a challenge and inspiration to us as Friends in our personal lives and in our life as a religious community, and as a concise expression of our faith and practice readily available to enquirers and to the wider world.

Their use will vary in different meetings according to the needs of the members. Generally it will be helpful to arrange for the reading of the advices and queries in meetings for worship over a specified period, while taking care that such reading should not be carried out within too limited a time. Friends may wish to consider during the year one or more of the sections in their meetings for church affairs or to hold special meetings and discussion groups for their consideration. The only duties laid down are as follows:

Area meetings

1.06 Area meetings should consider regularly the use made of *Advices and queries* in their constituent meetings. This consideration should be undertaken annually or triennially as each area meeting determines. Local meetings should be asked to report on the use made of this document so that area meetings may be fully informed. It is hoped that out of such sharing of experience area meetings may be enabled to give advice and encouragement where necessary in order to ensure that this document is used to the best advantage.

Area meetings should also consider whether it would be helpful to arrange for the reading of sections of *Advices and queries* during their own periods of worship, and to make suitable arrangements for such reading. Some area meetings may also wish to arrange periodically for the discussion of appropriate sections.

Local meetings

1.07 Local meetings should give periodic consideration to the ways in which advices and queries can be used and they are to report to their respective area meetings annually or triennially, as directed, on the use made of them.

Chapter 2

Approaches to God – worship and prayer

Experience and nature of worship

2.01 Worship is the response of the human spirit to the presence of the divine and eternal, to the God who first seeks us. The sense of wonder and awe of the finite before the infinite leads naturally to thanksgiving and adoration.

Silent worship and the spoken word are both parts of Quaker ministry. The ministry of silence demands the faithful activity of every member in the meeting. As, together, we enter the depths of a living silence, the stillness of God, we find one another in 'the things that are eternal', upholding and strengthening one another.

1967; 1994

2.02 On one never-to-be-forgotten Sunday morning, I found myself one of a small company of silent worshippers who were content to sit down together without words, that each one might feel after and draw near to the Divine Presence, unhindered at least, if not helped, by any human utterance. Utterance I knew was free, should the words be given; and, before the meeting was over, a sentence or two were uttered in great simplicity by an old and apparently untaught man, rising in his place amongst the rest of us. I did not pay much attention to the words he spoke, and I have no recollection of their purport. My whole soul was filled with the unutterable peace of the undisturbed opportunity for communion with God, with the sense that at last I had found a place where I might, without the faintest suspicion of insincerity, join with others in simply seeking His presence. To sit down in silence could at the least pledge me to nothing; it might open to me (as it did that morning) the very gate of heaven. And, since that day, now more than seventeen years ago, Friends' meetings have indeed been to me the greatest of outward helps to a fuller and fuller entrance into the spirit from which they have sprung; the place of the most soul-subduing, faith-restoring, strengthening, and peaceful communion, in feeding upon the bread of life, that I have ever known.

Caroline E Stephen, 1890

2.03 Some Friends are able to recall with clarity the first occasion on which they attended a Quaker meeting. While I cannot remember when or where I did so, I do have a vivid recollection of the meeting which I began to attend regularly.

It was held in a rather hideous building: the meeting room was dingy. We sat on rickety chairs that creaked at the slightest movement. The whole place gave little hope that those who worshipped there might catch a glimpse of the vision of God. It was in stark contrast to the splendour of the Anglican churches to which I had been accustomed, where through dignified ritual the beauty of holiness was vividly portrayed.

However, it was in this unlikely setting that I came to know what I can only describe as the amazing fact of Quaker worship. It was in that uncomfortable room that I discovered the way to the interior side of my life, at the deep centre of which I knew that I was not alone, but was held by a love that passes all understanding. This love was mediated to me, in the first place, by those with whom I worshipped. For my journey was not solitary, but one undertaken with my friends as we moved towards each other and together travelled inwards. Yet I knew that the love that held me could not be limited to the mutual love and care we had for each other. It was a signal of transcendence that pointed beyond itself to the source of all life and love.

George Gorman, 1973

2.04 *Daniel Wheeler (1771–1840) went to St Petersburg as agricultural adviser to tsar Alexander I and helped with the draining of marshes; he later spent four years sailing the South Seas as a missionary.*

Last First Day, in our little meeting, the Master was pleased to preside, and it was indeed a 'feast of fat things'; and the language which arose in my heart was, 'Take, eat, this is my body'. I never remember being under such a covering, and my desire is, that I may never forget it; and oh! that the fear of the Lord may so prevail amongst us, as to entitle us to His Love, which can alone enable us to 'run through a troop, or leap over a wall': and which at this time enableth me to call every country my country, and every man my brother.

Daniel Wheeler, written in Ochta near Petersburg, 1818

2.05 A'r pryd y gwelo Duw yn dda roddi gair yng ngenau neb ohonynt, mae hwnnw i ddywedyd y peth y byddo yr Arglwydd wedi ei ddatguddio a'i ddysgu iddo. Felly mae ef i roddi allan yn eglurhad yr ysbryd a'i nerth, ac yn y rhinwedd a'r bywyd, fel y byddo er adeiladaeth yn yr eglwys; canys mae dyfnder yn galw ar ddyfnder, a bywyd yn cyrraedd at fywyd, a'r gynulleidfa yn cyd fyned i'r dyfroedd i yfed yn rhad. Yna os datguddir dim i'r un a fyddo yn eistedd ger llaw, mae y cyntaf i ddistewi, oblegid mae y ffrwd honno o ddawn ysbrydol yn cael ei throi ar olwyn y dyn arall; canys mae y rhyddid ysbrydol hwnnw, yn y wir eglwys, i bob un, i lefaru megis ag y cynhyrfer hwynt, gan yr Ysbryd Glân.

Ellis Pugh, *c.*1700

An English translation 'from the British tongue' was published in 1732:

And when God sees meet to put a Word into the mouth of any one of them, he is to speak what the Lord hath revealed and taught him (I Cor 2:4). So is he to give it forth in demonstration and power, and in the virtue and life of the Spirit, that it may be to edification in the church; for deep calleth unto deep, and life reacheth unto life, and the congregation go together to the waters to drink freely (Ps 42:7). And if anything be revealed to one that sits by, when the first is silent, that stream of the spiritual gift is turned to the other, because that spiritual liberty is in the true church, for every one to speak as they are moved by the Holy Spirit.

2.06 The treasure I had found [in meeting for worship] seemed startlingly simple, and I held this treasure quietly to myself, exploring its significance, feeling it almost too good to be true. Part of its simplicity was that I and others were to start just where we were at the moment and proceed at our own pace from there. How blessed that there were no restraints of belief. The promptings of love and truth were the starting places and we could move at our own pace to recognise them as the leadings of God – the beyond which drew me and others on from our limitations and despairs and smallnesses.

Ruth Fawell, 1987

2.07 Worship is essentially an act of adoration, adoration of the one true God in whom we live and move and have our being. Forgetting our little selves, our petty ambitions, our puny triumphs, our foolish cares and fretful anxieties, we reach out towards the beauty and majesty of God. The religious life is not a dull, grim drive towards moral virtues, but a response to a vision of greatness.

Thomas F Green, 1952

2.08 To me, worship is recognising and communing with the divine, whether it is within myself, in others, or in the world. The pre-condition of worship is my belief in worth-ship, my own and that of other people.

A member of the Quaker Women's Group, 1986

2.09 All true worship is inspired by God. The place of worship is the place of dependence, the place of wonder and of power, the place of fellowship and of communion... Worship links us to God and implies faith in a God who is in some sense personal. Personality is the highest category we know and we cannot worship a Being who is less than the highest of which we conceive... Thus the act of worship presupposes on our part a sense of dependence on God and the acknowledgment of our need of him, and this means that the element of adoration and thanksgiving should always be present in worship. Worship in Christian experience is our response to the God of Love.

Robert Davis, 1933

2.10 *Thomas Kelly (1893–1941) was a scientist from Ohio who taught philosophy at Earlham and Haverford colleges. Towards the end of his life he had vivid experiences of the love of God, of which he spoke and wrote, in his* Testament of devotion.

In this humanistic age we suppose man is the initiator and God is the responder. But the living Christ within us is the initiator and we are the responders. God the Lover, the accuser, the revealer of light and darkness presses within us. 'Behold, I stand at the door and knock.' And all our apparent initiative is already a response, a testimonial to His secret presence and working within us. The basic response of the soul to the Light is internal adoration and joy, thanksgiving and worship, self-surrender and listening.

Thomas R Kelly, 1941

2.11 True worship may be experienced at any time; in any place – alone on the hills or in the busy daily life – we may find God, in whom we live and move and have our being. But this individual experience is not sufficient, and in a meeting held in the Spirit there is a giving and receiving between its members, one helping another with or without words. So there may come a wider vision and a deeper experience.

1925; 1994

Silent waiting

2.12 In silence which is active, the Inner Light begins to glow – a tiny spark. For the flame to be kindled and to grow, subtle argument and the clamour of our emotions must be stilled. It is by an attention full of love that we enable the Inner Light to blaze and illuminate our dwelling and to make of our whole being a source from which this Light may shine out.

Words must be purified in a redemptive silence if they are to bear the message of peace. The right to speak is a call to the duty of listening. Speech has no meaning unless there are attentive minds and silent hearts. Silence is the welcoming acceptance of the other. The word born of silence must be received in silence.

Pierre Lacout, 1969

2.13 True silence ... is to the spirit what sleep is to the body, nourishment and refreshment.

William Penn, 1699

2.14 We highly prize silent waiting upon the Lord in humble dependence upon him. We esteem it to be a precious part of spiritual worship, and trust that no vocal offering will ever exclude it from its true place in our religious meetings. Let not the silence ... be spent in indolent or vacant musing but in patient waiting in humble prayerful expectancy before the Lord.

Yearly Meeting in London, 1884; 1886

2.15 I know of no other way, in these deeper depths, of trusting in the name of the Lord, and staying upon God, than sinking into silence and nothingness before Him... So long as the enemy can keep us reasoning he can buffet us to and fro; but into the true solemn silence of the soul before God he cannot follow us.

John Bellows, 1895

2.16 [The early Friends] made the discovery that silence is one of the best preparations for communion [with God] and for the reception of inspiration and guidance. Silence itself, of course, has no magic. It may be just sheer emptiness, absence of words or noise or music. It may be an occasion for slumber, or it may be a dead form. But it may be an intensified pause, a vitalised hush, a creative quiet, an actual moment of mutual and reciprocal correspondence with God.

Rufus Jones, 1937

2.17 Meeting is the chance to escape from the trivial thoughts of everyday living, and to find answers from yourself or from God. Some people are scared of the silence. Without the noise that serves to reassure us, that blocks out thoughts we'd rather not have, we're vulnerable and find it's time to face ourselves. We can never hide from God, but it's easy to minimise the effect he has on our lives – except in the silence where he can be heard. Don't feel restricted by the silence, it is there to set you free from the pressures of life. No-one is judging your movements, your thoughts... Freedom of expression is the freedom to worship God on your own terms. Value the opportunity to think unguided by the world. Learn what you feel you need to know, let other information pass. No moment of silence is a waste of time.

Rachel Needham, 1987

Prayer

2.18 Be still and cool in thy own mind and spirit from thy own thoughts, and then thou wilt feel the principle of God to turn thy mind to the Lord God, whereby thou wilt receive his strength and power from whence life comes, to allay all tempests, against blusterings and storms. That is it which moulds up into patience, into innocency, into soberness, into stillness, into stayedness, into quietness, up to God, with his power.

George Fox, 1658

2.19 *William Leddra of Barbados on the day before he was martyred in 1661 wrote:*

As the flowing of the ocean doth fill every creek and branch thereof, and then retires again towards its own being and fulness, and leaves a savour behind it; so doth the life and virtue of God flow into every one of your hearts, whom he hath made partakers of his divine nature; and when it withdraws but a little, it leaves a sweet savour behind it; that many can say they are made clean through the word that he hath spoken to them. In which innocent condition you may see what you are in the presence of God, and what you are without him... Stand still, and cease from thine own working, and in due time thou shalt enter into the rest, and thy eyes shall behold his salvation, whose testimonies are sure, and righteous altogether.

2.20 Do you make a place in your daily life for reading, meditation, and waiting upon God in prayer, that you may know more of the presence and guidance of the Holy Spirit? Do you remember the need to pray for others, holding them in the presence of God?

Queries, 1964

2.21 I read that I was supposed to make 'a place for inward retirement and waiting upon God' in my daily life, as the *Queries* in those days expressed it... At last I began to realise, first that I needed some kind of inner peace, or inward retirement, or whatever name it might be called by; and then that these apparently stuffy old Friends were really talking sense. If I studied what they were trying to tell me, I might possibly find that the 'place of inward retirement' was not a place I had to go to, it was there all the time. I could know the 'place of inward retirement' wherever I was, or whatever I was doing, and find the spiritual refreshment for which, knowingly or unknowingly, I was longing, and hear the voice of God in my heart. Thus I began to realise that prayer was not a formality, or an obligation, it was a *place* which was there all the time and always available.

Elfrida Vipont Foulds, 1983

2.22 How, then, shall we lay hold of that Life and Power, and live the life of prayer without ceasing? By quiet, persistent practice in turning all our being, day and night, in prayer and inward worship and surrender, towards Him who calls in the deeps of our souls. Mental habits of inward orientation must be established. An inner, secret turning to God can be made fairly steady, after weeks and months and years of practice and lapses and failures and returns. It is as simple an art as Brother Lawrence found it, but it may be long before we achieve any steadiness in the process. Begin now, as you read these words, as you sit in your chair, to offer your whole selves, utterly and in joyful abandon, in quiet, glad surrender to Him who is within. In secret ejaculations of praise, turn in humble wonder to the Light, faint though it may be. Keep contact with the outer world of sense and meanings. Here is no discipline in absent-mindedness. Walk and talk and work and laugh with your friends. But behind the scenes keep up the life of simple prayer and inward worship. Keep it up throughout the day. Let inward prayer be your last act before you fall asleep and the first act when you awake. And in time you will find, as did Brother Lawrence, that 'those who have the gale of the Holy Spirit go forward even in sleep'.

Thomas R Kelly, 1941

2.23 Prayer is experienced as deeper than words or busy thoughts. 'Be still and cool in thy own mind and spirit from thy own thoughts', said Fox. It is marked by a kind of relaxed readiness, a 'letting-go' of the problems and perplexities with which the mind is occupied, and a waiting in 'love and truth': the truth about oneself, the truth about the world, deeper than the half-truths we see when we are busy in it about our own planning and scheming, the love in which we are held when we think of others more deeply than our ordinary relations with them, the love that at root holds us to the world. Prayer is not words or acts, but reaching down to love: holding our fellows in love, offering ourselves in love; and being held by, being caught up in love. It is communion, an opening of the door, an entry from the beyond. This is the point where secular language fails, for this cannot be spoken about at all: it can only be known.

Harold Loukes, 1967

2.24 Consider now the prayer-life of Jesus. It comes out most clearly in the record of St Luke, who leaves us with the impression that prayer was the most vital element in our Lord's life. He rises a great while before day that he may have some hours alone with His Father. He continues all night in prayer to God. Incident after incident is introduced by the statement that Jesus was praying. Are we so much nearer God that we can afford to dispense with that which to Him was of such vital moment? But apart from this, it seems to me that this prayer-habit of Jesus throws light upon the *purpose* of prayer.

I think of those long hours alone with God. Quite obviously *petition* can have had a very small place in our Lord's thoughts. We cannot suppose that He whose chief desire was that God's will should be done in all things could have been incessantly asking, asking. There must have been a sacred interchange far deeper than this. Especially are we sure that He was not praying for material blessings to be enjoyed by Himself alone. On the only occasion recorded in which He asked (in perfect submission) something for Himself, at Gethsemane, His request was not granted.

My own belief is that outward circumstances are not often (I will not say *never*) directly altered as a result of prayer. That is to say, God is not always interfering with the working of the natural order. But indirectly by the working of mind upon mind great changes may be wrought. We live and move and have our being in God; we are bound up in the bundle of life in Him, and it is reasonable to believe that prayer may often find its answer, even in outward things, by the reaction of mind upon mind. Prayer is not given us to make life easy for us, or to coddle us, but to make us strong ... to make us masters of circumstance and not its slaves. We pray, not to change God's will, but to bring our wills into correspondence with His.

William Littleboy, 1937

2.25 Prayer is not an occasional nod
Given in passing to God.
It's more like marriage – a closeness of living,
A constant receiving and giving.

Louie Horne, 1987

2.26 Prayer, we learn gradually, has far more to do with listening than with talking. In emotional stress the thoughts are so obsessive that they leave one no opportunity to listen. So, when we know someone is in trouble, we can and must listen (pray) for them. A Friend who had missed meeting for several weeks told us that she knew we had been praying for her before we said so; she had felt it and been sustained by it. She had thought there was no point in prayer or belief in God, but she had been helped by the knowledge that we still prayed and believed. It seems that one can do no less than this. We are seldom given guarantees that it is effective, just hints along the way; but they are hints we cannot ignore. We cannot prove the effectiveness of prayer, but nor can we cast scorn on examples of the kind I have given.

A friend tells me that when she prays for someone she does not so much pray *to* God for them as *for* God for them. This seems to me a vital clue about prayer. It is God that the troubled person needs, not our advice and instructions. As we learn more about worship we learn to listen more deeply so that we can be channels through which God's love reaches the other person. It is God at work, not we ourselves; we are simply used.

Diana Lampen, 1979

2.27 Prayer is an act of sharing with God, the Spirit, and not an attempt to prompt God to action. It is a promise that I will do my best, even if what I am able to do seems too insignificant to be worthwhile. When I pray for peace, and that the hearts of those in authority may be changed, it is a promise that I shall do such things as write to those in power, share in vigils, and above all lead my own life, as far as possible, in such a manner as to take away the occasion for strife between individuals and between peoples. When I pray for others who are in need, it is a promise to make my own contribution, perhaps by writing, by visiting, by a gift, by telling someone whom I know could help. When I pray for forgiveness, for strength and courage, I try to open my heart, making it possible for me humbly to receive.

'Anna', 1984

2.28 There is little point in praying to be enabled to overcome some temptation, and then putting oneself in the very position in which the temptation can exert all its fascination. There is little point in praying that the sorrowing may be comforted and the lonely cheered, unless we ourselves set out to bring comfort and cheer to the sad and neglected in our own surroundings. There is little point in praying for our home and for our loved ones, and in going on being as selfish and inconsiderate as we have been. Prayer would be an evil rather than a blessing if it were only a way of getting God to do what we ourselves will not make the effort to do. God does not do things for us – he enables us to do them for ourselves.

Elisabeth Holmgaard, 1984

2.29 The sick and those caring for them have need of our prayers. But let us not imagine ... that a few sentimental good wishes from a distance are all that is needed. Whenever we intercede in prayer we must be prepared for an answer which places a practical obligation upon us. A prayer is always a commitment.

Thomas F Green, 1952

2.30 A silent pause before meals is the Friends' equivalent for 'saying grace' – a practice which I own I think has much to recommend it. Here again there is, of course, the opportunity for words, should words spontaneously arise to the lips of any of those present.

Caroline E Stephen, 1890

2.31 Do not let us be discouraged because we find the path of silent prayer difficult or because we do not experience that joy of conscious communion which is given to some. The sunlight shines through the cloud; even when the cloud is so thick that we cannot see the sun at all, its rays carry on their healing work, and it does us good to go out into the open, even on a grey day. The experience of many of the greatest saints points to the traversing of a dark night of the soul before the light of full communion dawns, and to times of dryness of spirit coming at intervals to test the faith and perseverance of the seeker.

T Edmund Harvey, 1929

2.32 There is no use trying to conceal how difficult it is to find time for private prayer in the congested schedules under which most modern people live. But at the bottom it is not a question of finding time ... [but] of the depth of the sense of need and of the desire. Busy lovers find time to write letters to one another, often ... long letters; although what really matters is not the length of the letter any more than it is the length of the prayer. In this life we find the time for what we believe to be important.

Douglas Steere, 1938

2.33 Prayer is not just a matter of the feelings, but of the will. When we least feel like praying and when prayer seems pointless because there appears to be no-one to accept it – when God indeed seems absent, then is the time to call our will into action and refuse to give up. There will be occasions when our desert will seem only dry and barren. But refreshment is not far away, and we must persevere, holding on to the promise that the parched ground shall become a pool and the thirsty land springs of water.

Jack Dobbs, 1984

2.34 Prayer, then, is *communion*, whether it takes the form of petition, intercession, thanksgiving, or whether it be just the quiet unveiling of the heart to a trusted friend, the outpouring of the soul to the one who is nearest of all.

William Littleboy, 1937

See also 20.01–20.14

Meeting for worship

2.35 Friends, meet together and know one another in that which is eternal, which was before the world was.

George Fox, 1657

2.36 In worship we have our neighbours to right and left, before and behind, yet the Eternal Presence is over all and beneath all. Worship does not consist in achieving a mental state of concentrated isolation from one's fellows. But in the depth of common worship it is as if we found our separate lives were all one life, within whom we live and move and have our being.

Thomas R Kelly, 1938

2.37 Friends have never regarded [worship] as an individual activity. People who regard Friends' meetings as opportunities for meditation have failed to appreciate this corporate aspect. The waiting and listening are activities in which everybody is engaged and produce spoken ministry which helps to articulate the common guidance which the Holy Spirit is believed to give the group as a whole. So the waiting and listening is corporate also. This is why Friends emphasise the 'ministry of silence' and the importance of coming to meeting regularly and with heart and mind prepared.

John Punshon, 1987

2.38 In a gathered meeting there may be few spoken words, but there is rich ministry. An hour passes quickly. Other meetings are lifeless. They may be full of words, but there is little ministry, little that is of service. Time drags and people feel the need to fill the silence.

A gathered meeting has the strength to absorb the differences and support the needs of those who attend it; this is easier when the meeting is a community of people who know and trust each other, who are not afraid to share their experience of worship and to learn from one another.

Conference: *Exploring the fundamental elements of Quakerism*, 1986

2.39 A Friends' meeting, however silent, is at the very lowest a witness that worship is something other and deeper than words, and that it is to the unseen and eternal things that we desire to give the first place in our lives. And when the meeting, whether silent or not, is awake, and looking upwards, there is much more in it than this. In the united stillness of a truly 'gathered' meeting there is a power known only by experience, and mysterious even when most familiar. There are perhaps few things which more readily flow 'from vessel to vessel' than quietness. The presence of fellow-worshippers in some gently penetrating manner reveals to the spirit something of the nearness of the Divine Presence. 'Where two or three are gathered together in His name' have we not again and again felt that the promise was fulfilled and that the Master Himself was indeed 'in the midst of us'? And it is out of the depths of this stillness that there do arise at times spoken words which, springing from the very source of prayer, have something of the power of prayer – something of its quickening and melting and purifying effect. Such words as these have at least as much power as silence to gather into stillness.

Caroline E Stephen, 1908

2.40 What is the ground and foundation of the gathered meeting? In the last analysis, it is, I am convinced, the Real Presence of God.

Thomas R Kelly, 1940

The individual in meeting

2.41 The first that enters into the place of your meeting ... turn in thy mind to the light, and wait upon God singly, as if none were present but the Lord; and here thou art strong. Then the next that comes in, let them in simplicity of heart sit down and turn in to the same light, and wait in the spirit; and so all the rest coming in, in the fear of the Lord, sit down in pure stillness and silence of all flesh, and wait in the light... Those who are brought to a pure still waiting upon God in the spirit, are come nearer to the Lord than words are; for God is a spirit, and in the spirit is he worshipped... In such a meeting there will be an unwillingness to part asunder, being ready to say in yourselves, it is good to be here: and this is the end of all words and writings to bring people to the eternal living Word.

Alexander Parker, 1660

2.42 Come with heart and mind prepared. Pray silently as you gather together that you may all be drawn into the spirit of adoration and communion in which fellowship with one another becomes real. Yield yourselves and all your outward concerns to God's guidance, that you may find the evil weakening in you and the good raised up.

Advices, 1964

2.43 'Where two or three', saith our Lord, 'are gathered together in my name, there am I in the midst of them' (Mt 18:20). In these words he ... invites us not only to meet one with another but, in so doing, with himself also... Shall the poor perishing gratifications of sense and self-love, or any inconveniences of a trivial nature, be suffered to prevent our dutiful attendance upon him, in whom alone stands our everlasting interest? Shall a cloudy sky, a little wet, a little cold, a little ease to the flesh, a view to a little earthly gain, or any common incident, furnish an excuse for declining this duty, and thereby depriving ourselves of the blessed advantage, often vouchsafed to the faithful, of enjoying heavenly communion together in spirit with the Lord of life and glory?

Yearly Meeting in London, 1765

2.44 There are times of dryness in our individual lives, when meeting may seem difficult or even worthless. At such times one may be tempted not to go to meeting, but it may be better to go, prepared to offer as our contribution to the worship simply a sense of need. In such a meeting one may not at the time realise what one has gained, but one will nevertheless come away helped.

Berks & Oxon QM Ministry & Extension Committee, 1948

2.45 It is the individual faithfulness of each Friend which is needed if our meetings for worship are to be held to the glory of God. Each one of us must come expecting not only to receive but to be used. This involves a preparation of spirit, but many interpret the phrase 'Come with heart and mind prepared' too narrowly. The preparation needed is the living of our daily lives in constant awareness of the presence of God. In the rush of living we may miss the true Life. We must face realities, however, and try to overcome the practical difficulties which we do encounter. Our lives are sometimes inevitably rushed. This means that we may come to meetings for worship in turmoil or trouble. We may be tired, irritable or sleepy. We should not in such cases turn away from the meeting for worship, but should realise the value of such occasions as training times.

Important though our part of preparation, dedication and faithfulness is, we have always to remember that our part is dependent upon that power which comes to us, unlooked-for and undeserved, the power of the grace of God.

Berks & Oxon QM Ministry & Extension Committee, 1947

2.46 Regular attendance at your own meeting, leading to a deeper knowledge of the members and their needs, will contribute to the quality of its corporate life. We recognise and encourage concerned visitation of other meetings and opportunities of worship with those of other communions, but continued casual or undisciplined attendance sometimes at one place of worship and sometimes at another is a source of weakness both to the individual and to the meeting.

1959; 1994

See also 13.21–13.32 Travelling in the ministry and intervisitation

2.47 Does punctuality matter? It is not merely a question of disturbing the peace and quiet of those already assembled... What is on my mind is more than that. If we were coming together to worship individually, each to enter into his or her own private meditation, then it wouldn't much matter whether all arrived by the appointed time. In private meditation the worshippers could each 'settle' separately, training themselves not to be disturbed by latecomers. But if our goal is to achieve a group mystical experience, deepening and enriching our individual experience, then, it seems to me, we need to start the process at the same time.

A 'gathered' Quaker meeting is something more than a number of individuals sitting down together but meditating individually. So long as each sits in meditation in the way one does when worshipping by oneself, the worship will seldom reach that greater depth which a Quaker meeting at its best achieves. The goal of a truly 'gathered' meeting is to become fused into something bigger than the sum of the parts...

As a meeting 'gathers', as each individual 'centres down', there gradually develops a feeling of belonging to a group who are together seeking a sense of the Presence. The 'I' in us begins to feel like 'we'. At some point – it may be early in the meeting or it may be later, or it may never occur at all – we suddenly feel a sense of unity, a sense of togetherness with one another and with that something outside ourselves that we call God.

Thomas R Bodine, 1980

2.48 Heed not distressing thoughts when they rise ever so strongly in thee; fear them not, but be still awhile, not believing in the power which thou feelest they have over thee, and it will fall on a sudden. It is good for thy spirit and greatly to thy advantage to be much and variously exercised by the Lord. Thou dost not know what the Lord hath already done and what he is yet doing for thee therein.

Isaac Penington

2.49 The mind wanders and the will falters again and again... But it is foolish to allow failures in concentration to plunge us into profitless self-condemnation. A mother does not condemn her child who is struggling with many a failure to learn how to walk, but rather she is pleased by each successful effort... I like to believe that God is similarly pleased with our efforts and understanding of our many failures. What matters is whether or not the will, like a compass needle when deflected, is so pivoted that it can swing back to the true direction.

St Francis de Sales is reassuring:

> When your heart is wandering and distracted, bring it back quickly to its point, restore it tenderly to its Master's side, and if you did nothing else the whole of your hour but bring back your heart patiently and put it near our Lord again, and every time you put it back it turned away again, your hour would be well-employed.

Thomas F Green, 1952

2.50 At meeting for worship relax and let your baby be with you; my small daughter called it 'the best cuddle of the week' when I couldn't rush off and do something busy. It's not easy for the parents to believe that their child's gurglings actually help the meeting rather than interrupt it. Nonetheless, that is true, and you shouldn't give way to the temptation to take a happily babbling child out of the meeting (though howling is something different!).

Anne Hosking, 1986

2.51 When meeting for worship begins, I like to look around and see who is there, and this normally leads to a feeling of gratitude for the friendship, warmth, and support I've found among Friends. If I know of any difficulties or problems being experienced by anyone present, I would think along these lines. Or perhaps I would think of someone missing from their usual seat, and this might lead me to think of others who were ill, bereaved, anxious or overworked. I might then reflect on my own many and great blessings, and seek direction in using my time and talents. Or I might see someone unemployed, and be led to think of some of our social problems. It's a sort of chain reaction.

Dorothy Marshall, 1987

2.52 When I sit down in meeting I recall whatever may have struck me freshly during the past week. This is in part, initially at least, a voluntary and outward act… It means that the will is given up to service; and it is quite possible to stop everything by taking an opposite attitude. So thoughts suggest themselves – a text that has smitten one during the week – new light on a phrase – a verse of poetry – some incident, private or public. These pass before the door whence shines the heavenly light. Are they transfigured? Sometimes, yes; sometimes, no. If nothing flames, silence is my portion.

John William Graham, 1920

2.53 A score of years ago a friend placed in my hand a little book which became one of the turning points of my life. It was called *True peace*... It had but one thought ... that God was waiting in the depths of my being to talk to me if only I would get still enough to hear his voice.

I thought this would be a very easy matter, and so I began to get still. But I had no sooner commenced than a perfect pandemonium of voices reached my ears, a thousand clamouring notes from without and within, until I could hear nothing but their noise and din. Some of them were my own voice, some were my own questions, some of them were my very prayers. Others were the suggestions of the tempter, and the voices of the world's turmoil. Never before did there seem so many things to be done, to be said, to be thought; and in every direction I was pushed and pulled, and greeted with noisy acclamations of unspeakable unrest. It seemed necessary for me to listen to some of them, and to answer some of them, but God said, 'Be still, and know that I am God'. Then came the conflict of thoughts for the morrow, and its duties and cares; but God said 'Be still'. And as I listened, and slowly learned to obey, and shut my ears to every sound, I found, after a while, that when the other voices ceased, or I ceased to hear them, there was a still, small voice in the depths of my being that began to speak with an inexpressible tenderness, power and comfort.

John Edward Southall, *c.*1900

2.54 As I silence myself I become more sensitive to the sounds around me, and I do not block them out. The songs of the birds, the rustle of the wind, children in the playground, the roar of an airplane overhead are all taken into my worship. I regulate my breathing as taught me by my Zen friends, and through this exercise I feel the flow of life within me from my toes right through my whole body. I think of myself like the tree planted by the 'rivers of water' in Psalm 1, sucking up God's gift of life and being restored. Sometimes I come to meeting for worship tired and weary, and I hear the words of Jesus, 'Come unto me, all that labour and are weary, and I will give you rest'. And having laid down my burden, I feel refreshed both physically and spiritually. This leads me on to whole-hearted adoration and thanksgiving for all God's blessings. My own name, Tayeko, means 'child of many blessings' and God has surely poured them upon me. My heart overflows with a desire to give him something in return. I have nothing to give but my own being, and I offer him my thoughts, words and actions of each day, and whisper 'Please take me as I am'.

Tayeko Yamanouchi, 1979

Vocal ministry

2.55 Remember that to every one is given a share of responsibility for the meeting for worship, whether that service be in silence or through the spoken word. Do not assume that vocal ministry is never to be your part. If the call to speak comes, do not let the sense of your own unworthiness, or the fear of being unable to find the right words, prevent you from being obedient to the leading of the Spirit. Ask wisdom of God that you may be sure of your guidance and be enabled humbly to discern and impart something of his glory and truth. Pray that your ministry may rise from the place of deep experience, and that you may be restrained from unnecessary and superficial words. Faithfulness and sincerity in speaking, even very briefly, may open the way to fuller ministry from others. Try to speak audibly and distinctly, with sensitivity to the needs of your fellow worshippers. Wait to be sure of the right moment for giving the message. Beware of making additions towards the end of a meeting when it was well left before.

Advices, 1964

2.56 Jane Fenn, a young woman who migrated to Philadelphia in 1712 and became in time a travelling

Quaker minister of note, describes sitting in meeting one day and hearing an inner voice declare that she had been chosen for the ministry:

> Yet I must confess, this awful word of Divine command shocked me exceedingly, my soul and all within me trembled at the hearing of it; yea my outward tabernacle shook insomuch that many present observed the deep exercise I was under. I cried in spirit, 'Lord I am weak and altogether incapable of such a task, I hope thou wilt spare me from such a mortification; besides I have spoken much against women appearing in that manner.'

For six or seven months, Jane Fenn continued to resist the command to speak in meeting, until she could withstand the pressure no longer. She stood up to utter a few broken words and returned home rejoicing. Nevertheless, for many years thereafter, she continued to struggle with her own sense of inadequacy when confronted with the growing demands of the Spirit that she not only preach to local meetings, but also travel through the colonies and eventually back to England.

Margaret Hope Bacon, 1986

2.57 I went to meetings in an awful frame of mind, and endeavoured to be inwardly acquainted with the language of the true Shepherd. And one day, being under a strong exercise of spirit, I stood up, and said some words in a meeting, but not keeping close to the divine opening, I said more than was required of me and being soon sensible to my error, I was afflicted in mind some weeks, without any light or comfort, even to that degree that I could take satisfaction in nothing. I remembered God and was troubled, and in the depth of my distress he had pity upon me, and sent the Comforter. I then felt forgiveness for my offence, and my mind became calm and quiet, being truly thankful to my gracious Redeemer for his mercies. And after this, feeling the spring of divine love opened, and a concern to speak, I said a few words in a meeting in which I found peace. This I believe was about six weeks from the first time, and as I was thus humbled and disciplined under the cross, my understanding became more strengthened to distinguish the language of the pure spirit which inwardly moves upon the heart, and taught me to wait in silence sometimes many weeks together, until I felt that rise which prepares the creature to stand like a trumpet, through which the Lord speaks to his flock.

John Woolman, 1741

2.58 For some weeks before this particular Sunday I had been puzzling over and questioning in my mind various problems connected with my work. It was one of those episodes of spiritual upheaval which most of us go through from time to time when we seem to question our normal certainties, poke around the foundations of our normal life and discover to our alarm that some of them are very shaky. I had been in this highly charged state for several weeks.

On this Sunday morning though, I went quietly to meeting with the family, my recent preoccupations submerged by the business of getting us all dressed and breakfasted and to the meeting house on time. But as the minutes ticked by and I sat in the healing peace, I began to be aware that something inside me was formulating a question which urgently needed to be asked. I say 'something inside me' because it seemed at the same time to be both me and not me. I discovered to my horror that this something was urging me to get up and ask my question. My heart was pounding uncomfortably and I began to shiver (I don't know whether this was obvious to those around me; I was certainly aware of this shivering but shyness prevents one from asking afterwards whether these physical symptoms are visible to others). To start with I resisted this prompting. I looked round the room and noticed several Friends before whom I was reluctant to make a fool of myself. I could not get up and speak in front of them. I would rather die first. The shaking and pounding diminished a little as I decided this. But not for long. Soon it started up again, insistent, not to be denied. This time I told myself 'I'll count twenty and then if no one else has spoken I shall have to.' Again a slight abatement of the symptoms. But to no avail. I counted twenty and then fifty and still no one spoke. Now I sat conscious only of this overpowering force which was pushing me to my feet until finally I had to give in to it.

Afterwards I found it difficult to believe that I had spoken. It was all over so quickly. Had I really stood up in front of all those people and testified? Well, hardly testified, but yes, I had been driven by some inner prompting which, for want of a more precise word, one might well call spirit; and yes, I had quaked, most fearfully, with something which was more than just the fear of making a fool of myself before family and friends.

Elisabeth Salisbury, 1968

2.59 Some think, through a mistaken judgment, that they must be doing something every meeting, (like the preachers of the letter, who must either be singing, preaching or praying all the time) and by such a conduct they lose their interest and place in the hearts of friends by too long and too frequent appearing in both preaching and prayer: For the avoiding of which, keep close to thy gift, intently waiting to know thy place, both when to speak and when to be silent; and when thou speakest, begin under a sense of divine influence, whether it be in preaching or praying; and without it, do not either preach or pray.

Samuel Bownas, 1750

2.60 All true ministry springs from the reality of experience, and uses our gifts of heart and mind in its expression. But ministry is not the place for intellectual exercise. It comes through us, not from us. Although we interpret the Spirit it is that Spirit which will lead us to minister. The Spirit will decide which experiences are relevant and which will speak to the condition of the meeting. If you have to decide whether it is right to speak, consider that it isn't. If your words are important the meeting will find them anyway.

Conference: *Exploring the fundamental elements of Quakerism*, 1986

2.61 Ministry should be of necessity, and not of choice, and there is no living by silence, or by preaching merely.

John Churchman, 1734

2.62 In Friends' meetings also, from the fact that everyone is free to speak, one hears harmonies and correspondences between very various utterances such as are scarcely to be met elsewhere. It is sometimes as part-singing compared with unison. The free admission of the ministry of women, of course, greatly enriches this harmony. I have often wondered whether some of the motherly counsels I have listened to in our meeting would not reach some hearts that might be closed to the masculine preacher.

Caroline E Stephen, 1890

2.63 When language is used unthinkingly, without being related to the experience of either the speaker or the listener, it is meaningless. Words are only symbols and when there is no shared experience the symbolism breaks down. When we speak of our own experience, our feelings are always involved. The same is true when we listen to others: we may read into their words meanings which are not intended but which reflect our own emotions. Certain words or kinds of language may arouse such strong emotions that we are only able to relate them to our own experience and not to that of the speaker. Speakers too may be unaware of the effect of their words. The more important and profound the subject matter, the greater the need for sensitivity in choosing our words. This is no excuse for playing safe in what we say, or for not listening to others when what they say makes us uncomfortable.

Conference: *Exploring the fundamental elements of Quakerism*, 1986

2.64 Each Friend who feels called upon to rise and deliver a lengthy discourse might question himself – and herself – most searchingly, as to whether the message could not be more lastingly given in the fewest possible words, or even through his or her personality alone, in entire and trustful silence. 'Cream must always rise to the surface.' True. But other substances rise to the surface besides cream; substances that may have to be skimmed off and thrown away before bodies and souls can be duly nourished. 'Is my message cream or scum?' may be an unusual and is certainly a very homely query. Still it is one that every speaker, in a crowded gathering especially, should honestly face. Some of the dangers of silent worship can best be guarded against by its courtesies.

Violet Holdsworth, 1919

2.65 *In the Life*

My piece was pat and all ready to say,
She rose first. I threw my piece away.
    My well-turned stuff
    Was not so rough
As hers, but easy elegant and smooth.
    Beginning middle end
    It had and point
And aptly quoted prophet priest and poet.
    Hers was uncouth
    Wanting in art
Laboured scarce-audible and out of joint.
    Three times she lost the thread
And sitting left her message half unsaid.

'Why then did thee throw it
Into the discard?'
        Friend,
It had head
(Like this). Hers oh had heart.

Robert Hewison, 1965

2.66 Ministry is what is on one's soul, and it can be in direct contradiction to what is on one's mind. It's what the Inner Light gently pushes you toward or suddenly dumps in your lap. It is rooted in the eternity, divinity, and selflessness of the Inner Light; not in the worldly, egoistic functions of the conscious mind.

Marrianne McMullen, 1987

2.67 To some are granted deeper spiritual discoveries and revelations than to others, but to all, waiting in expectancy, at moments and in some measure is given a sense of the living touch of God. At such moments there may come the kindling of mind and heart which impels obedience to speak under the immediate promptings of the Holy Spirit. This is the ministry of inspiration, the prophetic ministry in the true sense, when the spoken word pierces to the heart of our relationship with God, unveils the living presence of Christ in the midst of the worshipping group and in its separate members, opens to our sight the way we must tread if we would realise that Spirit in and through our ordinary daily activities and find the creative response to the challenges of our time. In ministry of this character and depth something is given in the utterance which is beyond the intellectual and emotional capacity of the human being speaking, but which uses and enhances and transcends the natural gifts, the acquired knowledge, the hard and honest thoughts or the reaches of the speaker's imagination.

There is also the ministry of teaching which combines 'the potency of prayer and thought'. It recalls the meeting to the discoveries of truth, the perception of the acts of God in the lives of individuals. It includes the effort to understand and to interpret the central fact of Jesus Christ and his place in history, and the searchings and findings of men and women down the ages and in our own day as they have sought to relate new discoveries and insights to their understandings of eternal truth.

1967; 1994

2.68 In my young tempestuous days I heard many things in the Friends' meeting that I disliked and some that seemed to me quite false, and I felt the need to answer them. I was taught, and I believe correctly, that to insist on answering there and then would be to destroy the meeting; and that we all sit under the baptising power of the spirit of Truth, which is its own witness. We sit in silence so as not to trip over words; and we trust the good in each other which is from God, so that we may be kept from the evil.

J Ormerod Greenwood, 1980

2.69 A Friends' meeting for worship finds no room for debate or for answering (still less for contradicting) one another; if this is desirable, it will be left for another occasion. And if anything should seem to be spoken amiss, the spiritually minded worshipper will have the wit to get at the heart of the message, overlooking crudity and lack of skill in its presentation, and so far from giving way to irritation at what seems unprofitable, he will be deeply concerned for his own share in creating the right spiritual atmosphere in which the harm fades out and the good grows. Many a meeting has known this power, transforming what might have been hurtful into a means of grace.

A Neave Brayshaw, 1921

2.70 I think that learning to move in the exercise of the meeting, so that one is a part of it, yet taken beyond it and brought to see some new light as a result of it, is most important in creative ministry. The cluster of messages, with a fair interval of silence between each of them to let its message sink in; the cluster that goes on down, with each message deepening and intensifying and helping to light up a further facet of the communication, can be most effective. But for this to happen those sharing in it cannot be in a discussional frame of mind or in a debating stance, or yield to the ruthlessly critical mind, or all is lost and the meeting is pulled into a forum. It can only be done if there is a willingness to be led by each of the ones ministering into a deeper level of what they were not only saying but what they were meaning to say, and perhaps even beyond into what something beneath us all was meaning to have said through what we were saying... When a cluster ministry moves in this way, we all know that we are moving in the life, that we are breaking the cerebral barrier and being released ... and we are ourselves ignited by what is taking place.

Douglas Steere, 1972

2.71 It should be the care of elders to foster the spiritual life of all members and to give caution and advice to Friends who share in the vocal ministry. They should look out for Friends who may be likely to help the ministry and lead them to make their right contribution to the life of their meeting, and to encourage our members to think deeply on the great issues and problems of life and the fundamentals of our faith.

This, however, is not the duty of elders alone; as any Friends may hinder the work of the ministry by a critical or unloving spirit, so their sympathy and prayers for those who speak will help to create an atmosphere in which an inspired and inspiring ministry may grow. A friendly word of thankfulness from one who has been helped is often a great source of encouragement to the minister.

1925; 1959

For more about eldership see chapter 12 Caring for one another

2.72 He had an extraordinary gift in opening the Scriptures. He would go to the marrow of things and show the mind, harmony and fulfilling of them with much plainness and to great comfort and edification... But above all he excelled in prayer. The inwardness and weight of his spirit, the reverence and solemnity of his address and behaviour, and the fewness and fullness of his words have often struck even strangers with admiration, as they used to reach others with consolation. The most awful, living, reverent frame I ever felt or beheld, I must say, was his in prayer. And truly it was a testimony that he knew and lived nearer to the Lord than other men; for they that know him most will see most reason to approach him with reverence and fear.

William Penn writing of George Fox, 1694

2.73 The intent of all speaking is to bring into the life, and to walk in, and to possess the same, and to live in and enjoy it, and to feel God's presence.

George Fox, 1657

Children in meeting

2.74 Children have an uncanny knack of knowing the difference between living ministry, as opposed to words that are injected into the meeting for their good. This is why I feel Friends should at any time avoid deliberately speaking to children, for it usually means speaking down to them. In fact it is an excellent discipline for anyone who speaks in meeting to try to use words and ideas that can be understood by children, and yet speak to the condition of all present, because they arise from the profound depths which, in fact, produce things that are truly simple.

George Gorman, 1973

2.75 We had two daughters who were the only children to attend on Sundays. That they continued to come with us, and still retain affectionate memories of that, is due entirely to the loving care given by Friends in teaching them and making them feel part of the meeting. We need to instruct our children in the widest sense, so that they can use the knowledge we pass on, both in relation to the Bible and to our Quaker heritage... We do our children (not only those biologically ours) a disservice if we do not pass on to them our concerns, beliefs and ideas. It is a mistake to imagine that children taught nothing positive will then be able to evaluate everything for themselves. But we teach them what we have experienced, in the knowledge that they will incorporate it and use it in their own way, accepting or rejecting it for a world that is of their making, not ours. In the life of the Quaker meeting there is a tradition of equality and respect for individuals that I have found to be of pure gold in value. It is expressed in love and affection between the generations. I know that my daughters, now young adults, have truly felt part of the family of the meeting because they have respected and been respected in an atmosphere that is unusual even among Christian churches. When elderly Friends have died, they too have wept because they have valued the companionship of people who saw them as individuals in their own right and gave them a true sense of belonging.

Jean Brown, 1984

2.76 I recall a family weekend, when the children, about twenty-four of them, aged three and upwards, had their own sessions in parallel to the adults. On the first evening, after the getting-to-know-you games, we sat down on the carpet to worship. We lit some candles on the hearth, turned off the lights, asked two children to be elders, and were still. The meeting went on for over a quarter of an hour, and was very deep. Then the two elders shook hands, but the silence continued. After another five minutes, I started a conversation, but no one responded to my cheerful comments. I was the one who had lost touch. When the children did speak, it was slowly, thoughtfully, with long spaces between. This was when I realised that children do minister... That meeting lasted until someone entered the room and interrupted us – about forty minutes.

Anne Hosking, 1984

See also 2.50, 10.09, 10.10, 12.01 paragraph 6 & 19.35

Enriching worship

2.77 The depth of Quaker worship, its richness, its power and its ability to meet the needs of each worshipper as well as the gathered group, depends on the commitment of every participant, and on the way we all come to our meetings with hearts and minds prepared.

Jack Dobbs, 1982

2.78 I think that we suffer from lack of biblical study both individually and in groups; I do not urge that this should be done in the regular gatherings for worship, but rather in groups during the week. To restrict our fellowship to the single hour on Sunday mornings is, under ordinary conditions, to impoverish our times of worship. The over-busyness resulting from the changed and difficult home conditions has, I fear, told on this side of our lives and does need distinct attention.

Joan Mary Fry, 1947

See also 10.07 & 27.33

2.79 Friends are not usually noted for their art and in earlier periods of their history they objected to paintings, theatre, music and novels. But they did adopt one distinctive art form and made it their own – the spiritual journal. It became the characteristic way in which early Friends told the story of their journeys, both their inward pilgrimage and their outward travels. It is from his journal that we learn that John Woolman was not always pacific or self-controlled and had to wrestle with his desire to impose his own will on others. And we take comfort from the fact that self-doubt and uncertainty were part of his journey as they are of ours.

In this century the practice of journal keeping is being explored as a way of becoming aware of the patterns of our inner life, of growing in self-knowledge and discovering our own gifts and possibilities... Keeping a journal is just one way ... of beginning to re-create your life. At its most basic it is a decision that your life has value and meaning and deserves the effort of recollection and reflection. It is also a decision that what you are living and learning is worth recording. That decision has its roots in a very deep layer of gospel truth.

Jo Farrow, 1986

2.80 I have valued most during my time at Woodbrooke the opportunities to participate in worship-sharing groups. I believe that these are of fundamental importance to one's individual spiritual growth and well-being and to the health of the community of which one is an active member. I am developing a capacity to listen more attentively to disclosures of sorrow and joy as others recount to me their spiritual journeys. Tenuous at first is the hope that we will receive understanding in response to our awkward efforts to communicate. Courage grows though as we experience the concern of others touching us where we feel the pain most deeply. Compassionate listening involves the total engagement of the heart. It is through strength and grace that we are enabled to achieve trust and spiritual intimacy.

Kathy Tweet, 1993

2.81 Power of the inner kind increases with use. It is not unusual for telepathy to develop between those who are close to each other in love. Again, prayer groups increase prayer power, and as the bonds of friendship and trust develop, charismatic healing gifts arise. This type of spiritual study and prayer fellowship has been the most precious part of my life for many years. Such groups sustain and bind people together so that when one falls ill, feels depressed or suffers a bereavement, he or she may count upon the friendship of the others. It is this kind of relationship, where there is both giving and receiving at an inner level, which sometimes extends beyond the grave.

Damaris Parker-Rhodes, 1985

2.82 We have seen the need to evolve a meeting that is a preparation for meeting for worship, a meeting which is similarly open, personal and democratic but which is implicitly educational and uses a wide range of modes of interaction. The touchstone of its success is its ability to generate richer fellowship between participants as they come to know each other and themselves in the deepest things. Learning, in this use of the word, is not head and fact learning, but whole-self learning where feelings and spirit find equal room with thinking and reason.

There is no one way of going about meetings for learning; nor is there one content nor one single aspect of self that they might enrich. As well as intuition there is also information; as well as creative listening and role play and music there is also discussion and guidance. But yet all meetings for learning are about growth in that territory of the self which touches on ultimate meanings, about those things which we feel the deepest, about our shadow as much as about our light, about our being accepted and held in the group and not judged for being found wanting, about new community. Such meetings demand as much discipline as meetings for worship or our business meetings.

Alec Davison, 1982

See also 21.31

2.83 The importance, both for ourselves and for our children, of active association with our fellow members in work and worship has led our Society in the past strongly to encourage Friends to live near meetings. We [urge] Friends in fixing their places of residence to bear this in mind. But we are aware that there are many whose duties oblige them to reside where there is no meeting. We do not desire in any way to discourage these from associating in worship with members of other religious denominations. It is our concern that Friends thus situated should [consider holding] meetings of a simple spiritual character with their neighbours, either on first-day or during the week. The world needs this message, and it is one for which many souls are hungering. Where a meeting on first-day may not seem a wise arrangement a quiet hour of worship with neighbours of other religious denominations on a weekday may be found mutually helpful, and may serve to draw away from too great a dependence on the outward in religion.

London Yearly Meeting, 1905

2.84 If we met more often for worship in each other's homes, it would remind us that God is with us in every place, at the kitchen sink and at the table; we should get to know one another more intimately, and could break bread together; the home atmosphere might make it easier to invite our acquaintances to join us; and any increase in numbers would lead to multiplication by cell-division; and an expanding coverage of the community.

David W Robson, 1971

In addition to the regular meeting for worship on Sundays, and/or perhaps other days of the week, meetings are held on particular occasions, such as marriages and funerals. For extracts concerning meetings for worship on particular occasions, see 10.12 for a meeting held in the home of one who is ill, chapter 16 for Quaker marriage procedure, 17.01–17.06 for funerals and 22.44–22.46 for celebration of commitment.

Meetings for church affairs

2.85 The meeting for business cannot be understood in isolation; it is part of a spiritual discipline.

John Punshon, 1987

2.86 Are your meetings for church affairs held in the spirit of worship and dependence upon the guidance of God? Do you take your right share in them? Do you maintain your respect for others as persons however strongly you may differ from their opinions? Do you refrain from using hurtful and provocative language? Are you sufficiently conversant with our Christian discipline to be able, when difficult questions arise, to consider them with an informed mind as well as a loving and tender spirit?

Queries, 1964

2.87 Being orderly come together, [you are] not to spend time with needless, unnecessary and fruitless discourses; but to proceed in the wisdom of God, not in the way of the world, as a worldly assembly of men, by hot contests, by seeking to outspeak and over-reach one another in discourse as if it were controversy between party and party of men, or two sides violently striving for dominion, not deciding affairs by the greater vote. But in the wisdom, love and fellowship of God, in gravity, patience, meekness, in unity and concord, submitting one to another in lowliness of heart, and in the holy Spirit of truth and righteousness all things [are] to be carried on; by hearing, and determining every matter coming before you, in love, coolness, gentleness and dear unity; – I say, as one only party, all for the truth of Christ, and for the carrying on the work of the Lord, and assisting one another in whatsoever ability God hath given.

Edward Burrough, 1662

2.88 We see our meetings for church affairs not as business meetings preceded by a period of worship, but as 'meetings for worship for business'. Ideally the sacred and the secular are interwoven into one piece. Believing that all our business is brought before God for guidance we deprecate all that may foster a party spirit or confrontation. We therefore seek for a spirit of unity in all our decision making.

London Yearly Meeting, 1986

2.89 In all our meetings for church affairs we need to listen together to the Holy Spirit. We are not seeking a consensus; we are seeking the will of God. The unity of the meeting lies more in the unity of the search than in the decision which is reached. We must not be distressed if our listening involves waiting, perhaps in confusion, until we feel clear what God wants done.

London Yearly Meeting, 1984

2.90 What is required is a willingness to listen to what others have to say rather than to persuade them that one's own point of view represents what is right and proper. It also requires restraint. The reiteration of one point by several Friends each in their own way lends no weight to the point. What the meeting must learn to discern is its rightness, not how many people support it...

When conflict comes, as it does, and the temptation to compromise – to seek consensus – is resisted, the sense of divine guidance is unmistakably registered. New possibilities for a way forward which nobody has thought of emerge out of discussion. Postponement and delay settle minds and assist the process of coming to a united mind. Above all, those who take opposing views come to find that the discipline of waiting has mysteriously united them.

John Punshon, 1987

2.91 It has been the experience of this yearly meeting in the past to know that Friends have met in division and uncertainty, and that then guidance has come, and light has been given to us, and we have become finders of God's purpose. This gives us ground for confidence. We shall not be held back by the magnitude of the questions which are to come before us, nor by a sense of our own unworthiness.

London Yearly Meeting, 1936

2.92 The day was Friday, and we were mindful that within a few hours we would be going in separate directions, never to be gathered under the same circumstances again. As we met for worship that morning we were faced with the decision, whether or not to approve the epistle. We had laboured for several hours the day before, and it looked as though preferences for wording and other concerns would make it impossible to approve the final draft.

However, something happened which transformed the feeling of our meeting... [A New England Friend] said something like 'I know that the blood of Christ and the Atonement are very important issues for some Friends, and I don't see anything in the epistle which addresses those convictions...'

In the discussion that followed, [an] evangelical Friend expressed his concern that the number of references to Christ might be difficult for Friends not used to Christ-language. What had begun as an act of loving concern for other Friends transformed the meeting into a unified whole. The discussion had changed from persons wanting to ensure that their concerns were heard to wanting to ensure that the concerns of others were heard and that their needs were met. We had indeed experienced the transforming power of God's love.

Paul Anderson, *Report of the World Gathering of Young Friends*, 1985

The text of the epistle may be found at 29.17

See also chapter 3 General counsel on church affairs

Chapter 3

General counsel on church affairs

Introduction

3.01 This chapter refers especially to our main meetings for church affairs, and in particular to area and local meetings. Attendance at these meetings is the right, and indeed the responsibility, of all Friends. The principles governing our Quaker business method, however, are equally relevant to less regular meetings for church affairs held by recognised meetings and to the committees appointed by any of our meetings. Committees should appoint clerks, if this has not been done by the parent meeting, and minutes should be made during the course of each committee meeting. The general advice in this chapter will be helpful in enabling these meetings too to be rightly held.

See also 2.85–2.92

The sense of the meeting

3.02 In our meetings for worship we seek through the stillness to know God's will for ourselves and for the gathered group. Our meetings for church affairs, in which we conduct our business, are also meetings for worship based on silence, and they carry the same expectation that God's guidance can be discerned if we are truly listening together and to each other, and are not blinkered by preconceived opinions. It is this belief that God's will can be recognised through the discipline of silent waiting which distinguishes our decision-making process from the secular idea of consensus. We have a common purpose in seeking God's will through waiting and listening, believing that every activity of life should be subject to divine guidance.

This does not mean that laughter and a sense of humour should be absent from our meetings for church affairs. It does mean that at all times there should be an inward recollection: out of this will spring a right dignity, flexible and free from pomp and formality. We meet together for common worship, for the pastoral care of our membership, for needful administration, for unhurried deliberation on matters of common concern, for testing personal concerns that are brought before us, and to get to know one another better in things that are eternal as in things that are temporal.

3.03 Our meeting communities vary in size and in the circumstances and experience of their members. Sometimes we may need to vary the ways in which we manage our meetings for church affairs in order to make better use of the talents, time and energy of our members. Co-clerkship, for instance, has been beneficial in a number of meetings; sometimes the monthly pattern of business meetings has been varied to good effect. We should be open to learning from the experiments undertaken by other meetings. Being set in an unsatisfactory routine 'because we've always done it this way' may be as detrimental to seeking God's guidance as throwing our traditions to the wind. We are enjoined to live adventurously, but experiment must be grounded in the experience of generations of Friends, which offers us a method, a purpose and principles for the right conduct of our business meetings.

If we sometimes think things are wrong with our meetings for church affairs, it would help us to look at the situation in perspective if we could realise how many troubles arise not from the system, but from our human imperfections and the variety of our temperaments and viewpoints. These meetings are in fact not merely occasions for transacting with proper efficiency the affairs of the church but also opportunities when we can learn to bear and forbear, to practise to one another that love which 'suffereth long and is kind'. Christianity is not only a faith but a community and in our meetings for church affairs we learn what membership of that community involves.

3.04 Our method of conducting our meetings for church affairs is an experience which has been tested over three hundred years. In days of hot contest and bitter controversy the early Friends, knit together by the glorious experience of the Holy Spirit's guidance in all their affairs, came into the simple understanding of how their corporate decisions should be made.

We have learned to eschew lobbying and not to set great store by rhetoric or clever argument. The mere gaining of debating points is found to be unhelpful and alien to the spirit of worship which should govern the rightly ordered meeting. Instead of rising hastily to reply to another, it is better to give time for what has been said to make its own appeal. We must always be ready to give serious, unhurried and truly sympathetic consideration to proposals brought forward from whatever part of the meeting. We should neither be hindered from making experiments by fear or undue caution, nor prompted by novel suggestions to ill-considered courses.

3.05 The right conduct of our meetings for church affairs depends upon all coming to them in an active, seeking spirit, not with minds already made up on a particular course of action, determined to push this through at all costs. But open minds are not empty minds, nor uncritically receptive: the service of the meeting calls for knowledge of facts, often painstakingly acquired, and the ability to estimate their relevance and importance. This demands that we shall be ready to listen to others carefully, without antagonism if they express opinions which are unpleasing to us, but trying always to discern the truth in what they have to offer. It calls, above all, for spiritual sensitivity. If our meetings fail, the failure may well be in those who are ill-prepared to use the method rather than in the inadequacy of the method itself.

It is always to be recognised that, coming together with a variety of temperaments, of backgrounds, education and experience, we shall have differing contributions to make to any deliberation. It is no part of Friends' concern for truth that any should be expected to water down a strong conviction or be silent merely for the sake of easy agreement. Nevertheless we are called to honour our testimony that to every one is given a measure of the light, and that it is in the sharing of knowledge, experience and concern that the way towards unity will be found. There is need for understanding loyalty by the meeting as a whole when, after all sides of a subject have been considered, a minute is accepted as representing the discernment of the meeting.

Not all who attend a meeting for church affairs will necessarily speak: those who are silent can help to develop the sense of the meeting if they listen in a spirit of worship.

3.06 The unity we seek depends on the willingness of us all to seek the truth in each other's utterances; on our being open to persuasion; and in the last resort on a willingness to recognise and accept the sense of the meeting as recorded in the minute, knowing that our dissenting views have been heard and considered. We do not vote in our meetings, because we believe that this would emphasise the divisions between differing views and inhibit the process of seeking to know the will of God. We must recognise, however, that a minority view may well continue to exist. When we unite with a minute offered by our clerk, we express, not a sudden agreement of everyone present with the prevailing view, but rather a confidence in our tried and tested way of seeking to recognise God's will. We act as a community, whose members love and trust each other. We should be reluctant to prevent the acceptance of a minute which the general body of Friends present feels to be right.

As a worshipping community, particularly in our local and area meetings, we have a continuing responsibility to nurture the soil in which unity may be found.

In a meeting rightly held a new way may be discovered which none present had alone perceived and which transcends the differences of the opinions expressed. This is an experience of creative insight, leading to a sense of the meeting which a clerk is often led in a remarkable way to record. Those who have shared this experience will not doubt its reality and the certainty it brings of the immediate rightness of the way for the meeting to take.

3.07 The meeting places upon its clerk a responsibility for spiritual discernment so that he or she may watch the growth of the meeting toward unity and judge the right time to submit the minute, which in its first form may serve to clear the mind of the meeting about the issues which really need its decision. In a gathering held 'in the life' there can come to the clerk a clear and unmistakeable certainty about the moment to submit the minute. This may be a high peak of experience in a meeting for church affairs, but for the most part we have to wrestle with far more humdrum down-to-earth business. It must always be remembered that the final decision about whether the minute represents the sense of the meeting is the responsibility of the meeting itself, not of the clerk.

Sometimes it will be right to leave the decision to a later meeting, but the clerk should bear in mind that this can be the 'lazy' option. Sensitivity is required in recognising when the meeting is really too tired to proceed further. It may be realised that more background work would be beneficial, or that time is needed for everyone to consider the options more carefully. A decision to come back to the subject on a later occasion will then be a positive and important part of the process.

Friends should realise that a decision which is the only one for a particular meeting at a particular time may not be the one which is ultimately seen to be right. There have been many occasions in our Society when a Friend, though maintaining her or his personal convictions, has seen clearly that they were not in harmony with the sense of the meeting and has with loyal grace expressed deference to it. Out of just such a situation, after time for further reflection, an understanding of the Friend's insight has been reached at a later date and has been ultimately accepted by the Society.

We have a responsibility to uphold our clerks in prayer as they try to discern unity in sharply divided meetings. We must not expect to be delivered from differences of opinion – and indeed our life as a religious community would be dull and unprofitable if we were; but we do need to hold firmly to our conviction that divine guidance is there to be found.

Participation in meetings for church affairs

3.08 Are your meetings for church affairs held in loving dependence upon the spirit of God, and are they vigilant in the discharge of their duties? ... Do you individually take your right share in the attendance and service of these meetings so that the burden may not rest upon a few?

Queries, 1928

3.09 It is not expected that any Friend should attend every meeting or sit upon innumerable committees. Decide what is within your physical and spiritual capacity, and be responsible in your attitude to what you do select.

Be as regular, faithful and punctual as possible in your attendance.

All members are entitled to attend their local, area and general meetings, which are the units of Britain Yearly Meeting's regional organisation, and Yearly Meeting itself. You are encouraged to do so as regularly as you are able, because our business method depends on the widest possible participation by our members. Friends may be appointed to attend area and general meetings in order to ensure that enough Friends will be present but this does not excuse or prevent others from being there. It is recommended that those appointed be asked to report back to their own meetings.

When you are appointed to attend a meeting, you attend with local knowledge which may be of assistance: you are not there as a delegate with an inflexible brief to put over on behalf of another body of Friends which is not itself going through the exercise of the meeting.

On taking your seat, try to achieve quietness of mind and spirit. Try to avoid having subcommittees or conversations just as the meeting is about to begin. Turn inwardly to God, praying that the meeting may be guided in the matters before it and that the clerk may be enabled faithfully to discern and record the mind of the meeting.

For regulations on attendance of non-members at meetings for church affairs see 4.08 for area meetings, 4.32 for local meetings, 5.03 for General Meeting for Scotland, 5.04 for Meeting of Friends in Wales & 6.15 for Britain Yearly Meeting.

See also 11.28 for sojourning membership

3.10 Remember the onerous task laid upon the clerk and do all you can to assist. Submit information about matters to come before the meeting in good time and preferably in writing. Avoid if you possibly can any last-minute messages to the clerk.

Give your whole attention to the matter before the meeting. If you want to speak, try to sum up what you have to say in as few words as possible. Speak simply and audibly, but do not speak for effect. A pause after each contribution will enable what has been said to find its right place in the mind of the meeting. Do not repeat views which you have already expressed. Do not address another Friend across the room but speak to the meeting as a whole. Be ready to submit to the direction of the clerk. Except in very small meetings, those able to stand to speak should do so.

On some matters before the meeting you may feel very strongly. Listen as patiently as you can to all other points of view. Even Friends you consider ill-informed or wrong-headed may make positive or helpful points: watch for them. Do not put into other Friends' mouths things which they did not say. Be certain of your facts. Avoid stating as facts things which are matters of opinion.

Do not take offence because others disagree with you. Be chary of ascribing, even in your mind, unworthy motives to others. Try not to take things personally. Promote the spirit of friendship in the meeting so that Friends may speak their minds freely, confident that they will not be misinterpreted or misunderstood.

Value the meeting as a social occasion. Introduce strangers to one another. Be approachable; be cheerful. If you are an experienced Friend, invite newcomers to come with you. Help them to understand the business and to get to know the membership.

3.11 If, when all that is necessary has been said, the clerk is not ready to submit a minute, uphold those at the table in prayerful silence. If the minute is in general acceptable, do not harass the clerk by raising several minor corrections at once. Do not, under the pretext of altering the minute, raise new matter for discussion or reiterate your original contribution.

Clerkship

3.12 The clerk needs to have a spiritual capacity for discernment and sensitivity to the meeting. In conducting the meeting and drafting minutes on its behalf, the clerk's abilities are strengthened by an awareness of being supported by the members of the meeting. Friends who have not known the unforeseen joy which comes from this experience may gain encouragement from this knowledge, should they be invited to serve. If the clerk's service is under concern in the certainty of God's presence and help in the meeting, then strength beyond her or his normal powers will be given.

The service of the assistant clerk can be of great benefit both to the clerk and to the meeting. The clerk bears the final responsibility for preparing the business, conducting the meeting and drafting the minutes. It is recommended, however, that the assistant clerk be enabled to share in all the clerk's duties as much as possible. Consultation will often help the clerk to come to a right judgment. The assistant clerk will gain experience and maybe the confidence to accept nomination as clerk in due course. Planning for a period of apprenticeship through assistant clerkship can provide for a smooth transition. Some meetings have found that co-clerkship can be highly successful. This may involve two or more Friends, with or without an assistant clerk, and enables Friends' differing abilities and skills to complement each other, particularly when time and energy are at a premium. Such a departure from tradition usually takes place after careful consideration and planning, and can result in a lively and varied interpretation of the clerk's responsibilities.

The following advice to clerks should be seen as being equally relevant to co-clerks and assistant clerks, and to conveners whose responsibilities are similar to those of clerks. (For further information about conveners see 3.21.)

Advice to clerks

3.13 Remember that while you, as clerk, are the servant of the meeting, you do, by your very attitude and your arrangement of the agenda, set the pattern of worshipful listening which should characterise our meetings for church affairs. The meeting is likely to repose great trust in you, and you bear an important responsibility in enabling the meeting to listen and wait for God's guidance in its deliberations. Your experience in the ways of Friends and your understanding of the Quaker business method are very important in helping the meeting to discern God's will and to recognise the way forward. Help Friends to remember that the period of silent worship at the beginning of the meeting prepares for and opens the way to the consideration of the business; the worship does not finish as the business begins, and the clerks do not shake hands until the close of the business. The meeting has given you a measure of authority which includes an expectation and an acceptance of leadership and firm guidance. At the same time it will usually respond willingly if you find yourself at a loss and ask for help. Above all, it is your responsibility to come with heart and mind prepared.

Do not leave all your preparations to the last minute. Before the meeting discuss the business with your assistant clerk if possible. Check beforehand all facts which may be in question, so as to avoid plunging the whole meeting into fruitless and time-wasting speculation. It will save time in the meeting to bring at least the factual part of your minutes in draft form.

When introducing business into the meeting try briefly to provide sufficient background information to set the meeting purposefully on its course. In the subsequent deliberations you may need to advise on procedure or make a suggestion if none is forthcoming on a routine matter. A very small meeting may wish you to participate on occasion. Remember, however, that your main task is to discern the meeting's united mind and that it may be much harder to do this if you try at the same time to be a participant in the discussion. Be chary, therefore, of making known your own views. You may well find that this very discipline of detachment leads to a new and deeper relationship with the other members of the meeting. If you are deeply involved in a decision to be reached, the meeting should be invited to ask another Friend to act as clerk for the occasion.

3.14 Do not be afraid to ask the meeting to wait while you prepare your minute. You will then usually be able to complete it and have it accepted in that meeting. In some cases you may need to have time for reflection and to bring in a minute after an interval in the meeting.

Make sure that the minute covers all the points on which a decision is required and remember that reference may need to be made to it in the future. Where minutes record the presentation of reports which will be filed with them, it should not usually be necessary to quote the contents at length in the minutes themselves.

You may be required to draft a minute of record concerning a past event, a minute of exercise, which indicates the area and range of the discussion and records the experience or progress of the meeting, or a minute of decision.

Remember that any minute you present is only a draft minute until the meeting has accepted it as its own. If you have drafted alternative decisions, be ready to minute a decision of the meeting which is different from all the possibilities you had in mind. Accept with good grace improvements to your draft made by the meeting. The drafting of a minute is a spiritual exercise. Every clerk needs the full support and attention of the meeting, so that together they may achieve high standards of clarity and accuracy.

3.15 Acceptance of a minute must be a deliberate act. Even if it is not thought necessary to read out the whole of an agreed draft minute again at the moment of acceptance, the meeting must be sufficiently aware of its terms from the preceding exercise to be conscious of uniting to accept it. It is at the moment of accepting each minute that the united meeting allows you to record it as a minute of the meeting. It is good practice for the rough minutes to be signed at the meeting's conclusion. This also gives the clerk authority to sign any fair copy once it is certain it has been correctly transcribed. Very minor amendments such as punctuation and points of style may be made, but any alteration of the sense should be avoided most carefully. It is undesirable that minutes should be prepared afterwards for presentation to a later meeting when the membership may not be the same as that which originally deliberated.

The sending of copies of the relevant minutes to those who are required to take follow-up action after the meeting is the responsibility of the clerk.

You are responsible for the safekeeping of the minutes once the meeting has accepted them. They belong to the meeting, and only the meeting has authority to amend, countermand or supersede them by a subsequent minute. If minor corrections or annotations of a factual nature are necessary, these must be indicated as such in the margins or as footnotes in order to safeguard the integrity of the minutes.

For the safekeeping of records see 4.39–4.41

3.16 Remember that the Friend with particular gifts of judgment is not necessarily the one whose opinion is most needed on all matters; seek to assess the value of individual contributions. Do not forget that the silence of some is often of greater significance than the speech of others.

Be aware, however, that silence does not necessarily mean consent. When conflicting views have been expressed, leave time and opportunity for those who have previously disagreed to indicate whether they are ready to unite with the minute.

When strong division of opinion seems to be threatening the worshipful basis which should prevail in meetings for church affairs, a period of silent and prayerful waiting on the will of God may well have a calming and unifying effect.

3.17 When a Friend accepts an invitation to speak at your meeting, remember your responsibilities towards her or him. Try to ensure that the agenda is arranged to allow adequate scope for the introduction and consideration of the subject at a time when the meeting is not tired or overburdened with other matters. Try also to give the speaker quiet before the meeting, recognising that this service may be costing in nervous energy. If the speaker comes from a distance, be sure to advise her or him about travelling arrangements, including the time and place of arrival, and see that travelling and other expenses are quickly and graciously reimbursed.

3.18 Be careful to maintain a right balance in exercising the authority which the office lays upon you. Use discretion in deciding which matters should be brought before Friends and which may be dealt with by yourself. Beware, however, of the dangers of exceeding your authority in making decisions yourself on matters which should be referred to the meeting. In cases of doubt you may find it helpful to confer with Friends of experience. In the meeting deal courteously but firmly with those who speak at too great length or too frequently stray from the point under discussion. Remember that the right exercise of the clerk's authority is of great service to the meeting in promoting the smooth and expeditious handling of its business.

3.19 In preparing the business for the area or local meeting, you should try to be in regular contact with the various committees of the meeting. It is important that committees report regularly to their parent meeting. It may be possible to save the meeting's time by adequate preliminary discussion. With regard to nominations, for example, you may be able to avoid having to make appointments 'subject to consent'. It is also important that, in minuting appointments, the term of service and the date of termination be clearly stated.

Area meeting clerks are advised to be in close touch with elders and overseers, for example, when applications for membership are being considered. More generally, you should be aware of the responsibilities laid upon elders and overseers for the spiritual life of the meeting, for encouraging full participation in meetings for church affairs, and for the right holding of meetings for worship including meetings for church affairs.

Keep a sense of proportion and a sense of humour. Be sensitive to the tempo of the meeting. Do not be over-brisk nor allow matters to drag tediously. Be alert to those who may need encouragement to speak.

3.20 Apart from the preparation and conduct of the business, as clerk you are also responsible for the general administration of the meeting. You need to follow up previously agreed minutes and ensure that tasks undertaken are carried out, that enquiries are dealt with, and that committees are functioning satisfactorily. You may be involved in some committees ex-officio, and by sensitive awareness of the different activities in the meeting, you can help the meeting to function smoothly and steadily. Giving notices and welcoming visitors are important tasks. You need skill in deciding what to include in the notices, and sensitivity to the concerns and interests of members of the meeting.

Think affectionately between meetings of the needs of the community which has appointed you and how they can best be met; ask guidance of God continually in the performance of your task.

Conveners

3.21 The term *convener* is sometimes used as an alternative to clerk as, for example, in committees of area or meetings, and of elders and overseers, where either term may be used according to local custom and practice. It is often preferred in the case of a group or subcommittee which has been appointed for a task of limited duration and is directly responsible to a more permanent committee or meeting for church affairs. In such a case the convener is expected to perform the functions of a clerk and should conduct meetings of the group in accordance with our Quaker principles and practice.

Alternatively conveners may be appointed in the first instance with the specified responsibility for bringing together the appointed members of a group. It should always be made clear at the outset if this is the intention, since the first job of the convener at the initial meeting will then be to enable the group to appoint a clerk from among its members. When no convener or clerk has been designated, convening the first meeting of a group is by Quaker tradition the responsibility of the Friend named first in the minute setting up the group. It should not be assumed that the convener will necessarily be appointed as clerk.

Nominations and appointments

3.22

> Now there are varieties of gifts, but the same Spirit; and there are varieties of services, but the same Lord; and there are varieties of activities, but it is the same God who activates all of them in everyone. To each is given the manifestation of the Spirit for the common good. (I Cor 12:4–7)

It is a responsibility of a Christian community to enable its members to discover what their gifts are and to develop and exercise them to the glory of God.

3.23 Much of the work of meetings for church affairs and committees will be undertaken by Friends especially appointed by the meeting or committee responsible for the work, most often on the recommendation of a nominations committee. The process of appointment starts when the meeting identifies the need for a task to be performed. It is good practice for a meeting to have a clear view of the tasks that need to be accomplished on its behalf and to fix the length of service required so that both the meeting and the Friend appointed understand the commitment.

Many of our gifts are latent. A particular appointment may enable one Friend to exercise unsuspected abilities. Other Friends may find themselves overburdened by being appointed to service beyond their capacity and experience. It requires great discernment to know the right moment to ask a particular Friend to undertake or lay down a particular task.

Most appointments should be for either one or three years. It is generally undesirable for someone to hold an appointment for more than six years continuously although there may be exceptions. Meetings should give thought to the training of replacements for existing officers and it will help in this process if those appointed try to give the meeting some notice of wishing to be released from service.

Meetings will differ widely in the appointments they need to make. In some meetings, there may be a shortage of people willing to undertake the work that is needed. In others there may be many who are anxious to serve and some may feel excluded from the busy life of the meeting if not offered appointment. It is important that the whole process be open and clearly understood by all who attend.

3.24 The following suggestions for good practice are intended to apply to all our meetings and committees and to the appointment of Friends and, where appropriate, attenders.

a. In general a nominations procedure should be used when the appointment is to an office in the meeting, or for any other service of importance. Receiving nominations from the body of the meeting is not generally a good method of making appointments.
b. The great responsibility resting on nominations committees and their clerks cannot be too strongly stressed. Nominations committees should be large enough to be representative; impulsive Friends may need to be questioned, whilst the cautious and conservative may need to be encouraged to consider new ideas. The committee needs a balance of experience and age-groups. Members will need to have knowledge of the meeting and be prepared to take pains to understand the qualifications needed for the required appointments. They will need to be clear about the requirements of the office and where appropriate should consult the requesting body. They will also need to be discerning in judgment and tactful in manner. It is important that the members meet in a spirit of worship. Some meetings have found it helpful to survey the gifts of their members in a systematic way.
c. Nominations committees are appointed on behalf of the meeting, and suggestions for their consideration put forward by other members of the meeting may well be helpful to them. Such suggestions are best made directly to members of the nominating group. A nominations committee should act when asked to by its meeting or committee and only in exceptional circumstances on its own initiative.
d. Nominations committees are appointed in many ways. Sometimes names are suggested from the body of the meeting, on other occasions a special committee is asked to bring forward names of Friends to serve on the nominations committee. In some circumstances participating bodies send

forward representatives. It is important to ensure openness and to prevent any suggestion of an inner group; thus membership should be for a limited duration. Many meetings retire one-third of their nominations committee every year on a rotating basis.

e. A nominations committee should think carefully before bringing forward the name of one of its own members for appointment. Any such nominee should withdraw from the meeting when her or his name is being presented.

f. A nominations committee should meet in a worshipful manner. Committee members will occasionally need to consult each other by telephone, but this should not be the normal means of conducting the committee's business.

g. The nominations committee is not the appointing body and must bring the suggested names to the body for which it acts. Members of this body have the responsibility for approving the names or not and must be given the opportunity to express any doubts they might have. Sometimes it may seem impossible to find someone to serve. Nominations committees should not hesitate to bring their problem back to the meeting to ask for both guidance and practical help.

h. The duration and scope of an appointment should be explained to all who are asked to accept nomination; the approach should not be made casually or acceptance taken for granted. It will be helpful to ask those nominated if they would consent to serve if the meeting required it. When a nominations committee brings forward a name it should not then be necessary to appoint 'subject to consent'. However it is important that it is made absolutely clear that the appointment would be made by the meeting in its discernment and not by the nominations committee. It will be helpful to indicate when the appointment is likely to be made.

i. Those nominated to serve as clerk of a meeting, elder, overseer, treasurer, registering officer or as a member of any nominations committee should be in membership. In case of difficulty the Recording Clerk may be consulted. (For further guidance on the appointment of elders and overseers see 12.07–12.09.)
j. Where two Friends would be expected to work together (e.g. as a clerk and assistant clerk) care should be taken to talk the proposal over informally with them before making any firm approach.
k. When it is decided not to renominate any Friend holding an appointment, care should be taken to convey this information sensitively in person or by letter well before nominations are submitted.
l. Nominations committees should be required to report from time to time on their thinking and their way of working.

3.25 Despite being made prayerfully appointments do not always turn out as planned. It is at the discretion of a meeting to end an appointment at any time if it is necessary to do so. Loving and tender care will be essential. An appointed Friend who finds the service inappropriate should be released.

Responsibility for an appointment does not end when it is made. Having been fully involved in the making of the appointments, the meeting must support and uphold those carrying out the tasks. Some may be disappointed that they themselves were not asked to carry out a particular function; humility and prayerful support for those chosen will be better than a continuing resentment.

Our ability to discern the gifts of others is not perfect and we will recognise an element of God's grace in our deliberations. Be bold; welcome the chance to give opportunities to younger Friends and to those more recently arrived, and encourage those who underestimate their own potential for service.

The use of small groups in identifying needs and reaching decisions

3.26 The focus of this chapter has been the working of our Quaker business method through the tried and tested structures of our meetings for church affairs. It is however important to be aware of the contribution that groups other than our meetings for church affairs and their committees can make to our decision-making process. These might include discussion meetings, threshing meetings or meetings for clearness. From time to time a meeting may benefit from looking at itself and identifying specific areas needing attention: pastoral care, outreach, or major changes such as rebuilding or developing premises. The discussion of such matters in small groups, properly constituted, can help to involve the whole meeting and prepare it for decisions which must eventually be taken in the regular meeting for church affairs. Valuable suggestions and solutions may come from individuals who would not feel able to voice them in the more formal meeting. The terms of reference and limits of the group's decision-making responsibility must be made clear at the outset.

For further guidance on the use of small groups see 12.20–12.21; for general guidelines about meetings for clearness see 12.22–12.25; for threshing meetings see 12.26.

For meetings for clearness see also relevant sections:
4.23 on the amicable settlement of disputes;
11.11 in relation to applications for membership;
13.01 on testing personal leadings;
13.08 & 13.11 on the process of discernment of concern;
16.19–16.21 in relation to intentions of marriage.

Authority for public statements

3.27 Individuals and groups must be careful not to claim to speak for Friends without explicit authority. Any activity or statement made in public which claims to be undertaken in the name of Friends and relating to the corporate life and witness of the Religious Society of Friends must be authorised by the appropriate meeting for church affairs. Any public statement which claims to be given on behalf of Friends in Britain Yearly Meeting as a whole will require the judgment of a more widely representative body than a meeting, area meeting or ad hoc group; it should be considered and agreed by Meeting for Sufferings or by Yearly Meeting before publication. It must be made clear when local initiatives relate solely to local meetings. Similarly, individual Friends or ad hoc groups should make it clear that they speak only for themselves unless their local or area meeting has agreed a minute supporting their action.

On occasion it may be necessary for the clerk of a meeting, or another appointed Friend, to take urgent action to correct misleading reports in the press or other misunderstandings in the public domain. This section is not intended to hamper such necessary action undertaken responsibly in the interests of a meeting.

Conclusion

3.28 The ensuing chapters contain regulations governing procedure for our various meetings for church affairs. There will inevitably be cases not covered by a particular regulation, and meetings should seek always to appreciate the general principle behind the regulations. Meetings are counselled, however, against too easily admitting exceptions where circumstances do not warrant them, for these regulations are the fruit of the Society's experience in its corporate life. Friends are encouraged to get to know the relevant regulations before taking an active part in meetings for church affairs.

In our meetings for church affairs an effective continuing life can be secured only if there is at least a strong nucleus of Friends attending with regularity, willing to accept responsibility and to give judgments based on informed minds as well as spiritual wisdom. There are few things which tend to destroy interest and loyalty in any business so easily as prolonged and unnecessary discussions on trivia: such discussions are very often provoked and kept up by those who do not trouble to inform themselves adequately of the facts, or who use their occasional attendance to re-open matters already decided. The meeting should expect and encourage its clerk to take firm action in such circumstances.

3.29 There is no justification for wasting precious time in our meetings for church affairs under the excuse or delusion that we may safely do so because it is God's work. But they should be times of enjoyment as well as of hard work, times when we can see old friends and make new ones over tea, when we can be stimulated by other people's ideas and insights as we deliberate together, when we can discover our own gifts and those of other members as we work together. It was said of Gilpin Gregory that 'when his health failed and he was daily seen by his doctor, he would frequently appear at monthly meeting against his doctor's orders and contrary to the advice of his friends, and if remonstrated with he would say, "It does me good; I shall be none the worse for it, and it may be for the last time".' All our meetings for church affairs should be used imaginatively so that they are not 'business' meetings to be attended from duty or neglected with a sense of guilt but real meetings for church affairs which build us up in Christian love – and do us good.

3.30 Keep your meetings in the power of God... And when Friends have finished their business, sit down and wait a while quietly and wait upon the Lord to feel him. And go not beyond the Power, but keep in the Power by which God almighty may be felt among you... For the power of the Lord will work through all, if ... you follow it.

George Fox, 1658

Chapter 4

Area meetings and local meetings

Area meetings

Constitution and functions

4.01 Until 2007 area meetings were known as monthly meetings. The change was made to give more emphasis to the area meeting as a spiritual community rather than a regular event, and in the interests of accuracy because many monthly meetings no longer met monthly.

Monthly meetings were an important part of the gospel order established by George Fox, which played a large part in ensuring the survival of the young Society of Friends. From 1659 onwards monthly meetings were set up, first for men only, then for women and finally joint; they combined business with social ties, caring for the poor and prisoners, education and ministry. By 1676 they were the unit of authority for membership, marriages, property, records, the recognition of ministers (until 1924) and the recognition and laying down of local meetings; most of these functions continue today. So too does their formal responsibility, completed by 1789, for the appointment of elders and overseers.

4.02 The area meeting is the primary meeting for church affairs in Britain Yearly Meeting. Its role is to develop and maintain a community of Friends, a family of local meetings who gather for worship and spiritual enrichment. It should provide that balance between worship, mutual support, administration, learning, deliberation and social life which can make its meetings enjoyable occasions and build up the spiritual life of its members.

Area meetings act as facilitators and co-ordinators, ensuring that their constituent local meetings have access to opportunities for fellowship, spiritual development, and spiritual and pastoral care, including the care of children and young people. They also provide mutual support through the shared testing of concerns.

Area meetings also carry responsibilities for ensuring the right stewardship of local and area resources. Each area meeting is a separate charitable entity and it may be required to be registered as such with the relevant charity regulator (see 15.01). Area meetings which are registered or preparing for registration will operate under a formal governing document, which amongst other matters should set out the arrangements for trusteeship (see 15.03–15.05). A model document suitable for charitable registration is available from the Recording Clerk and at www.quaker.org.uk/qfp.

The area meeting consists of those who are by minute recorded as its members.

4.03 The organisation of area meetings will vary, depending on their size. Each area meeting should decide how to manage local business to suit local needs and resources.

Area meeting time can often be used more efficiently if detailed matters can be prepared in advance. However, the whole meeting should deal with matters which are fundamental to its identity as a spiritual community.

Area meetings may wish to work with other meetings to carry out certain functions such as managing property (see for example 5.08). Not all area meetings will need to set up a complex committee structure. Meetings should bear in mind the importance of balancing the benefits of flexible patterns with the need to be accountable. Whatever business arrangements are adopted, it is helpful if they are regularly reviewed, to ensure that they are practical and workable. It is also important that certain specific responsibilities are considered carefully.

4.04 Each area meeting should appoint members to serve as:

a clerk and assistant clerk, or Friends to share these responsibilities;

a treasurer;

a registering officer (see 16.10);

a nominations committee;

a body of trustees (see 15.03–15.05);

a custodian of records or a committee for the purpose (see 4.39).

Meetings may when appropriate appoint a member of another area meeting, but in such cases advance consultation between the meetings is advisable, and the decision must be communicated by minute.

Area meetings are responsible for eldership and oversight and most will also appoint from their membership an appropriate number and distribution of elders and overseers (see 12.05–12.06 and the notification requirements in 12.09).

The Recording Clerk should be kept informed also of the names and addresses of clerks, clerks to trustees, treasurers and registering officers.

4.05 Other appointments which may be found helpful are:

an additional assistant clerk to deal with membership matters;

an assistant treasurer or finance committee;

a children and young people's committee;

an outreach committee;

a warden(s) and premises committee, where the area meeting is the employing body (and see 13.39);

Friends to advise on funerals (see 17.07, 17.08, 17.14).

Other appointments may also be helpful to the area meeting. In addition appointments will be needed to other bodies with which the area meeting has a relationship (see in particular 4.16, 4.17).

4.06 The meeting should also consider which matters are left to the discretion of elders, overseers, trustees or the clerks as appropriate.

It is important that detailed guidelines be drawn up for the officers appointed by the area meeting, so that those who undertake these tasks are fully aware of what is involved. Area meeting appointments should be made for a fixed period, generally not more than three years, after which they should be reviewed.

See 3.22–3.25 Nominations and appointments

4.07 Each area meeting shall meet at such frequency, times and places as the meeting itself may direct.

The clerk may arrange for a special area meeting to be held if necessary. Such a meeting must be arranged by the clerk if a written request from five members is received. As wide notice as possible of a special area meeting should be given in each constituent local meeting. Formal notice must be given at the close of each meeting for worship held on the previous Sunday.

4.08 The area meeting is open to all its members. Other Friends should notify their presence to the clerk before the meeting begins and, if drawn to speak, should be sensitive to the fact that it is not their area meeting (see also 11.27). Attenders may be present only with permission of the clerk, which should be sought well in advance of the day of meeting. It should be borne in mind that some matters, particularly membership, are confidential and cannot easily be discussed with non-members present.

4.09 Area meetings will from time to time have to consider minutes or papers from Yearly Meeting, Meeting for Sufferings, Britain Yearly Meeting Trustees or the standing committees through which they work. Other new area meeting business will normally come through a local meeting or through an area meeting committee or a representative of the area meeting on another body. It will usually be appropriate for an individual Friend with a concern to bring that concern to her or his own local meeting before approaching the area meeting. If the local meeting recognises the concern, it should forward a minute to the area meeting (see 13.09–13.18).

4.10 The area meeting shall keep the following matters under regular review:

a. the right and regular holding of meetings for worship in its constituent local meetings (4.33.a);
b. the right ordering of meetings for church affairs within its constituent meetings (4.32);
c. agreement with each constituent local meeting as to how responsibilities are to be fulfilled (4.34);
d. the appointment and service of elders and overseers; the level and nature of pastoral care in the area meeting (12.06,12.16);
e. the use of *Advices and queries* (1.05–1.07);
f. the maintenance and revision of its official register of members (11.38) and its list of attenders and children not in membership associated with its several meetings for worship (11.39);
g. the maintenance and revision of any published list of members, attenders and children not in membership (11.40);
h. the preparation of the annual tabular statement, recording membership changes, marriages and deaths, which is to be forwarded to the Recording Clerk as early as possible in the following year (6.07, 11.37);
i. the arrangements for forwarding notices of change of address (11.22–11.23) and certificates for transfer of membership (11.25–11.26);

j. the proper custody of its records (4.39–4.45) including deeds (15.09);
k. the care of trust property, including the appointment of trustees (15.03–15.04) and the right application of capital and income (15.07);
l. the stewardship of financial resources and maintenance of accounts, including those of its committees and its constituent meetings, in accordance with the general rules set out in 14.20–14.23: they must be examined by an independent person (who must satisfy the conditions set out in 14.22) before the annual statement of accounts is considered by the meeting and, if approved, accepted;
m. the provision of the relevant financial accounts and property records to the Quaker Stewardship Committee in order to enable it to fulfil its responsibilities (14.28) including annual certification to the Yearly Meeting;
n. the advice to Friends on their outward affairs and the timely making and revision of their wills (4.22);
o. the supervision (16.11–16.21) and recording (16.51) of marriages according to our usage; the prompt forwarding to the Recording Clerk of the name of any newly appointed registering officer (16.10); any delegation to specific local meetings of responsibility for appointing meetings for worship for the solemnisation of marriage (16.27);
p. the recording of deaths of members of the area meeting (11.41); the provision of advice on funerals (17.07); the appointment of Friends responsible for the arrangement of funerals (17.08); the production and revision of memoranda (17.15) to ensure that a sufficient number of Friends are familiar with the practical arrangements for funerals and memorial meetings in their area (17.14);
q. the supervision and recording of burials (including the interment or scattering of ashes after cremation) in burial grounds belonging

to the area meeting (15.17, 17.11–17.13); the supervision of the use of gravestones in its burial grounds (15.20); the care of burial grounds (15.10, 15.19);

r. the maintenance and use of libraries in local meetings (13.41–13.42);

s. the nomination, where appropriate, in England and Wales, of Quaker prison ministers, in accordance with 13.49–13.50;

t. the relevance of new legislation to their activities and the compliance of their constituent meetings with the law: current concerns include matters as diverse as charity law, Criminal Records Bureau procedures for work with children, young people and vulnerable adults (4.14), data protection (4.45) and disabled access.

This list will doubtless change over time.

Area meetings will, according to particular circumstances, have other areas of responsibility (e.g. local homes for elderly people) and should always keep them under regular review.

Reference should also be made to the following paragraphs concerning other responsibilities of area meetings: representation on Meeting for Sufferings (4.17, 7.05–7.07), on Quaker Life Representative Council (4.17, 8.13–8.14) and at the Annual Conference of Treasurers (14.16–14.17); attendance at Yearly Meeting (6.12); assistance in the amicable settlement of disputes (4.23); discernment in concern (13.05–13.07 & 13.09–13.18).

4.11 It is important that the area meeting give full and prayerful support to everyone who is appointed to serve it, whether on its own committees, or as a representative on another body, or in an individual capacity (see 3.25).

This is particularly important when the post to be filled involves heavy and perhaps lonely responsibility. The roles of registering officer (see chapter 16 *Quaker marriage procedure*) and Quaker prison minister (13.45–

13.52), which both have specialist and legal aspects, are good examples, and Friends nominated should be fully aware of the responsibilities involved. Area meetings are encouraged to pay proper attention to the spiritual support and nurture of those who give what may be costly although often rewarding service. (See 12.27 for advice on support groups.)

Reorganisation: transfer of local meetings

4.12 Some area meetings may consider that they are too large or too small, have geographical constraints or have insufficient resources to form a supportive and effective community. Area meetings are encouraged in these circumstances to propose changes, which may result in a transfer of a local meeting from one area meeting to another, or amalgamation or division of area meetings. Any changes should stem from local needs. When area meetings are considering reorganisation it is recommended that they bear in mind the value of groupings which correspond to any relevant regional, ecumenical or other institutions. Any proposals for reorganisation shall, after agreement between the area meetings concerned, be presented to Meeting for Sufferings for endorsement. Area meetings should note that the consent of the relevant charity regulator may also be required.

Pastoral care and outreach

4.13 Each area meeting is responsible for nurturing the spiritual life of its constituent meetings for worship and for the oversight, pastoral care and religious education of people of all ages. See also chapter 12 *Caring for one another*. It should consider regularly the opportunities available for local outreach and service.

The potential contribution of meeting house wardens to outreach should be borne in mind, particularly when the rebuilding and reorganisation of meeting houses is being considered (see 13.34).

4.14 Area meetings need to consider, agree and regularly review their own meeting policy on the safety of children, young people and vulnerable adults, taking into account current relevant legislation, the requirements of their insurers, and current guidance on good practice from Quaker Life, available at www.quaker.org.uk/qfp. Meetings are advised to have policies in place whether or not they currently have children, young people or vulnerable adults in their constituent local meetings.

Membership

4.15 Area meetings are responsible for membership matters. They have the responsibility of admitting new members into the Society and of terminating membership, and the duty of keeping the appropriate records of membership (see chapter 11 *Membership*). They also have the authority to recognise local meetings as part of Britain Yearly Meeting (see 4.31).

Relationship to other meetings for church affairs

4.16 An area meeting shall provide Britain Yearly Meeting and Meeting for Sufferings, and any general meeting or Quaker gathering (see 5.02) to which it belongs, with such nominations or information as may from time to time be required.

4.17 An area meeting is required to nominate Friends to serve on Meeting for Sufferings, the standing representative body of the whole yearly meeting (7.02). This is the main channel of communication between area meetings and Yearly Meeting, so area meeting business should give a high priority to preparation of its representatives and receiving reports from them. Another opportunity for regular involvement with the wider work of Britain

Yearly Meeting is provided by the appointment of area meeting representatives to Quaker Life Representative Council (8.13). The terms of reference of these bodies and the duties of the area meeting representatives to provide an effective two-way channel of communication should be made clear to those being nominated. Conferences and other occasional gatherings which provide further opportunities for wider communication and fellowship will benefit from a wide representation from area meetings.

4.18 An area meeting may communicate formally by minute with its constituent local meetings, with any general meeting or Quaker gathering (5.02) to which it belongs (including the General Meeting for Scotland (5.03) or the Meeting of Friends in Wales (5.04–5.05) where appropriate), with Yearly Meeting (6.06.a, 6.25), with Meeting for Sufferings (7.02) and with meetings with which it does business through its representatives appointed to joint committees. The area meeting has an obligation to receive minutes from those bodies. There may occasionally be circumstances in which it will be helpful to circulate other minutes for information only.

4.19 In considering concerns which their members may bring before them, area meetings should exercise care to ensure that their own consideration is adequate and that in forwarding the matter to another meeting they are truly recognising a leading that the subject be considered further. Area meetings should also consider what action they themselves could take before forwarding the concern to another meeting. Area meetings must beware of evading their own responsibility for reaching a united judgment. This responsibility may involve consideration at more than one session of the area meeting. It is essential that before forwarding a concern the area meeting should consult at an early stage with the relevant standing committee or department (see 8.08–8.11 and 8.16–8.17) in order to find out what facts and experience can be offered to its consideration of a concern. (See 13.09–13.18.)

4.20 The relationship between area meetings, Meeting for Sufferings and Britain Yearly Meeting Trustees and committees is delicate and complex.

> If there is sometimes tension in the relationships this is not necessarily unhealthy. It is unhealthy when a matter is shunted from one body to another because a group of Friends lack the spiritual energy and courage to wrestle with a matter which they know may result in uncomfortable plain speaking to a fellow member whose concern, however deeply held, is not shared by the meeting. It is equally unhealthy when any individual or meeting is preoccupied with status, with 'getting things through', with efforts to predetermine how another body shall act. We can only be delivered from these dangers by a constant relearning of the nature of true concern.
>
> Meeting for Sufferings, 1978

Junior Yearly Meeting

4.21 Area meetings have an important relationship with Junior Yearly Meeting, which is the largest national gathering of 16–18-year-old Friends within Britain Yearly Meeting. This gathering is arranged by Quaker Life (8.10) but is representative of, and its participants financed by, area meetings. Most young people have only one opportunity to participate. Being selected as an area meeting representative can be a formative and affirming experience, giving these young Friends an opportunity to meet others in their age group and to become more aware of their Quaker identity.

Advice on outward affairs

4.22 Area meetings should periodically bring to the attention of members their responsibility for the right ordering of their outward affairs. Such advice on outward affairs has traditionally reminded Friends of the importance of keeping their financial affairs in good order, and of making and revising their wills in time of health. The proper acquisition and use of income, conduct in business and employment and the stewardship of money held for others have also been included, but area meetings need not feel themselves limited to these subjects. Area meetings also have discretion as to how they discharge this corporate responsibility for advising on individual conduct. Local traditions vary. Some include a regular reminder from overseers in a newsletter, while others address a special letter of counsel on outward affairs to all adult members. Whatever the method preferred, the purpose is the same: to remind members of the area meeting of the guidance to be found in our discipline on matters of honesty and integrity (see chapter 20) as they relate to the personal life of every Friend.

Disputes among Friends

4.23 Area meetings are recommended to appoint a group of experienced and knowledgeable Friends who would be available to give general assistance in the amicable settlement of disputes. If help from outside the area meeting is needed, enquiry should be made of the clerk of Meeting for Sufferings, who may suggest Friends qualified to give it. Techniques of problem-solving, mediation, counselling or meetings for clearness may be appropriate in particular instances where disputants wish to mitigate the consequences of confrontation. It should be borne in mind that Friends were among the pioneers of conflict resolution as a distinct activity and have constantly sought to promote reconciliation in the wider world.

See also 10.21–10.24 Conflict within the meeting & *20.67–20.75* Conflict

Legal action

4.24 Legal action by Friends, and in particular legal disputes between Friends, should if possible be avoided. However, there may arise differences which might best be resolved by obtaining a legal ruling or definition from a court of law. (See 20.67–20.75 *Conflict.*)

Right of appeal against decisions

4.25 If a member is dissatisfied with a final decision of an area meeting affecting her or him (e.g. if membership has been terminated) and feels that the area meeting has acted unjustly, unreasonably, with insufficient knowledge or not in right ordering, the member may appeal in writing to the area meeting clerk. The nature of the appeal and name of the appellant should be kept confidential as far as is possible or is desired by the appellant. The area meeting shall then appoint a small group of disinterested Friends to try to settle the matter (see 4.23). If this fails, the area meeting shall then ask a neighbouring area meeting or meetings to appoint a small group of disinterested elders, or one drawn from those exercising eldership, to act as an appeal group. The appeal group should meet with the appellant and representatives of the respondent area meeting and issue a judgement to that area meeting, as far as possible without breaking the confidentiality of the parties. The area meeting should accept the judgement of the appeal group, at which stage the decision should become as public as is needed for the matter to be acted upon.

If the appellant remains dissatisfied with the decision of the appeal group, he or she may then appeal to Meeting for Sufferings against the decision of the area meeting. On receiving such an appeal, the clerk of Meeting for Sufferings shall report this to the area meeting and shall request Meeting for Sufferings to appoint an appeal group of five Friends, who should be independent of the area meeting concerned, to make all such enquiries as seem to them desirable, from the member concerned and from others having relevant knowledge, to consider and determine whether or not the appeal should be allowed and whether any further recommendations should be made. In conducting such enquiries the healing power of worship will be helpful. The decision of the Friends so appointed shall be final and be communicated directly to the parties concerned. The appeal group shall inform Meeting for Sufferings that they have reached a decision and communicated it to the parties concerned, and Meeting for Sufferings shall record this in its minutes without breaking the confidentiality of the parties concerned. Guidelines for the conduct of an appeal group are obtainable from the Recording Clerk and at www.quaker.org.uk/qfp.

4.26 If an area meeting is dissatisfied with a final decision of another area meeting that affects it, the dissatisfied area meeting may appeal to Meeting for Sufferings against such decision. The procedure on such an appeal shall be similar to that on an appeal by a member personally, but prior notice shall be given by the dissatisfied area meeting to the other area meeting concerned before invoking this appeal procedure.

Testimonies concerning deceased Friends

4.27 The possibility of writing a testimony concerning the life and service of a deceased Friend has been a valued part of our tradition. A testimony should not be a formal obituary or eulogy, but should record in thankfulness the power of divine grace in human life.

4.28 *Testimony concerning Hannah Brown (1711?–1779):*

The purpose of a testimony concerning our deceased, worthy Friends [is] intended as a memorial, that they have walked as children of the Light, and of the Day, and to excite those that remain to take diligent heed, and yield obedience to the teachings of the still small voice, that they may follow them as they followed Christ, the great captain of their salvation.

Hertford Monthly Meeting, 1780

4.29 It is the responsibility of the area meeting to arrange for the preparation of a testimony, but it is sometimes difficult to be clear during a session of area meeting whether a spontaneous request for one is in right ordering. It is suggested that local meetings should write a brief passage for their own records on every member who dies. The writing of a testimony by the area meeting should be undertaken on the recommendation of the local meeting or other group such as elders. If a spontaneous suggestion is made during area meeting, this should be referred to the local meeting or to a small group for advice. Meetings deciding to prepare a testimony, and particularly those Friends doing the drafting, are encouraged to consult the advice in the paper *Testimonies to the grace of God in lives – an enduring presence* available from the Recording Clerk and at www.quaker.org.uk/qfp. If the testimony is considered likely to be of benefit to a wider group of Friends or to the Society as a whole, it may be forwarded to the relevant general meeting or Quaker gathering or to Yearly Meeting (see 6.06.g & 6.25). This should not, however, be an automatic decision. Its value as an inspiration to other Friends is not dependent only on its relevance in a wider rather than a local context.

4.30 If a Friend belonged to several area meetings during her or his lifetime, it may be appropriate for more than one area meeting to contribute to a testimony. Any such meeting should feel free to take the initiative, but should be particularly sensitive to the need to consult beyond its own boundaries. The area meetings concerned should agree on which of them should take responsibility for producing the testimony.

It may be right in a few cases for more than one testimony to be written. One or more such testimonies may be from other yearly meetings, in cases where the Friend spent part of her or his life abroad.

Local meetings

4.31 The area meeting may contain a variety of meetings for worship differing in size and practice. Any group of Friends may meet to worship at any time. The area meeting should encourage worshipping groups, as they evolve into regular meetings for worship, to adopt practical arrangements suited to their circumstances. The existence of a new local meeting or the laying down of an existing local meeting should be formally recognised by the area meeting and recorded by minute, which should be sent to the Recording Clerk.

4.32 The membership of a local meeting consists of those on the area meeting list of members who are attached to that meeting. Meetings for church affairs should be held when most people can attend, non-members attending by permission of the clerk. Most meetings will encourage regular attenders at meeting for worship to participate in meetings for worship for church affairs on suitable occasions. Friends in membership of other meetings may be present, but should notify their presence to the clerk before the meeting begins, and, if drawn to speak, should be sensitive to the fact that it is not their own meeting. However, any Friends who have been accepted as sojourning members of the area meeting (11.28) are expected to share as fully as they are able in the life of their local meeting.

Local meetings are at all times subordinate to their area meeting.

Much helpful advice and experience in exercising the care of the worshipping community is found in chapter

10 *Belonging to a Quaker meeting* and in chapter 12 *Caring for one another*. All members should be familiar both with these parts of our discipline and with chapter 3 *General counsel on church affairs*.

4.33 Local meetings differ greatly in size. Thus the scope of work undertaken will vary but every local meeting will give due respect to Quaker values, testimonies and practice and will provide regular opportunities for public worship.

The following responsibilities need to be considered by every local meeting although some of them may best be fulfilled in conjunction with another local meeting, or through the area meeting.

a. Make arrangements for the regular holding of public meetings for worship, which will normally be held at least once a week. Suitable premises will need to be arranged. If, after careful thought, a local meeting wishes to meet less frequently then, with the agreement of its area meeting, it may do so but there should be meetings at least once each month; this should be reviewed each year. The area meeting must be kept informed of the days and times when meetings for worship are held.
b. Use Advices and queries (1.05–1.07).
c. Nurture and sustain the spiritual life of the meeting and the pastoral care of those associated with it; the welcoming of newcomers is of particular importance. Enquirers should be helped to explore and understand the Society.
d. Take a special responsibility for the children within its care and for their parents. The continuing religious education of all, including regular attenders as well as members, should be of real concern to the meeting.
e. Conduct all its own business and hold regular meetings for church affairs, which should be planned to involve all members of the meeting.

These meetings should include preparation for area meeting business.

f. Encourage, by appointment or otherwise, an attendance of local Friends at the area meeting (see 10.06); Friends should be encouraged to take a full part in the activities of their area meeting.
g. Make sure that the financial needs of the meeting and the yearly meeting are properly understood by its members and that channels exist for giving in a convenient way. Accounts of any financial activities must be kept in accordance with the general rules set out in 14.20–14.23 and the guidance given by the area meeting; they must be examined by an independent person (who must satisfy the conditions set out in 14.22) before the annual statement of accounts is considered by the meeting and, if approved, accepted and reported to the area meeting.
h. Prepare such statistics, returns and reports as are required.
i. Preserve certain records (see 4.40).
j. Monitor the relevance of new legislation to its activities, as advised by the area meeting (see 4.10.t).
k. Consider local outreach; as a minimum the advertising of the times and places of meetings in the local press and placing an entry in the telephone directory should be arranged in conjunction with the area meeting.
l. Support other local meetings to carry out their responsibilities when requested and support the formation and nurture of new local worshipping groups and occasional meetings for worship.
m. Appoint correspondents (see 8.15) to Quaker Peace & Social Witness and other bodies as appropriate.
n. Maintain a library and encourage the reading of Quaker publications (see 13.41–13.42).
o. Form links with other churches and faith communities in the area and where possible

jointly undertake service in the community (see 9.14–9.20).

p. Seek to exert a Christian influence in the neighbourhood both as a meeting and in co-operation with others.

4.34 Each local meeting should agree with its area meeting the duties and responsibilities which the local meeting undertakes on behalf of the area meeting. This agreement should be formally recorded as part of a memorandum of understanding. The local meeting should report regularly, as required, to its area meeting on the discharge of these responsibilities. In the case of smaller meetings which are not able to carry forward all the responsibilities listed above, the recorded agreement should make clear the work that they are able to do themselves and what is done in co-operation with another local meeting.

4.35 For a local meeting to carry out its duties and other activities, certain appointments will need to be made (see 3.22–3.25 *Nominations and appointments*). The meeting must at least appoint a clerk or convener and also a treasurer if it has any financial activities, or alternatively, Friends to share these responsibilities. The Recording Clerk should be informed of the names and addresses of the current holders of these offices in all local meetings.

4.36 Other appointments which may be found helpful are:

an assistant clerk (3.12–3.20);

a collector (13.44);

a librarian (13.41);

a nominations committee;

a premises committee;

a children's committee;

a committee responsible for hospitality and domestic arrangements;

doorkeepers;

correspondents.

Whilst elders and overseers are appointed by the area meeting, much of their service will be within the framework of the local meeting (see 12.06).

Some meetings will have wardens or resident Friends (see 13.33–13.40). Our dealings with those we employ or who live on our premises need care and knowledge.

4.37 Local meetings should rely on their area meeting for the trusteeship, charitable accountability, and if necessary, charitable registration of their affairs, except in special circumstances, which will require the agreement of the area meeting. (See 14.28, 14.30, 15.03.)

4.38 A very large local meeting may well unbalance an area meeting. Members of such a meeting will need to exercise considerable care with respect to what is local meeting and what is area meeting business. They will need to consider tenderly those in the smaller meetings who may feel distanced from some of the activities of the area meeting. Being too large a meeting can also cause problems within the meeting itself, with difficulties in pastoral care and in achieving a sense of community. Sometimes when a local meeting grows very large it may wish to consider starting a new meeting. Early consultation with the area meeting will be in order.

Records

4.39 Area and general meetings should appoint a Friend to act as a custodian of their records, or else appoint a committee for the purpose. Area meetings should take responsibility for the records of their constituent meetings, ensuring their timely transfer to the custodian of records. They are advised in particular to ensure that the records of any local meeting which has been laid down are collected together. The Library Committee of Quaker Life publishes guidance for clerks and custodians on the creation, care and custody of records (4.43), and see www.quaker.org.uk/qfp.

4.40 It is advised that the following be preserved in Friends' ownership:

a. minute books of yearly, general, area and local meetings;
b. minute books of elders and overseers and of standing committees of meetings for church affairs;
c. official registers of members (11.38), printed lists of members and attenders (11.40), marriage registers (16.45), registers of burials (17.12), burial ground plans (15.17), registers of properties and trusts (15.09);
d. such other documents as it is reasonable to expect may be needed for future reference.

It is an essential part of the stewardship of the meeting's assets that the custodian should maintain a full catalogue of records and where they are located, whether kept in meeting house safes or strongrooms or elsewhere. It is advised that area meetings should check the accuracy and completeness of their catalogues at least triennially.

4.41 The attention of area and general meetings is drawn to the many advantages of depositing older records with an appropriate national or local record office or repository. Records not in current use should be deposited on loan. Such documents, deposited under suitable conditions, remain the property of the area or general meeting concerned, while benefiting from the care of professional archivists.

4.42 It is the responsibility of area meetings to decide which records shall be available to students, whether Friend or non-Friend, and to stipulate the conditions for their release. The Library at Friends House and many meetings make available records more than fifty years old, subject to exceptions where particular discretion is needed (e.g. overseers' minutes).

4.43 Meetings requiring advice or information on the handling of their records are encouraged to get in touch with the Library Committee through the Librarian at Friends House. The Library Committee maintains a central catalogue of local meeting records, and it should be notified of any change in the place where they are deposited.

4.44 Meetings have sometimes been approached by an outside body and offered the opportunity to put old records on microfilm. This may be primarily for the benefit of those making the offer. The area meeting is responsible for deciding whether it would also be of benefit to the meeting and is strongly advised to seek guidance from the Library Committee (4.43). The Library Committee should be kept informed of decisions made so that the relevant experience may be shared with other area meetings.

Data protection and confidentiality

4.45 Meetings storing information about their members and attenders on computers or other electronic devices or in manually processed paper files should be sensitive to the need to protect such information from unauthorised use and must comply with all legal requirements for data protection. Basic factual information on members such as addresses can be kept by the area meeting on the official register of members (11.38) without notification of those concerned. Such information may be passed to the yearly meeting database, except that members may then request that information other than their names be withheld.

Information on attenders and the non-member partners of members may only be held with their explicit consent. Information on children not in membership (11.39) may only be held with the explicit consent of their parent or guardian. Consent forms for inclusion in the area meeting lists should be drafted to enable such persons to opt for their information to be passed on to the yearly meeting database.

Friends should be made aware of the difficulty of maintaining perfect security of the printed lists made available to members and, frequently, to attenders, and should be given the opportunity of deleting some or all of their personal details (11.40).

If meetings record any other information on members and attenders, whether electronically or in paper-based records, for example in connection with nominations work or with applications for membership, the persons concerned must be informed that the information is held and that they may see and approve their own record.

Further advice can be obtained from the Recording Clerk (see also 8.06).

Chapter 5

General meetings and other gatherings

General meetings: descriptions and functions

5.01 The origin of regional gatherings, each embracing several monthly meetings, goes back to 1660 when George Fox was 'moved to set up the men's quarterly meetings throughout the nations'. These were followed by women's quarterly meetings. From the middle of the eighteenth century these progressively became mixed. They gradually took on considerable responsibilities for discipline, inspiration, pastoral care and records of membership. They also nominated members for service on Meeting for Sufferings. Overall they functioned as a link in the chain of responsibilities joining local meetings to the yearly meeting. With reorganisation in 1967 the title and function of quarterly meetings disappeared and they were renamed 'general meetings'. In the years following some became inactive and were held in suspense pending any further changes in the structure of Britain Yearly Meeting. All continuing meetings concentrated mainly on their functions of being places of wider fellowship, holding meetings for conference, inspiration and extension work, and offering a broad support of Quaker life and witness within their region. Some retained administrative responsibilities, particularly in relation to Quaker schools and the care and nurture of children and young people.

5.02 The name general meeting is now used for several different kinds of organisation, usually based on a geographical grouping of several area meetings. The General Meeting for Scotland (see 5.03) and Meeting of Friends in Wales (see 5.04 and 5.05) have certain delegated powers from Yearly Meeting. Yearly Meeting in 2005 recognised that some geographic general meetings wished to be laid down and with effect from Yearly Meeting in 2007 the eighteen regional general meetings in England and Wales were removed from the administrative structure. There are two other distinct types of general meeting, one being any Quaker school general meeting that functions solely as that school's responsible body, the other being Young Friends General Meeting (see 5.09).

General Meeting for Scotland

5.03 General Meeting for Scotland has national responsibilities, on behalf of Britain Yearly Meeting, to represent and advance the life and witness of Quakers in Scotland. It consists of all Friends in membership of the Scottish area meetings, and meets at least quarterly. Provision is made for members of other meetings and attenders to be present at meetings as in 4.08. The responsibilities of General Meeting for Scotland include:

a. promoting spiritual life and witness, facilitating contact between Friends of all ages, and providing opportunities for training and mutual support for those with special responsibilities, in conjunction with the associated area meetings and Quaker bodies;
b. representing Britain Yearly Meeting in Scotland, including: acting on behalf of Britain Yearly Meeting in relation to ACTS (Action of Churches Together in Scotland) (see 9.09–9.12) and other church and faith groups; acting on behalf of Britain Yearly Meeting and of Friends in Scotland in dealings with

the Scottish parliament, the Scottish government and the Scotland Office, and on such procedures as may be required by the Scottish legal system;

c. encouraging communication from Scottish area meetings on matters which in their judgement merit interchange of views (see 4.18) including testimonies to the life and service of deceased Friends, discerning whether the latter be forwarded to Yearly Meeting for the benefit of the Society as a whole (see 4.27–4.30);
d. representing Scotland to Britain Yearly Meeting, liaising with yearly meeting committees and departments where appropriate.

General Meeting for Scotland will provide information and nominations or appointed representatives to Quaker and other bodies when required. The meeting may communicate by minute with Yearly Meeting through its Agenda Committee (6.18) and Meeting for Sufferings (7.04), as well as with area meetings in Scotland. It also has the obligation to receive minutes from these bodies.

Meeting of Friends in Wales

5.04 Meeting of Friends in Wales has national responsibilities, on behalf of Britain Yearly Meeting, to represent and advance the life and witness of Quakers within Wales. The meeting consists of all Friends who live in Wales or who are members in local meetings within Wales. Provision is made for members of other meetings and attenders to be present at meetings as in 4.08. The responsibilities of Meeting of Friends in Wales include:

a. promoting spiritual life and witness, facilitating contact between Friends of all ages, and providing opportunities for training and mutual support for those with special responsibilities, in conjunction with associated area meetings and Quaker bodies;
b. representing Britain Yearly Meeting in Wales, including: the appointment of Friends to serve

on Cytûn (Churches Together in Wales) and its committees (see 9.09–9.12), communication with the National Assembly for Wales, and with other public and voluntary organisations in Wales, especially those concerned with social witness, peace and interfaith relations;

c. encouraging communication from associated area meetings on matters which in their judgement merit interchange of views (see 4.18) including testimonies to the life and service of deceased Friends, discerning whether the latter be forwarded to Yearly Meeting for the benefit of the Society as a whole (see 4.27–4.30);
d. responding to issues which relate to living in a bilingual society, including outreach in Wales and commissioning, translating and publishing Quaker material in the Welsh language;
e. representing Wales to Britain Yearly Meeting, liaising with yearly meeting committees and departments where appropriate.

The Meeting of Friends in Wales will provide information and nominations or appointed representatives to Quaker and other bodies when required. The meeting may communicate by minute with Yearly Meeting through its agenda committee (6.18) and Meeting for Sufferings (7.04), as well as with area meetings which include parts of Wales. It also has the obligation to receive minutes from these bodies.

The following is a translation into Welsh of 5.04

Cyfarfod y Cyfeillion yng Nghymru

5.05 Mae gan Gyfarfod y Cyfeillion yng Nghymru gyfrifoldebau ar ran Cyfarfod Blynyddol Prydain, i gynrychioli ac hyrwyddo bywyd a thystiolaeth y Crynwyr yng Nghymru. Mae'r cyfarfod yn cynnwys pawb o'r Crynwyr sydd yn byw yng Nghymru neu yn aelodau o gyfarfodydd lleol yng Nghymru. Gwneir darpariaeth i aelodau o gyfarfodydd eraill fynychu cyfarfodydd yn unol â 4.08. Mae cyfrifoldebau Cyfarfod y Cyfeillion yng Nghymru yn cynnwys:

a. ar y cyd â chyfarfodydd rhanbarth perthnasol a chyrff Crynwrol eraill hybu bywyd a thystiolaeth ysbrydol, hwyluso cyswllt rhwng Cyfeillion o bob oed a chynnig cyfleoedd am hyfforddiant a chyd gefnogaeth i'r rhai sydd â chyfrifoldebau arbennig;
b. cynrychioli Cyfarfod Blynyddol Prydain o fewn Cymru, gan gynnwys: penodi Cyfeillion i weithredu ar Cytûn (Eglwysi Ynghyd yng Nghymru) a'i bwyllgorau (gweler 9.09–9.12), cyfathrebu gyda Llywodraeth Cynulliad Cymru a gyda chyrff cyhoeddus a gwirfoddol eraill yng Nghymru, yn enwedig y rhai sydd yn ymwneud â thystiolaeth gymdeithasol, heddwch ac amlffydd;
c. annog cyfathrebu oddiwrth y cyfarfodydd rhanbarth perthnasol ar faterion sydd, yn eu tyb hwy, yn haeddu cael eu cyd drafod (gweler 4.18), gan gynnwys tystiolaethau i fywyd a gwasanaeth Cyfeillion ymadawedig, gan ddirnad os dylid anfon rhain at y Cyfarfod Blynyddol er lles y Gymdeithas gyfan (gweler 4.27–4.30);
ch. ymateb i faterion sydd yn ymwneud â byw mewn cymdeithas ddwyieithog gan gynnwys ymestyn i'r gymuned yng Nghymru a chomisiynu, cyfieithu a chyhoeddi deunydd Crynwrol yn y Gymraeg;
d. cynrychioli Cymru i Gyfarfod Blynyddol Prydain, gan gysylltu â phwyllgorau ac adrannau y cyfarfod blynyddol fel bo'n addas.

Fe fydd Cyfarfod y Cyfeillion yng Nghymru yn darparu gwybodaeth ac enwebiadau neu benodiadau i gyrff Crynwrol a chyrff eraill yn ôl y galw. Gall y Cyfarfod gysylltu trwy gofnod â Chyfarfod Blynyddol Prydain trwy ei bwyllgor agenda (6.18) a'r Cyfarfod Dioddefiannau (7.04), ac hefyd â'r cyfarfodydd rhanbarth sy'n cynnwys rhannau o Gymru. Mae hefyd yn ofynnol i'r cyfarfod dderbyn cofnodion gan y cyrff hyn.

Other gatherings

5.06 Other Quaker gatherings, assemblies or associations provide a place of fellowship and a means for Friends to have a vital sense of being part of a larger Quaker body beyond their local meetings.

A number of Quaker gatherings are former geographic general meetings which wish to continue as gatherings, having been removed from the administrative and constitutional structure by Yearly Meeting (see 5.02). Yearly Meeting asked them at that time to consider renaming themselves. Other Quaker gatherings may be set up subsequently.

General meetings and gatherings provide for conference and inspiration, and for broad support of the life and witness of Quakers within their compass, considering regularly what is being done and what might be done to extend the service of their members and to reach out to those who are in need of spiritual guidance and friendship (see 12.06). They also find opportunities to consider the work of the yearly meeting and may link with ecumenical and interfaith activities in their area.

5.07 Quaker gatherings or conferences may be set up by two or more area meetings, by a mix of area and local meetings, or by two or more general meetings. The constituent meetings are those that choose to take the responsibility for organising and funding such gatherings or conferences. The members are the members of the sponsoring meetings.

If a newly formed gathering is intended to have an ongoing structure and regular meetings, it must inform Meeting for Sufferings and the Yearly Meeting of its existence and proposed mode of operation. All gatherings (including those that continue from pre-existing general meetings) must inform Meeting for Sufferings and the Yearly Meeting of any substantial changes in their mode of operation or constituent meetings.

General meetings or gatherings that wish to discontinue activity must ensure the appropriate winding up of their responsibilities and funds. They must notify Meeting for Sufferings and the Yearly Meeting of their intention to lay themselves down, then of the steps that they take to discharge or transfer their responsibilities and to deposit their records. Lastly they should forward to the Recording Clerk the minute by which they are finally laid down.

Six Weeks Meeting

5.08 Six Weeks Meeting, dating back to 1671, does not fit neatly into the modern pattern of area meetings, general meetings and gatherings. It is made up of representatives from the area meetings within the London region. Its main objective is to maintain, preserve and insure the places of worship of the constituent area meetings, and their contents. It is accountable to the constituent meetings for the stewardship of the funds and assets it holds on their behalf. It may communicate formally by minute with the constituent area meetings, Meeting for Sufferings and Yearly Meeting.

The names of constituent area meetings in 2009 were Kingston & Wandsworth; London West; North East Thames; North London; North West London; South London and South East London. Each appoints an agreed number of representatives to Six Weeks Meeting (currently three). The normal period of appointment or re-appointment is five years. The Friends appointed are individually managing trustees of the properties and financial assets in the care of Six Weeks Meeting (15.03).

Young Friends General Meeting

5.09 Young Friends General Meeting is open to Quakers between the ages of eighteen and about thirty, who need not be formally in membership of the Religious Society of Friends. Area meetings may appoint representatives to Young Friends General Meeting. At its meetings for business three times a year it organises a range of other events for young people. It may communicate formally by minute with area meetings, Britain Yearly Meeting and its Agenda Committee, Meeting for Sufferings and the standing committees of Yearly Meeting and Meeting for Sufferings.

Young Friends General Meeting nominates two representatives to Meeting for Sufferings, being officers or others able to speak in its name (see 7.05.c).

Chapter 6

Yearly Meeting

History

6.01 Our yearly meeting grew out of a series of conferences of ministering Friends, some regional, some national. We may think of that at Swannington in 1654 or Balby in 1656 (the postscript to whose lengthy letter of counsel is so much better known than the letter itself) or Skipton the same year, or the general meeting for the whole nation held at Beckerings Park, the Bedfordshire home of John Crook, for three days in May 1658, and attended by several thousand Friends. This in some ways might be considered the first yearly meeting were it not for the fact that the 1660s, through persecution and pestilence, saw breaks in annual continuity. The meeting in May 1668 was followed by one at Christmastime, which lasted into 1669, since when the series has been unbroken. 1668, therefore, we have traditionally chosen as the date of establishment of London Yearly Meeting. But many (though not all) of the meetings up to 1677 were select, that is, confined to 'publick' (or ministering) Friends: from 1678 they were representative rather than select in character. Minutes are preserved from 1672.

The life of the yearly meeting centred until the mid nineteenth century on the quarterly meeting answers to the queries and the 'Epistles Foreign and Domestick'. Epistles and travelling ministers between them made the Atlantic community of Friends a reality; smuggling in Cornwall or dissension in Nantucket received equal thought and attention. The education of Friends' children was a recurring theme, and with the establishment of Ackworth (1779) and Sidcot (1808) the reports of boarding schools made increasing claims on the time of the meeting. The answers (more and more stereotyped) to the queries, lengthy reports and other documents read aloud, the long-winded Friends, the narrow range of interest and minutiae of procedure – all must on occasion have been stifling to the rebels. 'And now for about an hour', wrote a young Friend in 1858, 'the YM talked to points of order. When 5 or 6 courses are mentioned and a good many friends speak to each, it does not seem difficult to spend an hour or more in this way.' 'It is difficult', he added charitably, 'to see how this is altogether to be avoided.'

In fact, however, Yearly Meeting was probably seldom as parochial as the cautious minutes show, and even they point to certain outstanding sessions – the 1783 one on the slave trade, for instance; or that in 1818 on capital punishment. Yearly Meeting was not merely preoccupied with introspective consideration of the state of the Society: it sought to awaken the public conscience. A statement in 1856 on liberty of conscience was translated into half a dozen languages and taken by deputations of concerned Friends to ecclesiastics and statesmen from Madrid to St Petersburg. Petitions to parliament and memorials to the monarch covered a wide range of concern. When in 1842 Caroline Fox with her brother and father called on Thomas Carlyle, 'he wanted to know what we were doing at the Yearly Meeting, and what were its objects and functions, and remarked on the deepening observable amongst Friends; but when we told of the letter to the Queen recommendatory of peace in Afghanistan, he was terribly amused. "Poor little Queen! She'd be glad enough to live in peace and quietness if the Afghans would but submit to her conditions".'

'Every Quakeress', wrote Charles Lamb, 'is a lily; and when they come up in bands to their Whitsun-conferences, whitening the easterly streets of the metropolis, from all parts of the United Kingdom, they show like troops of the Shining Ones.' Women Friends had from the seventeenth century taken opportunity during the men's Yearly Meeting to confer together, but it was not until 1784 that a Women's Yearly Meeting was established, with the right to communicate with women's quarterly meetings. From the 1880s some joint sessions of men and women Friends were held, and in 1896 Yearly Meeting decided that 'in future women Friends are to be recognised as forming a constituent part of all our meetings for church affairs equally with their brethren'. Some separate sessions still continued but the Women's Yearly Meeting was laid down in 1907.

After the yearly meeting was constituted on a representative basis in 1678 ministering Friends, and later, elders, found occasion to meet with members of the Second Day Morning Meeting (the weekly gathering of 'ministering Friends in and about the city') at the beginning and the close of Yearly Meeting. This gathering, therefore, assumed a measure of national authority – it issued, for instance, in 1702 'A brief memorial of some necessary things', which was the basis of the advices on ministry – and in 1754 it was constituted as the Yearly Meeting of Ministers & Elders. In 1876 the meeting was enlarged in membership and renamed the Yearly Meeting on Ministry & Oversight, but as part of the egalitarian movement of the late nineteenth century it was decided to discontinue the separate hierarchy of preparative, monthly and quarterly meetings on ministry and oversight, and, in consequence, the Yearly Meeting on Ministry & Oversight last met in 1906. Elders and overseers subsequently met separately for conference.

Until as recently as 1861 Yearly Meeting was in theory composed only of representatives, together with 'such ministering Friends as may be in town, and the correspondents or members of the Meeting for Sufferings'. From the mid-eighteenth century (if not earlier) the doors were in fact open to any man Friend, and much business was in consequence referred to the Large Committee, which was confined to those constitutionally entitled to be there. When at length the Yearly Meeting sessions were opened to all men Friends as a right there was one, at least, who took a mournful view. 'The Yearly Meeting', he wrote, 'will become less and less of a *religious,* and more and more of a merely *popular,* assembly. The fruit of its deliberations, even at its best, will be liable to fall, in an unripe state, as "untimely figs", by a want of constancy and settlement in the *root of life.* There is, besides, great cause to dread, *that the talkative, unstable part in man, which should be silent in the churches, will presume to speak therein with increasing boldness,* bringing forth confusion.'

Whether or not we feel Daniel Pickard's predictions have been justified, we can indeed be thankful that in almost every generation there has been a Right Holding of Yearly Meeting Committee, though the exact title may have varied from one occasion to another. Such a group has the opportunity of deciding whether we need to direct our attention to constitutional change, or to the shortcomings of our human nature. In 1902 John Wilhelm Rowntree and Edward Worsdell applied their minds to the conduct of Yearly Meeting with devastating remarks: 'Discussion confused and futile', 'discussion disproportionate and prolix', 'a demonstration not a conference'. It was two years before this outburst that the first memorandum of agenda had been issued, and it had been agreed to print some reports in advance.

In 1905 Yearly Meeting was held for the first time out of London. Meeting at Leeds it received at its opening session a message from the venerable patriarch J Bevan Braithwaite, who after sixty-four years of unbroken attendance, felt the journey inadvisable. 'Coming together as we do', wrote the Yearly Meeting in its response, 'amid such new surroundings, the thought of the faithful lives of service which have been given in the past to the work of our Society comes with peculiar power and helpfulness to us, and as we listened to thy letter and thought of the long years in which thou wast present during the sittings of the yearly meeting, the desire arose that we might be more faithful in giving ourselves to the work.' We too may re-echo the desire that we may be inspired by those who have gone before us in our yearly meeting but not fettered by their procedures.

In 1994 London Yearly Meeting agreed to change its name to the Yearly Meeting of the Religious Society of Friends (Quakers) in Britain, or in short form, Britain Yearly Meeting. This decision followed a recommendation by Meeting for Sufferings after a consultation with monthly meetings. The new name was chosen to express the identity of the yearly meeting in a more inclusive way, so that Friends who were physically distant from London could feel more fully part of the whole. It also reflects more accurately the geographical area which is covered: England, Scotland, Wales, the Channel Islands and the Isle of Man. The new name came into effect on 1 January 1995.

Yearly Meeting entered the twenty-first century with its sessions fulfilling a variety of purposes, including those listed here. It receives the annual report of Meeting for Sufferings and its committees. It provides an opportunity to scrutinise and affirms the work done in the name of Friends in our meetings and by our standing committees and staff. It lays matters of concern before the Yearly Meeting for divine guidance, testing or decision. It informs and educates us, as a meeting for learning. It agrees constitutional changes and amendments to our book of discipline. It strengthens our witness as a religious society and encourages us in our living of the testimonies. It inspires us to action, corporately in our meetings or individually and in groups. It searches our spiritual depths and refreshes our spiritual life as individuals and corporately. It reinforces the sense of community in our meetings and in Britain Yearly Meeting as a whole. It praises, gives thanks to God, and celebrates.

Purposes and functions

6.02 We did conclude among ourselves to settle a meeting, to see one another's faces, and open our hearts one to another in the Truth of God once a year, as formerly it used to be.

Yearly Meeting in London, 1668

6.03 The intent and holy design of our annual assemblies, in their first constitution, were for a great and weighty oversight and Christian care of the affairs of the churches pertaining to our holy profession and Christian communion; that good order, true love, unity and concord may be faithfully followed and maintained among all of us.

Yearly Meeting in London, 1718

6.04 Yearly Meeting is an occasion when the concerns of one group of Friends or another can be shared with the meeting as a whole, as it seeks God's guidance and relates each particular insight or service to the others brought before it. At different stages of its history its agenda and pattern have been built up in different ways. There was a time when the main exercise related to 'the state of the Society' as revealed by the answers to the queries or, after written replies were discontinued, by triennial reports from quarterly meetings. The twentieth century witnessed a considerable growth in the number of standing committees of the Yearly Meeting and Meeting for Sufferings, and in their size and work, and increasingly the agenda of Yearly Meeting was built up round their concerns. An Agenda Committee (6.18) is charged with the duty of considering and deciding upon the business to be put before the Yearly Meeting.

6.05 *In 1999 the Agenda Committee wrote:*

We see Yearly Meetings as events in the life of the institution of Britain Yearly Meeting which can involve:

constitutional decision-making;

annually overseeing and guiding the stewardship exercised between Yearly Meetings;

settling policy on major areas of work or witness;

promoting teaching and learning;

offering inspiration and leadership;

celebrating together;

re-dedicating ourselves;

calling us to action;

creating and sustaining a community, including those both under and over 19.

Yearly Meetings are also occasions in which we can learn, practise, improve, and take back to our local meetings ways of conducting business which are rooted in Quaker tradition and our own experience yet also meet contemporary challenges. They should be a focus for every facet of Quakerism, constantly reminding us of what it means to be a Quaker today.

We are aware that we do not always achieve these purposes in our Yearly Meetings as well as we might; and indeed that it may not be possible to fulfil all the purposes to an equal extent at an individual Yearly Meeting. Seeking the right balance at any one Yearly Meeting is a necessary though difficult task. Our experience is that Yearly Meeting is most fruitful when its programme includes some decision-making and 'doing together', alongside more reflective sessions; and when it focuses on doing what only Yearly Meeting can do.

6.06 The agenda may comprise:

a. minutes from area or general meetings and minutes or memoranda from standing committees of Meeting for Sufferings sharing with the yearly meeting as a whole some concern which has their united support;

b. proposals for amendments to our book of discipline forwarded by Meeting for Sufferings or Yearly Meeting Agenda Committee in accordance with the process currently approved; details of this process may be obtained on application to the Recording Clerk;
c. a summary of the proceedings of Meeting for Sufferings during the year, together with such reports as it may forward from committees on their work, together comprising the annual report (6.25);
d. the financial report and audited accounts of the Yearly Meeting Funds for the preceding year (6.25);
e. the tabular statement (6.07);
f. the report of the Agenda Committee (6.18);
g. testimonies to the grace of God in the lives of deceased Friends, forwarded by area and general meetings;
h. epistles received from other yearly meetings and other Friends' bodies, reminding us of our membership in a world family of Friends;
i. subjects initiated by the Agenda Committee (6.18);
j. the report of the Quaker Stewardship Committee, certifying that every part of Britain Yearly Meeting is producing proper financial accounts and property records (14.28).

Items b, c, d, e and j are presented for consideration and acceptance, the *Trustees' annual report & accounts* having been approved by Britain Yearly Meeting Trustees (8.03) and forwarded by Meeting for Sufferings.

6.07 The tabular statement is a factual account of changes over the preceding year in the status and membership of the constituent meetings of the yearly meeting, together with other information on the membership of the yearly meeting, compiled by the Recording Clerk from information supplied by area meetings (4.10.h, 11.37).

6.08 In the course of reflecting on his experience as secretary from 1940 to 1945 of Friends War Victims Relief

Committee and Friends Relief Service, Roger Wilson wrote in 1949:

> Yearly Meeting is not, in the last resort, made up of a body of experts. People who know a great deal about the matter in hand may do most of the talking, central committee members familiar with the complexities of translating convictions into practical terms may appear to be leading the meeting. But a few halting yet sincere hesitations, uttered by a Friend from a small meeting in a distant county may, in fact, be of more significance in revealing a matter in its true setting than all the sophistication of the committee worthies. Again and again on deep issues it is reality as known and experienced by the simple and single-minded meeting, that does not know too much to have lost its simple faith, that guides the Society; and the central committee or its administrator who knows that its service is, in the end, related to the life of the local meetings in the country, will have a deep respect for the weight of Yearly Meeting.

6.09 No organisation or planning can produce a good Yearly Meeting if those who attend come for an inadequate reason. When the Religious Society of Friends gathers for its annual assembly, it does so because it seeks to come to know the mind of God on the various affairs to be brought forward... We are ordinary people, with the shortcomings of ordinary people, and there is laid upon us the necessity of patience with one another in all our gatherings, and especially in Yearly Meeting, and the willingness to accept the imperfect arising from our human limitations. When therefore we find our Yearly Meeting falling short of the standard which it should reach, whether in worship or in deliberation, it behoves each of us to listen more intently for the voice of the Spirit, and to seek the more earnestly that every contribution, be it by spoken word or in silence, is that which is in accord with the divine leading. In our worship at Yearly Meeting, it is laid upon us with special weight to listen. It is not our ministry that is required in worship, nor our inspiration in deliberations, but we seek to hear the true word of God speaking through our frail humanity and leading us to the place where he would have us be. This is the right holding of Yearly Meeting.

Right Holding of Yearly Meeting Committee, 1960

6.10 *The service and counsel of John Morland (1837–1934):*

His attendance at Yearly Meeting was increasingly prized, and his personality felt to be a permeating influence. To the last his judgment retained its acuteness. How frequently in a few trenchant sentences he has cut through a problem or re-stated confused issues... The precepts laid down by him whilst clerk of Yearly Meeting (1899–1903) were scrupulously observed by himself: 'Do not speak without a sense of the imperative ought; speak audibly, not loudly but clearly; speak shortly.'

Testimony of Mid-Somerset Monthly Meeting, 1934

6.11 *Mary Hughes (1860–1941) comes with heart and mind prepared:*

Anyone who lived with her during April and May knew how intensely Friends' Yearly Meeting was on her mind. It was as important to her as 'going up to Jerusalem'. For weeks beforehand it came into her prayers in the morning, at meal times and with friends. She wished that God's power would be in the meetings, that people would go forth from them with a new vision of God's work for them, a new sensitiveness towards their fellows, especially the distressed.

Rosa Hobhouse, 1949

Constitution

6.12 Britain Yearly Meeting in session is the final constitutional authority of the Religious Society of

Friends in England, Scotland*, Wales†, the Channel Islands and the Isle of Man. Its membership consists of all those who belong to the several area meetings in Great Britain, the Channel Islands and the Isle of Man. All members of the yearly meeting have the right to attend and to take part in its deliberations. In order to provide for a due attendance, each area meeting is to ensure that a sufficient number of Friends will undertake to be present. Public statements to be made in the name of the Religious Society of Friends in Great Britain, the Channel Islands and the Isle of Man must be authorised by Britain Yearly Meeting or by Meeting for Sufferings (3.27).

Clerks

6.13 The Yearly Meeting shall at its first session appoint, on the nomination of the Committee on Clerks (6.19), a clerk and two assistant clerks. The clerks shall hold office until the first session of the ensuing Yearly Meeting.

Visiting Friends

6.14 Members of the Society not belonging to Britain Yearly Meeting may attend the sessions of the Yearly Meeting on producing a minute or letter of introduction signed by the clerk of their own meeting or otherwise satisfying the clerk of their membership. However, Friends in sojourning membership of an area meeting (11.28) are exempt from this requirement.

Permission to non-members

6.15 Permission for the attendance of non-members at one or more sessions may be given at the discretion of

* On the responsibilities of General Meeting for Scotland see 5.03.
† On the responsibilities of the Meeting of Friends in Wales see 5.04–5.05.

the clerk, if satisfied that their presence is likely to be of service to the Society. Such permission should be sought well in advance of Yearly Meeting and should be supported by one or more elders to whom the applicant is well known. Last-minute requests should not be made. Elders supporting applications should ensure that non-members receive suitable support and guidance to enable them to be of service and to benefit from attendance at Yearly Meeting. If called to speak in a Yearly Meeting session, non-members should be sensitive to the fact that they are not in membership and should make this known.

Time of meeting

6.16 Yearly Meeting shall normally meet in May, but approximately one meeting in four shall be held residentially in the summer. The dates and places at which Yearly Meeting is to be held shall be determined by Meeting for Sufferings on the recommendation of the Yearly Meeting Agenda Committee. Meeting for Sufferings shall have the power to summon a Special Yearly Meeting (7.02.f).

Yearly Meeting committees

6.17 The following committees are appointed in whole or in part by Yearly Meeting, for continuing work after its conclusion: Agenda Committee (6.18), Committee on Clerks (6.19), Central Nominations Committee (6.21), Quaker Stewardship Committee (14.29).

In order to facilitate the business of Yearly Meeting the following committees shall be appointed at an early session: Nominating Group (6.22), Epistle Drafting Committee (6.23), Committee to Examine Minutes (6.24). The service of these committees ceases at the close of Yearly Meeting, save only in the case of the Nominating Group, which shall serve until the first session of the ensuing Yearly Meeting. Additionally Yearly Meeting may appoint, on the nomination of the Central Nominations Committee, at an early session two Friends to serve on the Arrangements Committee (6.20) for the period of Yearly Meeting. Yearly Meeting may decide to set up, or request Meeting for Sufferings to set up, other committees or ad hoc groups for special tasks.

Agenda Committee

6.18 The planning of the agenda for, and the use of the premises during, Yearly Meeting shall be in the hands of the Yearly Meeting Agenda Committee, which shall consult as may be necessary with standing committees, general and area meetings and the Meeting of Friends in Wales.

The membership of the Agenda Committee shall be as follows:

a. the clerk and assistant clerks of Yearly Meeting together with any other Friend nominated by the Committee on Clerks to serve as clerk or assistant clerk of the next Yearly Meeting;
b. nine Friends appointed by Yearly Meeting for a three-year period on the recommendation of the Central Nominations Committee, one-third retiring annually though eligible for re-appointment;
c. nine Friends appointed by Meeting for Sufferings for a three-year period on the recommendation of the Central Nominations Committee, one-third retiring annually though eligible for re-appointment;
d. one Friend appointed by Yearly Meeting for a three-year period on the recommendation of Quaker Life Central Committee for the children and young people's programme (8.10).

The Agenda Committee shall:

e. appoint such subcommittees of its members as are from time to time required;

f. appoint annually three or more of its members to serve on the Arrangements Committee (6.20).

The Agenda Committee is responsible for liaison with the planning committee appointed by Yearly Meeting to oversee the arrangements for each residential Summer Gathering (6.26, 6.27).

The Agenda Committee works closely with Meeting for Sufferings and its standing committees to promote the right holding of Yearly Meeting, to foster the Agenda Committee's relationship with them, and to integrate the work of the committee into the budgeted programme of central work of the Britain Yearly Meeting. It keeps under review the longer-term evolution of the institution of Yearly Meeting in session and the pattern of its gatherings over time, in relation to organisational and spiritual development in the life of the Society. Its terms of reference may be obtained on application to the Recording Clerk.

Committee on Clerks

6.19 The Committee on Clerks is responsible for considering the short-, medium- and long-term clerkship needs of the Yearly Meeting.

The Committee on Clerks acts as the nominating body for clerks of Yearly Meeting, Meeting for Sufferings, Britain Yearly Meeting Trustees and Summer Gatherings. It brings forward:

a. to Yearly Meeting, annually, names of a Friend to serve as clerk and two Friends to serve as assistant clerks of Yearly Meeting;
b. to Meeting for Sufferings, annually, names of Friends to serve as clerk and assistant clerk of Meeting for Sufferings;
c. to Yearly Meeting, annually, names of Friends to serve as clerk and assistant clerk of the Trustees;

d. to Yearly Meeting, two years before each Summer Gathering, names of Friends to serve as clerks of the Summer Gathering.

The Committee on Clerks consists of thirteen members including a clerk appointed by the committee from within its number. One-third of the members other than the clerk will retire annually at the rise of Yearly Meeting, and are eligible for re-appointment. These Friends shall serve for no more than six continuous years. The clerk is appointed for a three-year period and may serve for a maximum of nine continuous years on the committee.

Arrangements Committee

6.20 The Agenda Committee shall appoint annually three or more of its members who shall, with the clerk and assistant clerks of Yearly Meeting, serve as an Arrangements Committee. Yearly Meeting may at an early session appoint, on the nomination of the Central Nominations Committee, two further Friends to serve on this committee for the period of Yearly Meeting.

The Arrangements Committee shall act on behalf of the Agenda Committee between meetings. It shall consider any alterations which may appear to be required in the agenda whether before or during Yearly Meeting, any application received too late for consideration by the Agenda Committee for the use of the premises during Yearly Meeting, and any questions referred to it for the better ordering of the Yearly Meeting. It shall decide which testimonies concerning deceased Friends (6.06.g) and epistles from yearly meetings and other Friends' bodies (6.06.h) are to be read in the sessions.

Central Nominations Committee

6.21 The Central Nominations Committee is a standing committee appointed by Yearly Meeting (6.22) to bring forward names for service as required both by Yearly Meeting in session and by Meeting for Sufferings. It consists of twenty-seven members, with one-third of the members retiring annually at the rise of Yearly Meeting and not eligible for immediate re-appointment. The clerk and assistant clerk are appointed by the committee from within its number and may serve a further year beyond the initial appointment period.

The Central Nominations Committee brings forward names to each Yearly Meeting for the following appointments:

a. Yearly Meeting Agenda Committee: three Friends to serve for three years (6.18);
b. Yearly Meeting Arrangements Committee: two Friends to serve during the period of Yearly Meeting (6.20);
c. Epistle Drafting Committee: five to seven Friends to serve during the period of Yearly Meeting, including one to act as convener (6.23);
d. Yearly Meeting Elders as required by the Yearly Meeting;
e. Yearly Meeting Overseers as required by the Yearly Meeting;
f. Yearly Meeting Accessibility and Support Group: numbers required by the terms of reference (which may be obtained on application to the Recording Clerk);
g. Yearly Meeting Publications Group for *Quaker faith & practice*: one Friend to serve for three years;
h. Quaker Stewardship Committee: three Friends to serve for three years (14.29);
i. Britain Yearly Meeting Trustees: five Friends to serve for three years (8.03).

When due or required, it also brings in names of Friends to serve on the Summer Gathering Planning Committee (6.27), on ad hoc groups or for any other appointments requested by Yearly Meeting.

When interim appointments to any of these bodies are required, the Central Nominations Committee may bring forward names to Meeting for Sufferings, which acts on behalf of Yearly Meeting.

The Central Nominations Committee acts for Meeting for Sufferings in bringing forward names for appointments of Meeting for Sufferings' representatives to Yearly Meeting Agenda Committee (6.18); for appointments to the central committees, standing committees and trusts appointed by Meeting for Sufferings (8.03–8.04; 8.08–8.11; 8.16–8.19); and as representatives to various bodies, for service on ad hoc groups or for any other appointments requested by Meeting for Sufferings.

The committee works closely with each body on which vacancies arise in order to clarify the requirements, which may include the need for representatives from other bodies.

Yearly Meeting Nominating Group

6.22 Nominations for appointment to the Central Nominations Committee and the Committee on Clerks are made by the Yearly Meeting Nominating Group. The group consists of six to eight Friends appointed in a Yearly Meeting session each year: a convener nominated by the previous Nominating Group and the remainder on nomination from the body of the meeting. The group meets and consults as necessary during the period up to the next Yearly Meeting, including with the Central Nominations Committee and the Committee on Clerks, to enable it to bring nominations to that Yearly Meeting, as follows:

a. annually, four Friends to serve on the Committee on Clerks for a three-year period from the rise of the Yearly Meeting (6.19);
b. annually, nine Friends to serve on the Central Nominations Committee for a three-year period from the rise of the Yearly Meeting (6.21);

c. Friends to fill casual vacancies on these two bodies;
d. one Friend to serve as convener of the next Yearly Meeting Nominating Group.

Epistle Drafting Committee

6.23 The Yearly Meeting shall at its first session appoint, on the nomination of the Central Nominations Committee, an Epistle Drafting Committee, of which one member shall be named as convener. Yearly Meeting shall, at an appropriate stage in its deliberations, offer guidance on the content of the epistle. The draft of the epistle shall be made available to Friends for written comment and shall be submitted to Yearly Meeting for approval, normally at the beginning of the final session. The epistle as approved shall be read in the concluding session of Yearly Meeting and signed by the clerk.

Committee to Examine Minutes

6.24 The Yearly Meeting shall at its first session appoint not more than ten Friends, who shall arrange a rota whereby two of their number shall examine the minutes of the meeting at the close of each session and correct any slight inaccuracies that may be found. If any substantial alterations appear to be required they are to be proposed at the next session prior to any other business.

Documents

6.25 Any communication to the Yearly Meeting from a general or area meeting, from the Meeting of Friends in Wales, Six Weeks Meeting or Young Friends General Meeting shall be in the form of a minute signed by the clerk of such meeting, as shall communications from Meeting for Sufferings and from committees of the Yearly Meeting.

The Agenda Committee, in arranging the subjects to be brought before Yearly Meeting, is encouraged to prepare concise but lucid memoranda which can be printed in *Documents in advance* and circulated in ample time to allow not only for individual study but for discussion in local meetings.

The *Proceedings* of the Yearly Meeting comprise *Documents in advance*, including the *Annual report of Meeting for Sufferings and its committees*, the *Trustees' annual report & accounts* for the preceding year, the tabular statement, the report of the Agenda Committee, testimonies to the grace of God in the lives of deceased Friends, the epistles received from other yearly meetings and Friends' bodies, and the printed minutes of Yearly Meeting.

Summer Gatherings

6.26 Yearly Meeting Summer Gatherings are residential events held from time to time, usually week-long every four years, as determined by Meeting for Sufferings on the recommendation of Yearly Meeting Agenda Committee. The first was held in Bradford in 1991.

6.27 During the 1970s and 1980s residential Yearly Meetings (6.16) were becoming increasingly popular, with Friends appreciating the events alongside the sessions as much as the business. Hence it was decided to try out a gathering without the formal Yearly Meeting business, answering the needs of Friends to live together in community and to explore issues and activities for which there was little programmed time at a meeting for church affairs. Summer Gatherings have clearly answered this need and they are now a valued part of the Britain Yearly Meeting schedule.

The aims of Summer Gatherings are:

> to strengthen and support the witness and activity of Friends by continuing the personal friendships, spiritual inspiration and momentum that residential gatherings provide;

to provide time, at a more leisurely pace than is normally possible during Yearly Meeting, for the exploration of those issues and concerns which by their nature require such time;

to provide the space for exploration of issues and concerns in groups or other diverse ways;

to provide the time and facilities for study and real learning;

to involve as many Friends and attenders of all ages as possible in active participation; this should include activities for all ages.

Attendance at a Summer Gathering is open to all Friends and attenders by application, within the numerical limits agreed beforehand.

The events are organised by a Summer Gathering Planning Committee appointed by Yearly Meeting (6.21) and working in liaison with the Agenda Committee (6.18). A copy of the terms of reference of the Planning Committee may be obtained on application to the Recording Clerk.

The clerks of Summer Gatherings are appointed by Yearly Meeting on the nomination of the Committee on Clerks (6.19), and serve also as the clerks of the Planning Committee.

The Summer Gathering may communicate by minute to Yearly Meeting via the Agenda Committee, or to Meeting for Sufferings.

Yearly Meeting and Meeting for Sufferings

6.28 Yearly Meeting delegates to Meeting for Sufferings, as its standing representative body (7.02–7.03) in the intervals between Yearly Meetings, deliberation, discernment and the oversight of our corporate religious life. Meeting for Sufferings also receives regular interim reports for information and consultation from the Britain Yearly Meeting Trustees.

Meeting for Sufferings is largely (7.05.a, b, c & d) appointed by Yearly Meeting in session, to which it reports annually. Yearly Meeting in session remains the final constitutional authority (6.12), to which Meeting for Sufferings is accountable.

Yearly Meeting also entrusts to Meeting for Sufferings the organisation and periodic revision of the structure of standing committees which oversee particular areas of the central work undertaken on behalf of Britain Yearly Meeting as a whole. However, it reserves to itself decisions affecting the existence and basic functions of Quaker Life (8.10) and Quaker Peace & Social Witness (8.11) as central committees. While Meeting for Sufferings may modify their composition and terms of reference, as for its other standing committees, the essential place of these two central committees and the work they represent in the yearly meeting organisation may not be altered without the approval of Yearly Meeting in session.

Other changes in the structure of standing committees through which Meeting for Sufferings works must be reported to Yearly Meeting (7.03); in such cases, any church government amendments proposed reflect decisions of Meeting for Sufferings already taken, and it is for Yearly Meeting to decide whether the proposed textual changes to our book of discipline accurately describe the new structure.

Meeting for Sufferings is entrusted with the general care of matters affecting Britain Yearly Meeting in its life and witness. It has a particular care for its central work organisation and church government, including the preparation of constitutional amendments for Yearly Meeting in session to consider.

Chapter 7

Meeting for Sufferings

History

7.01 The yearly meeting's local organisation was settled in the years 1667–9. The 1670s saw the development of central organisation. Apart from Yearly Meeting (1668), three bodies deserve special mention – the Six Weeks Meeting (1671), Morning Meeting (1673) and Meeting for Sufferings (1675). All were basically meetings of London Friends; all, to a greater or less extent, undertook national responsibilities. The Six Weeks Meeting was the most metropolitan of the three, though even it engaged on occasion in such national business as the wording of the marriage certificate. The Morning Meeting may have had its origin in the 'meeting of ancient Friends' said to have started about 1656 or the general meeting of ministering Friends in and about the city, established in 1661. It comprised men 'publick' (or ministering) Friends in and about the city, and when, later, elders were appointed, men elders became eligible for membership of the Morning Meeting, which met each Monday.

It was the Morning Meeting which took the initiative in calling a conference in October 1675 to consider what steps could be taken to secure redress from sufferings. At that meeting it was agreed 'that certaine friends of this Citty be heere nominated to keep a Constant Meeting about Sufferings 4 times a year, with the day and time of each meeting here fixed and setled'. Twelve Friends, two from each of the London monthly meetings, were then listed with 'as many as are free of the Second dayes morning meeting of publick Friends to meet togeather as aforesaid', and that 'at least one friend of each County be appointed by the quarterly meeting thereof to be in readyness to repaire to any of the same meetings at this Citty, at such times as theire urgent occasions or sufferings shall require'. The constitution of Meeting for Sufferings agreed by Yearly Meeting 1702 was set forth as: 'Publick Friends and such that are appointed or approved by the severall Quarterly Meetings of the Countyes & other Countrys that Correspond with this meeting in all Places, and are entred as such in the Correspondent Book.'

The full Meeting for Sufferings was to meet at the beginning of each law term and one quarter of the membership was to meet weekly (each Friday) until the next full meeting. The minutes begin on 22 June 1676. At the outset some eight to ten Friends attended the weekly meetings and the speed with which, backed by information from the quarterly meeting correspondents, the meeting was able to put Friends' case to good effect before members of both Houses of Parliament is indeed impressive. The meeting was not restricted to the efforts to obtain redress in particular 'Cases of Suffering' (though this was the first item in the minutes until about 1750). Yearly Meeting entrusted it with the task of trying to obtain relief from the oath, in which it was successful under the Affirmation Acts of the late seventeenth and early eighteenth centuries. Yearly Meeting likewise asked it to try to secure a reduction of the burden suffered under tithes, which the meeting attempted by the promotion of successive Quakers Tithe Bills in the 1730s. It was the same closely knit relationship of county quarterly meeting correspondents and London members of Meeting for Sufferings that enabled Friends to campaign with such success in the movement towards the abolition of the slave trade. Meeting for Sufferings, meeting weekly (as it continued to do until 1798), was able with great effect to carry out Yearly Meeting's instructions. So swift and smooth had its organisation become that it would be tempting to describe it as highly efficient parliamentary lobbying. Although it was primarily a London body its effective correspondent system enabled it to speak with an authoritative national voice.

The nineteenth century saw a steady increase in the work of Meeting for Sufferings and a corresponding growth of its committees. The Parliamentary Committee had existed from the early eighteenth century. The Slave Trade Committee of 1783–92 was followed by other and more permanent committees – the 1817 Minden & Pyrmont Committee became the Continental Committee, serving for over 100 years as a link between Friends in Great Britain and small groups on the continent of Europe, in Australasia, in Calcutta, southern Africa and other places; the administrative committees charged with the care of the premises and with printing were supplemented by others responsible for the library and for finance; other committees took up particular concerns of Friends – several undertook successive efforts at relief work, an anti-slavery committee was re-established, in 1888 the Peace Committee was formed, and subsequent committees were set up to express Friends' views on the opium traffic and on betting and gambling.

Alongside this steadily widening stream of interests, the constitution of the meeting was changing. The era of railway travel made it increasingly easy for Friends to attend, and the system of London and country correspondents gave place to that of quarterly meeting representatives. This was reflected in revised constitutions of 1856 and 1883. In 1884 the meeting had an appointed membership of 98 with representatives from all but six quarterly meetings. In 1898 (following a decision of Yearly Meeting 1896) the first women Friends took their seats in Meeting for Sufferings. Anna Littleboy, one of those then appointed, recalled thirty years later that 'while kindly and courteously received, it was evident that the presence of women was not exactly welcomed by most of the older members, and the clerk impressed upon them that the meeting was for the conduct of business and not for speeches'.

Perhaps a more drastic change than the admission of women Friends was the laying down in 1901 of the Morning Meeting and the transference of its functions to Meeting for Sufferings. Henceforward the consideration of personal concerns for service overseas and the welcoming of travelling Friends from other yearly meetings was added to already increasing business. Preoccupation with relief work, and still greater growth of the range of Friends' concern added to the length of agenda. The days of the meeting which began at eleven o'clock and was over by a late lunchtime had passed.

The twentieth century therefore witnessed a steady trend of delegation of routine matters to subcommittees, but it also saw a gradual growth in the meeting's function in drawing together and relating to one another the different strands in the yearly meeting's life and service. This process was helped as some of the nineteenth-century 'independent associations' (the Friends Foreign Mission Association and the Friends Tract Association for example) became or were merged with official committees of the yearly meeting, gradually accepting the responsibilities and discipline that this involved. It also became increasingly clear that the distinction between committees of Yearly Meeting and Meeting for Sufferings had outlived its usefulness, and Special Yearly Meeting 1965 agreed that all standing committees should be appointed by Meeting for Sufferings, which, in periodic review of their work, would be enabled 'to become more sensitive to the insights of the committees and thus ... promote that knowledge and understanding by means of which both the meeting and the committees should be able more effectively to enter into and to discharge their responsibilities'.

The additional tasks laid on Meeting for Sufferings as 'a central body which can act on behalf of the Society between Yearly Meetings' necessitated, in the words of

Special Yearly Meeting 1965, that 'such a body must be representative of Friends both geographically and as to diversity of our membership'. This led to representation from monthly meetings rather than quarterly meetings, to three-year appointments rather than annual, to a change in the day of meeting from Friday to Saturday and, in 1974, to the withdrawal of the automatic right of elders to attend. In furtherance of 'the essential unity of the work undertaken in the name of the Yearly Meeting', staff employed by the yearly meeting and by seven separate employing committees were unified and became employees of Meeting for Sufferings. The anomaly remained that while the yearly meeting's essential central services were funded by means of a 'quota' contributed by monthly meetings, standing committees were issuing separate financial appeals which had the effect of competing one with another. The financing of all the central work was unified between 1986 and 1988, placing further responsibility on Meeting for Sufferings for the testing of concern and for the allocation of available resources to the wide variety of religious service undertaken in the name of the yearly meeting.

In 1997 Meeting for Sufferings revived the practice of maintaining a register of Friends before the courts or imprisoned for matters of conscience.

Thus, albeit in different circumstances, Meeting for Sufferings attempts to fulfil its functions as defined by Yearly Meeting 1833: 'A standing committee of this meeting ... entrusted with a general care of whatever may arise during the intervals of this meeting, affecting our religious society and requiring immediate attention'.

Functions

7.02 Meeting for Sufferings is the standing representative body entrusted with the general care of matters affecting Britain Yearly Meeting and, in the intervals between Yearly Meetings, the making of decisions and the issuing of statements in the name of Britian Yearly Meeting. Within our church government it exercises discernment on priorities and receives regular interim reports for information and consultation on the Britain Yearly Meeting Trustees' work. It has a part to play in developing a visionary and prophetic role for the whole yearly meeting and in fostering communication throughout the yearly meeting.

The functions of Meeting for Sufferings are:

a. to set the priorities for the centrally managed work in its long-term plan, which would interpret the wishes of the Yearly Meeting and the concerns of the area meetings, taking into account its knowledge of the detailed aspirations and plans of the central and other standing committees, the advice of the Britain Yearly Meeting Trustees and the funds available;
b. to issue public statements in the name of Britain Yearly Meeting (3.27);
c. to receive regular interim reports for information and consultation on the work of the Britain Yearly Meeting Trustees (8.03);
d. to receive the Britain Yearly Meeting *Trustees' annual report & accounts* for information, as forwarded by the Trustees to Yearly Meeting (8.03);
e. to make a report on its own activities to Yearly Meeting each year;
f. to determine the dates of Yearly Meeting and where it will be held, on the recommendation of the Yearly Meeting Agenda Committee (6.16); it may summon a Special Yearly Meeting should occasion arise;
g. to deliberate on how best to support the spiritual life of the yearly meeting and to further the development of its visionary and prophetic role;
h. to keep under review and to test as appropriate the existing and new concerns referred to it by area meetings and others (4.19, 4.20, 13.13);

i. to foster communication throughout the yearly meeting;
j. to receive minutes from area meetings and, when thought appropriate, pass them to Britain Yearly Meeting Trustees and the central or other standing committees for attention;
k. to make appropriate entries in the prison and court register (7.01);
l. to appoint representatives to attend other Yearly Meetings as thought fit;
m. to receive information about changes in the composition or status of general meetings and gatherings (5.07);
n. to make changes in the composition of area meetings (4.12);
o. to give assistance to area meetings in the amicable settlement of disputes (4.23);
p. to hear appeals against area meeting decisions (4.25–4.26);
q. to give guidance on policy matters referred to it by the Britain Yearly Meeting Trustees from time to time;
r. to authorise action and minutes as required under other sections of *Quaker faith & practice*;
s. to set up an arrangements group and support and working groups to assist its own work as it sees fit.

7.03 The Britain Yearly Meeting Trustees shall furnish Yearly Meeting with annual reports on their work and the work of the central and other standing committees. They keep Meeting for Sufferings informed about their work by providing regular interim reports for information and consultation. The Britain Yearly Meeting Trustees and the central and other standing committees are reminded that they should consult with Meeting for Sufferings and have regard for its guidance in any of the following circumstances:

a. when proposing to enter upon some major new field of service, or to give up some significant long-term project;

b. when proposing to make some new pronouncement or envisaging a new relationship which involves some important question of principle for Britain Yearly Meeting;
c. when considering major appeals or commitments;
d. when it seems desirable to share with Friends the interpretation of some urgent need or of some unusually significant piece of service;
e. when some concern impinges on the work of other committees or aspects of the yearly meeting's wider work.

7.04 Area meetings, General Meeting for Scotland, the Meeting of Friends in Wales, Six Weeks Meeting, Young Friends General Meeting, the Britain Yearly Meeting Trustees and the standing committees appointed by Yearly Meeting or Meeting for Sufferings may communicate with Meeting for Sufferings by minute signed by or on behalf of their clerk. Such meetings or committees may request that Friends other than members of Meeting for Sufferings be allowed to speak to such minutes.

Constitution

7.05 Meeting for Sufferings comprises the following:

a. about 170 Friends appointed by the Yearly Meeting on the nomination of area meetings (7.07), in accordance with the schedule provided (7.06), serving for triennial periods from Yearly Meetings 2006, 2009, etc, with service normally limited to six years (3.23);
b. Friends appointed by the Yearly Meeting on the nomination of certain standing committees appointed by Meeting for Sufferings (7.08), being officers or other named representatives, in accordance with the following schedule:

Quaker Communications Central Committee (8.08)	2
Quaker Finance & Property Central Committee (8.09) (the clerk and one other)	2
Quaker Life Central Committee (8.10)	2
Quaker Peace & Social Witness Central Committee (8.11)	2
Quaker Committee for Christian & Interfaith Relations (8.16, 9.13)	1
Quaker World Relations Committee (8.17, 9.06)	1

c. two representatives appointed by the Yearly Meeting on the nomination of Young Friends General Meeting (5.09), being officers or others able to speak in its name;

d. up to two representatives each appointed by the Yearly Meeting on the nomination of General Meeting for Scotland (5.03) and Meeting of Friends in Wales (5.04–5.05), subject to review in due course;

e. the clerk and assistant clerk of Meeting for Sufferings, any previous clerk and assistant clerk of the meeting during the remainder of the triennial period in which their service ends, the clerk of Yearly Meeting, the clerk of the Britain Yearly Meeting Trustees (8.03), all other Britain Yearly Meeting Trustees, the clerk of the Central Nominations Committee (6.21), and any members of the Meeting for Sufferings Arrangements Group whose membership of the meeting would otherwise have ended, ex officio;

f. up to ten Friends co-opted by the meeting itself (7.09), the appointments ending at the close of each triennial period;

with the Recording Clerk, the Assistant Recording Clerk, and all members of the Management Meeting (8.21), ex officio.

In case of vacancy by death, release or resignation under a, b, c or d above, the nominating body may forward the name of a Friend to serve for the remainder of the triennial period to Meeting for Sufferings, which may make an interim appointment up to the next Yearly Meeting, which then can make an appointment to fill the vacancy.

Meeting for Sufferings shall regularly inform the Yearly Meeting of all changes in its membership under e and f above.

Permission for the attendance of other Friends at a particular meeting may be given at the discretion of the clerk of Meeting for Sufferings.

Area meeting representatives

7.06 Each area meeting may make two nominations from its membership for appointment to Meeting for Sufferings (4.17). Additional nominations may be made by larger area meetings in accordance with a schedule approved by the Yearly Meeting one year before each triennial appointment (7.05.a), modified as necessary by interim decisions necessitated by the division or amalgamation of area meetings. The schedule shall provide for one additional representative for every 300 members or part thereof in excess of 300.

Advice to area meetings as to nominations

7.07 In nominating Friends to serve on Meeting for Sufferings, area meetings are reminded of the variety and weight of the business which comes before that meeting, which must have the spiritual authority to speak in the name of Quakers in Britain.

A responsible sharing in the exercise of the meeting is essential. Britain Yearly Meeting requires Friends to serve on its behalf who are diligent within their own areas in the attendance of meetings both for worship and for church affairs, and able if occasion arises to interpret sensitively the views and judgment of their own area meetings to Meeting for Sufferings.

More important, however, is the duty of members to the meeting itself; if it is to reach right judgments it must be served by Friends of spiritual maturity and with a good grasp of our testimonies and structures.

Area meetings are therefore encouraged to nominate representatives who are well versed in Friends' business methods through participation at local level. It is also important that sufficient numbers of representatives are able and willing to act as trustees of Britain Yearly Meeting if asked to serve in that capacity. In making nominations, area meetings should bear in mind the need to balance experience and continuity with the value of fresh insight and wider involvement of the membership and the importance of reporting back as part of the communication between Meeting for Sufferings and area meetings (4.17).

Area meetings should bear in mind minute 27 of Yearly Meeting 2000 concerning the service of former members of staff: 'that care be taken to ensure that adequate time has elapsed between the ending of their employed service and the commencement of committee service, particularly where the work of the committee is directly related to their former work. We understand that "adequate time" should normally mean a minimum of one year, or longer in the case of Friends whose work was closely related to that of the committee concerned.' The Yearly Meeting commended this policy as good practice to area meetings in respect of their nominations to serve on Meeting for Sufferings.

Committee representatives

7.08 In order that the meeting may have immediately available to it authoritative information about the thinking or action of any of its principal committees which may appear to have a bearing on any subject under consideration, Yearly Meeting appoints representatives of certain standing committees, on the nomination of those committees, in accordance with the schedule provided (7.05.b). These committees are asked to ensure that there is a regular attendance of their representatives.

The representation of the Quaker Finance & Property Central Committee comprises its clerk and one other in recognition of the role of the clerk as Yearly Meeting Treasurer in relation to the centrally managed work as a whole.

Co-options

7.09 To secure or to retain the service of able and knowledgeable Friends, without disturbing local arrangements for selecting representatives, Meeting for Sufferings is empowered to co-opt up to ten Friends (7.05.f).

Time of meeting

7.10 Meeting for Sufferings shall normally be held on the first Saturday of a month. It meets as often each year as the business requires. The clerk shall have the power to call a special meeting and at least seven days' notice shall be given to all members of the meeting.

Clerks

7.11 Meeting for Sufferings shall annually appoint Friends to serve as clerk and assistant clerk on the nomination of the Committee on Clerks (6.19).

Chapter 8

The centrally managed work of the Religious Society of Friends (Quakers) in Britain

Introduction

8.01 Britain Yearly Meeting in session is the body with ultimate authority for church affairs for Quakers in Britain (6.12). The term 'Britain Yearly Meeting' refers also to the combined membership of the seventy or so area meetings that make up the Religious Society of Friends in Britain and it is used as well in its governing document to refer to the work carried out centrally on behalf of the membership. This work is overseen by committees with membership drawn from Friends throughout Britain. Whilst much of the work of the yearly meeting takes place at general, area or local meeting level, some work is more appropriately organised centrally, and it is that which is described in this chapter.

In the governing document for the centrally held and managed policy, property, employment and work adopted by Yearly Meeting, the charitable object of Britain Yearly Meeting is 'the furtherance of the general religious and charitable purposes of the Religious Society of Friends in Britain and beyond'. The full governing document and explanatory notes are obtainable on application to the Recording Clerk.

8.02 There are four aspects to the centrally managed work of Britain Yearly Meeting:

a. organising and maintaining the whole of the Religious Society of Friends in Britain as responsive to the leadings of the Holy Spirit; this entails calling, briefing and running decision-making meetings with all the facilities necessary for them to work efficiently and effectively, and also conducting relations with other churches and faiths and ecumenical bodies;
b. supporting Friends in their local organisation, by providing services and advice relevant to the current demands of the Quaker community: for example such work may relate to children, elderly people, those getting married, those looking after meeting houses, and those raising funds;
c. raising awareness and developing understanding about the basic tenets of Quaker faith and practice, such as spirituality, peace and human rights, within and without the Religious Society of Friends in Britain;
d. putting Quaker thinking into practice in relation to the problems and needs of people at home and abroad: for example through training, conferences, work with those in positions of power, and social and development projects.

Britain Yearly Meeting Trustees

8.03 Yearly Meeting appoints trustees to act on its behalf as managing trustees of the work, assets and property held directly by Britain Yearly Meeting.

The Trustees are responsible to the Yearly Meeting for the right stewardship of its work, assets and property; as charity trustees, they are also legally defined as responsible for the general control and management of the administration of the affairs of Britain Yearly Meeting.

Although the Trustees have powers and responsibilities set out in the Britain Yearly Meeting governing document, these are grounded in terms of service.

Trustees have a duty to account to the outside world for the conduct of their trust. Gathered meetings, both of the Trustees and of other bodies, provide the religious discernment that guides our actions in the world. Trustees recognise and listen carefully to the discernment of Yearly Meeting, Meeting for Sufferings and their committees and ensure that it is followed, within legal and financial constraints.

Trustees undertake, on behalf of Yearly Meeting, legal compliance, monitoring and scrutiny functions. They also ensure that the centrally managed work is being properly governed and managed in accordance with the religious and charitable objects of Britain Yearly Meeting (see 8.01), set out in the governing document approved by Yearly Meeting and available on application to the Recording Clerk. They oversee the work of the Management Meeting (8.21) and are the employers of Britain Yearly Meeting staff (8.05).

In order to achieve this, the Trustees approve annually an operational plan and budget for the forthcoming year. They also approve the *Trustees' annual report & accounts* for the past year, which is presented for information to Meeting for Sufferings before submission to Yearly Meeting and to the charity regulators in due course.

The membership, responsibilities and duties of the Trustees are set out in detail in terms of reference to be approved and revised from time to time by Yearly Meeting. A copy is available on application to the Recording Clerk.

The Trustees are appointed by Yearly Meeting on the nomination of the Central Nominations Committee (6.21.i) as set out in the Trustees' terms of reference. In making nominations for service as trustees, the Central Nominations Committee ensures that the Friends approached are aware of the legal responsibilities of trustees and of the legal position on eligibility (see 15.04). The clerk and assistant clerk are appointed by

Yearly Meeting on the nomination of the Committee on Clerks (6.19.c).

Yearly Meeting also entrusts to the Trustees the organisation and periodic revision of the structure of the standing committees which oversee particular areas of the centrally managed work. However, it reserves to itself decisions affecting the existence and basic functions of the Trustees, and of Quaker Life Central Committee (8.10) and Quaker Peace & Social Witness Central Committee (8.11).

The Trustees must report to Yearly Meeting any changes in the structure of standing committees through which they work (7.03); in such cases, any amendments to our church government reflect decisions already taken, and it is for Yearly Meeting in session to decide whether the proposed textual changes to our book of discipline accurately describe the new structure.

8.04 The centrally managed work of Britain Yearly Meeting (see chapters 6 & 7) is in large part carried out by several committees responsible to Yearly Meeting through the Trustees. Although these committees are responsible to the Yearly Meeting through the Trustees, for practical reasons they are appointed by Meeting for Sufferings acting on behalf of Yearly Meeting.

These committees are of two main types: standing committees, which are established for an unlimited duration, and ad hoc committees, which may be set up for a specific purpose as occasion requires and are usually expected to complete their task by a set date. (See also 6.17 & 6.28.)

The Trustees may delegate any of their powers to a committee that includes two or more of the Trustees.

Most of the work of Britain Yearly Meeting is undertaken by standing committees, including the four central committees (8.08–8.11) which are responsible for particular areas of work. All standing committees work to terms of reference approved by the Trustees and are accountable to them. The Trustees are accountable to Yearly Meeting and the charity regulators, as described in 8.03. (Committees appointed in whole or in part by Yearly Meeting in session are described in chapter 6.)

Standing committees may delegate certain work to functional committees and other subsidiary bodies, such as programme management groups. Standing committees are responsible for appointing all such subsidiary bodies, determining their respective terms of reference and membership within the overall guidance on nominations (3.23–3.25 & 7.07).

The Trustees and the standing committees may communicate by minute with Meeting for Sufferings and Yearly Meeting Agenda Committee, and with each other. Whilst standing committees may also communicate by minute with General Meeting for Scotland, the Meeting of Friends in Wales and area meetings on matters furthering their purposes, they should ensure that this is done in co-ordination with Trustees and other standing committees, liaising as required.

Employment of staff

8.05 The Trustees employ staff in order to service the centrally managed work. Most are based at Friends House in London. The staff provide many of the resources and much of the expertise required to carry out Britain Yearly Meeting's work effectively in a manner consistent with Friends' testimonies and beliefs. Much preparatory, ongoing and follow-up work falls to the staff, and they need the full support of all Friends.

The Trustees ensure that staff working for Britain Yearly Meeting and committee members are treated fairly and do not experience unjust discrimination. Staff and committee members should strive to 'answer that of God in everyone' by working as a community which fosters a spirit of toleration and mutual concern for each other. In carrying out the work of Britain Yearly Meeting, respect for truth and integrity should be paramount so that high ethical standards are maintained.

The Recording Clerk

8.06 The Recording Clerk acts as secretary to Yearly Meeting, Meeting for Sufferings and the Britain Yearly Meeting Trustees and is responsible for servicing these bodies and for ensuring that their work is carried out. As the senior member of staff employed by the Trustees, the Recording Clerk's main tasks include maintaining contact with meetings throughout the yearly meeting, leading the Management Meeting (8.21), being line manager of the general secretaries and certain senior staff, acting as 'keeper and interpreter' of the regulations laid down in our church government, and representing Britain Yearly Meeting to, and fostering good relations with, outside bodies.

The office of Recording Clerk has widened considerably since it was first established in about 1657. In those early days, the role was largely concerned with the sufferings of Friends, and up to 1703 included serving the Yearly Meeting as clerk. In more recent times, oversight of the management of the departments has become an important function of the Recording Clerk.

The Recording Clerk serves, for the purposes of the Data Protection Act 1998, as Data Compliance Officer and is responsible for ensuring that the recording and processing of data held by the Yearly Meeting conforms with the law (4.45).

Participation of staff in meetings of the Britain Yearly Meeting Trustees

8.07 Members of the Management Meeting (8.21) and other staff attending meetings of the Britain Yearly Meeting

Trustees are not trustees of the centrally managed work and are not responsible for the decisions of the meeting. They are present in order to be able to provide the meeting with information about their work, and in order for them to be able to interpret and carry out the Trustees' decisions more effectively. Friends' understanding of the Quaker business method is that God may speak through anyone present.

The four central committees

It is unlikely that the work of the central committees, as described here, will remain unchanged for the next generation. The existence and basic functions of Quaker Life and Quaker Peace & Social Witness may not be altered except with the approval of Yearly Meeting (8.03) but the more detailed outline of the work of the committees described below may change more frequently according to the emphasis given by Meeting for Sufferings, the Britain Yearly Meeting Trustees and the central committees.

Quaker Communications Central Committee

8.08 Quaker Communications Central Committee exists to support and strengthen local meetings and Quakers in Britain as a whole. It does this by helping to promote a dialogue through which the purposes and programmes of Britain Yearly Meeting's work are developed. It seeks to secure financial and other support to enable Quaker testimonies to be demonstrated in the world; the strength of our religious society rests on the quality of our shared understanding and the degree to which we are prepared in discussion, voluntary action and financial contribution to commit our support to common purposes. It is accountable to the Britain Yearly Meeting Trustees.

Quaker Communications works to increase and monitor income from meetings, Friends, other individuals and grant giving bodies, in the form of contributions, legacies and grants. It uses its marketing expertise to contribute to the effective planning of income-earning activities, including publishing and conference provision. It sponsors work on legacy development (14.09–14.10) and, on behalf of Britain Yearly Meeting, it makes proposals to appropriate bodies who might wish to provide grant aid to support approved initiatives. The committee oversees the arrangements for the Annual Conference of Treasurers (see 14.16–14.17) and provides services including the annual schedule (14.08) to assist local treasurers and collectors.

Quaker Communications works to improve information sharing amongst Friends. Its services include providing printed and audio-visual materials and exhibition materials, applying information technology, and arranging conferences, study visits and gatherings. It also liaises with the press and electronic media on behalf of Britain Yearly Meeting.

Quaker Finance & Property Central Committee

8.09 Quaker Finance & Property Central Committee is accountable to the Britain Yearly Meeting Trustees for the effective stewardship of finance and property for Britain Yearly Meeting's work. Its financial service involves responsibility to the Trustees for the Yearly Meeting Funds (see 14.12–14.15) and any associated funds, administration of the Meeting Houses Funds (15.15), receipt and oversight of any special funds given to Britain Yearly Meeting, and advice on financial and investment policy. The clerk of the committee (7.08) is appointed directly by Meeting for Sufferings and has a role as Yearly Meeting Treasurer in relation to the centrally managed work as a whole.

The committee is responsible to the Britain Yearly Meeting Trustees for preparing the accounts of the yearly meeting (8.03) and its associated funds (see also chapter 14 *Finance*). It also advises the Trustees on financial resource planning, for which it prepares forecasts and guidelines. Quaker Finance & Property Central Committee is responsible to the Trustees for the management of the property owned and used by Britain Yearly Meeting and provides advice to local meetings.

For Friends Trusts Limited see 8.18 & 15.02

Quaker Life Central Committee

8.10 Quaker Life Central Committee works with Friends in their meetings and with other local and national committees to help deepen experience of God's grace and its consequent expression in all our lives and in our meetings. It seeks to nurture the worshipping community of Quakers in Britain, developing it into an inclusive community.

Its purpose is to strengthen and sustain the fabric of Quaker life by offering programmes and opportunities that will empower Friends, individually and in their meetings, to deepen their spiritual lives and attract new people to their meetings. The committee carries out its work by support, training, developing skills, and sharing experience and good practice. It uses local and regional networks, publications and other communications, and the opportunities available through co-operation within the Christian church and with other faith groups.

The three main areas for which Quaker Life Central Committee is accountable to the Britain Yearly Meeting Trustees are: spiritual development, religious learning and pastoral care; support for the right holding of meetings for worship and for church affairs; membership matters and outreach. The committee works closely with Woodbrooke Quaker Study Centre, and through Charney Manor and Swarthmoor Hall, in many of these areas.

The committee works together with and for those taking special responsibilities such as clerks, wardens, librarians, registering officers, elders and overseers. It also supports those involved with nominations, work with children and young people, relations with other churches and outreach to those who may be interested in Quakers in Britain.

As part of its work with young people, the committee is responsible for the holding of Junior Yearly Meeting (4.21).

The Library Committee is a functional committee of Quaker Life Central Committee but may report directly to the Britain Yearly Meeting Trustees when appropriate.

Quaker Peace & Social Witness Central Committee

8.11 Quaker Peace & Social Witness Central Committee works for Britain Yearly Meeting to translate our faith into action. As Quakers we are impelled by our faith to make our lives an active witness for peace and justice. Our historic testimonies to equality, justice, peace, simplicity and truth challenge us to alleviate suffering and seek positive social change.

The committee aims to ensure that its work is clearly rooted in Quaker values, expresses Quaker testimonies and builds upon Quaker experience. It works to build the daily experiences and spiritual leadings of Friends in their meetings into our corporate work. With this foundation the committee seeks to support Friends individually in their lives, jointly in their meetings and in Britain Yearly Meeting, to witness on behalf of Quakers in the world. Our work should be primarily directed to areas where our Quaker witness can be best done corporately and where it has a particular contribution to make.

The committee is responsible to the Britain Yearly Meeting Trustees for promoting a committed and rigorous social and political engagement for the building of a just and peaceful world. The committee tries to address the causes of violence, locally, nationally and globally, by engaging in nonviolent peacemaking in areas affected by armed conflict, working for a culture of peace and justice based on nonviolent change. It works towards a society where diversity is appreciated and all people can fulfil their potential for fullness of life in harmony with others. It promotes social justice, the reduction of prejudice and the equal treatment of all people, and works against unjust systems. The committee also seeks to promote changes that will help us to live responsibly and in harmony with all life and the Earth itself.

Quaker Peace & Social Witness Central Committee works with individual Friends and meetings to make available advice, education and information as Friends seek to respond to their leadings.

The committee engages in dialogue locally, nationally, internationally and globally, to witness to Quaker values and testimonies; and to express the views of Quakers in Britain to governments, intergovernmental bodies and other political institutions. The committee seeks to promote truthfulness, integrity, openness and accountability in social and political institutions. Quaker Peace & Social Witness Central Committee works with other Quaker bodies nationally and internationally to share experience and expertise. It works with ecumenical and interfaith groups, and with other churches and faiths at home and abroad, to advance shared concerns.

Quaker Peace & Social Witness Central Committee seeks to express corporately our experience that the Holy Spirit moves people to serve and learn from their fellow human beings and to promote peace and social justice.

Constitutions of central committees

8.12 Within the limits set out in 7.03, each central committee is accountable to the Britain Yearly Meeting Trustees for formulating and presenting policy for its area of work in accordance with the long-term framework approved by Meeting for Sufferings. They determine priorities for, monitor, and evaluate the work within their departments' areas of responsibility. Each central committee is also responsible for:

a. establishing functional committees and working groups as required and reviewing their work (8.04);
b. establishing an effective nominations committee, working closely with the Central Nominations Committee (6.21) as appropriate;
c. keeping the Trustees (and through them, Meeting for Sufferings) informed about significant matters arising from its area of responsibility;
d. considering any matters that Meeting for Sufferings or the Trustees refer to it, either by consulting with an appropriate representative council, if relevant, or through urgent attention and action. (See also 8.20.)

Quaker Communications, Quaker Finance & Property, Quaker Life and Quaker Peace & Social Witness Central Committees work to terms of reference approved by the Trustees. Copies of all terms of reference may be obtained on application to the Recording Clerk. There are normally between ten and twenty members serving on each committee, appointed on a rolling triennial basis, with any re-appointment subject to a maximum service of three consecutive terms.

Representative councils

8.13 Quaker Life Central Committee has a representative council which provides a two-way channel of communication with Friends in their meetings, the main purposes being educational, inspirational and consultative.

The Annual Conference of Treasurers (14.16–14.17) acts in a similar way to a representative council in relation to Quaker Communications and Quaker Finance & Property Central Committees.

The role of the representative council member is also one of co-ordination and communication, in order to enhance links between local meetings, area meetings and the central committee. As detailed discussion of policy and review of working practices are often carried out by central committees in the light of feedback obtained by the representative councils, the role of council members is vital. They should:

a. attend (or arrange for their deputy to attend) each meeting of the representative council – area meetings will pay participation fees and reasonable travel expenses;
b. bring to the council news of activities or needs at local level in order to keep the central work relevant and appropriate, contributing to the discernment of priorities;
c. keep their local meetings informed about the breadth and depth of work undertaken centrally and in so doing support the fundraising effort necessary to sustain this work;
d. be in touch with any local members of the central committee;
e. make regular reports to area meetings, whether in full session or in special interest groups or through written reports and newsletters.

8.14 Representative council membership comprises:

a. the appointed representative, or appointed deputy, of each area meeting within Britain Yearly Meeting;
b. two representatives of Young Friends General Meeting;
c. the members of the central committee;
d. the clerk of Britain Yearly Meeting and the clerk of Meeting for Sufferings ex officio;
e. up to ten co-opted members.

The membership is reviewed triennially.

The Quaker Peace & Social Witness meeting correspondents

8.15 Local meeting correspondents (4.33.m) receive and distribute news of the work of Britain Yearly Meeting by keeping in touch with Quaker Peace & Social Witness Central Committee. It is equally important that correspondents send local news to Friends and others elsewhere through these central channels: communication is a two-way process.

Correspondents will receive regular mailings. Quaker Communications will provide advice on how to select and present relevant information effectively. The correspondent should agree a working method with the local meeting clerk.

The local meeting clerk or convener should send the name of the correspondent, upon appointment, to Quaker Peace & Social Witness Central Committee.

Other standing committees

Other standing committees of Meeting for Sufferings are indicated below. Terms of reference for each may be obtained on application to the Recording Clerk.

Quaker Committee for Christian & Interfaith Relations

8.16 Quaker Committee for Christian & Interfaith Relations is responsible for keeping Quakers in Britain informed of the various movements towards co-operation within the Christian church and opportunities for interfaith dialogue. Its work and constitution are described in 9.13.

Quaker World Relations Committee

8.17 Quaker World Relations Committee maintains contact with other yearly meetings and with Friends World Committee for Consultation and its Europe & Middle East Section to which Britain Yearly Meeting is affiliated. Its work and constitution are described in 9.06.

Bodies whose trustees are appointed directly by Meeting for Sufferings

Friends Trusts Limited

8.18 Friends Trusts Limited is a registered charity and a company limited by guarantee which acts as custodian trustee of property and investments held on behalf of Britain Yearly Meeting and the area meetings of the Religious Society of Friends (Quakers) in Britain and its component parts. Its work and constitution are described in 15.02.

Quaker Housing Trust Limited

8.19 Quaker Housing Trust Limited was formed in 1967 in response to Friends' concern about the provision of adequate and appropriate housing. The trust makes grants and loans, and offers advice to charitable organisations providing accommodation, particularly to vulnerable people. Independent of the Britain Yearly Meeting Funds, it is a channel whereby Friends may give or lend money for such provision. It is a registered charity and a company limited by guarantee.

Quaker Housing Trust Limited has between seven and twelve trustees appointed for terms of three years by Meeting for Sufferings, names having been submitted by the Central Nominations Committee, to form its council of management.

The work of committees and staff

8.20 It is the role of the standing committees, particularly the central committees, to use their leadings and discernment to advise the Britain Yearly Meeting Trustees and Meeting for Sufferings on policies and priorities for their work. In so doing they should draw on the experience, knowledge and concerns of area meetings and, where appropriate, representative councils so that local Friends are involved in the process.

Committees need to be aware of the different roles they may play in responding to items on their agendas. Central committees determine policies and priorities for their areas of responsibility within the limits described in 7.03. Their role is to determine the work to be done and ensure that it is manageable without attempting to do it themselves. Those who carry out the work may be functional committees, working groups, volunteers or staff, or combinations of these. Central committees primarily delegate work to staff, whose responsibility is to undertake the work under the co-ordination of the Management Meeting. Other standing committees, functional committees, ad hoc committees and working groups may do more of their own work without much direct staff involvement. Committees that do undertake work themselves need to ensure it is done in partnership with staff, who have the responsibility to co-ordinate its management.

The close working partnership between staff and committee members brings a wide range of talents and experience to bear on our work. Committee members need to remain free of routine administrative tasks if they are to have the time to exercise their important decision-making functions. However, committee members also need to be aware of how their decisions might affect, unsettle or fulfil the staff members involved. In turn, members of staff have to be aware of the delicate tension of being in a position of knowledge and ensuring that their committees benefit from their experience and preparation whilst being left in a position to make consequent decisions freely.

The Management Meeting

8.21 The Management Meeting is responsible for co-ordinating the management and overseeing the implementation of the work of Britain Yearly Meeting. It is accountable to the Britain Yearly Meeting Trustees, whom it advises on practical and technical aspects of the work and to whom it reports regularly and submits its minutes. The Management Meeting is responsible for the cohesion and consistency of the management of the centrally managed work, through the co-ordination of the work of individual managers, working to the vision and policies discerned by Meeting for Sufferings and following the operational plan agreed by the Trustees.

The meeting is composed of the Recording Clerk and other members of the senior staff designated by the Britain Yearly Meeting Trustees on the recommendation of the Recording Clerk. It meets as required under the leadership of the Recording Clerk (8.06). Members are collectively responsible for all its decisions, acting for Britain Yearly Meeting as a whole as well as the particular area for which they are responsible.

Conclusion

8.22 Each committee and department has arisen and developed in response to a particular need. Each generation of Friends has been faced with a structure in some respects untidy, and we may be thankful for the clear-minded among us who help us, from time to time, to set our house in better order. But order without life does not work and our continual task is to ensure that our structures are in harmony with the changing tides of life in Britain Yearly Meeting.

It is neither possible nor desirable for every Friend to take a detailed interest in the work of every committee. We are, however, called to a broad sympathy with, and understanding of, the extent of the work entrusted to the committees under the guidance of Meeting for Sufferings in the name of the whole yearly meeting.

8.23 The committees whose work has been described were all set up to carry through what Yearly Meeting or Meeting for Sufferings has considered important service which Friends should undertake. It is imperative, therefore, if they are to continue to be sensitive to the concern of the yearly meeting, that there shall be a living and two-way communication between them and local meetings. It is sometimes complained that committees issue statements or initiate policies and work of which local meetings remain largely ignorant or see as some far-distant event, little affecting them. If the complaint is even in part justified, what remedy is open to us? First, let us set our minds to see the committees not as some distant 'they' with documents emanating from an impersonal 'Friends House'. It is we who compose the committees and the document we dislike was, like as not, drafted by Friends in meetings not far from our own.

People are usually preferable to paper, though admittedly some Friends are more effective than others in transmitting experience in a concise and lively way. Friends accepting service on committees, whether by local nomination or not, might usefully share with their area meeting the interests and concerns which are claiming their committee's attention. And, since many Friends are diffident to a fault, clerks might seek them out, looking not to mere reporting but to the sensitive sharing of experience.

If committees are to be responsive to changing concern, they must be aware of local judgment, which in turn must be based upon knowledge. It is essential, therefore, that meetings should from time to time review the effectiveness of the ways in which they keep themselves informed of the activities of committees.

Our committees do not live to themselves. Their appointment by and reporting through the Britain Yearly Meeting Trustees to Yearly Meeting or Meeting for Sufferings reflect their responsibility. As the representatives of area meetings on Meeting for Sufferings attempt a disciplined understanding of the total work and witness of the yearly meeting, so the individual pieces of work of different committees will be seen in a right perspective.

Chapter 9

Beyond Britain Yearly Meeting

Introduction

9.01 Our meetings for church affairs, within the compass of the Yearly Meeting of the Religious Society of Friends in Britain, exist within a variety of contexts. Britain Yearly Meeting is part of the world family of Friends; Britain Yearly Meeting sees itself corporately, and is seen by others, as part of the Christian church both globally and locally; interfaith dialogue is increasingly part of contemporary religious life. Within the spectrum of Britain Yearly Meeting there is a wide range of individual understandings of these three contexts, but all three will impinge on the life of our meetings. We need to remain aware of the wider relationships involved, and to take them into account in the conduct of our church affairs.

This chapter describes the formal relationships into which Britain Yearly Meeting has entered, their constitutional foundations and the structures which foster those relationships. It also offers advice on some of the implications for our meetings of Friends' ecumenical involvement at different levels, and on how best to address the problems and opportunities which arise.

Friends do not share a single understanding of the nature of the church, or of our place within it; we tend to feel our way into relationships with which we are reasonably comfortable, rather than prescribe a particular arrangement of structures as correct. This places a heavy but necessary responsibility on our meetings for church affairs, at all levels, for the right conduct of their deliberations leading to decisions on their interchurch involvement.

It is hoped that the following paragraphs will help Friends, whatever our differing views of the nature of the church, towards a fuller understanding of the contexts within which our meetings exist, and will guide us in the conduct of our meetings for church affairs when challenged by relationships with other religious bodies.

Britain Yearly Meeting and the world family of Friends

9.02 In the world family of Friends there is a rich variety of experience, some of which is unfamiliar to Friends in Britain Yearly Meeting. Some Friends make frequent and joyful use of song and Bible study, and may be led by a pastor; for others silent waiting on God is the basis of worship, from which vocal ministry develops. Many Friends have a vivid experience of personal salvation through the teaching, life, death and resurrection of Jesus Christ; many hesitate to express their deepest spiritual experiences in words. It is important that Friends in Britain Yearly Meeting be aware that we are part of the world Quaker community, that we have a responsibility to learn about Friends in other parts, and that this can be done in local meetings as well as among yearly meetings.

Friends World Committee for Consultation (FWCC)

9.03 All Quaker groups in the world are invited to affiliate themselves to the Friends World Committee for Consultation. Most have done so. FWCC acts in a consultative capacity, serving as a channel of communication between Friends, helping us to explore and nurture our identity as Quakers, so that we can discuss and be faithful to our true place in the world as a people of God. It encourages joint conferences, intervisitation and the collection and circulation of information about Quaker literature, some of which it publishes itself. FWCC is recognised as a non-governmental organisation with consultative status at the United Nations and at some of its agencies. It is therefore able to accredit Quaker representatives to attend UN conferences on issues of Quaker concern, as well as to work on such issues full-time at the Quaker United Nations Offices in New York and Geneva.

9.04 Britain Yearly Meeting is committed to the support of FWCC and in particular of its Europe & Middle East Section (EMES), which has its own secretary and keeps in touch with European yearly meetings as well as Friends in the Middle East and in those European countries which have no yearly meeting. Britain Yearly Meeting contributes financially to FWCC, including EMES. Local meetings are also encouraged to consider how best they might express their support of Friends beyond the boundaries of our own yearly meeting, and enhance our contacts with such Friends.

9.05 Meeting for Sufferings, on the recommendation of the Central Nominations Committee, appoints up to seven representatives of Britain Yearly Meeting to serve on FWCC for three years. There will often be value in considering re-appointment for a second three-year term. The representatives are expected to attend the annual meeting of EMES and the triennial meetings of FWCC. They also serve on the Quaker World Relations Committee of Britain Yearly Meeting (see below).

Quaker World Relations Committee (QWRC)

9.06 QWRC is a committee appointed by Meeting for Sufferings to maintain contact with other yearly meetings and with FWCC. It must ensure that the FWCC representatives of Britain Yearly Meeting are well prepared to communicate the concerns of this yearly meeting in the wider Quaker context, and to report fully on the meetings they attend. QWRC is responsible for drawing the attention of Britain Yearly Meeting to issues and concerns raised at world and section meetings of FWCC and for offering suggestions on possible ways to respond.

QWRC acts on behalf of Meeting for Sufferings to prepare letters of greeting to be sent to other yearly meetings. It encourages a lively exchange of interest between Britain Yearly Meeting and FWCC, and intervisitation between this yearly meeting and other yearly meetings.

QWRC is composed of up to fifteen Friends appointed by Meeting for Sufferings, names having been submitted by the Central Nominations Committee. In addition the Britain Yearly Meeting representatives to FWCC serve on QWRC ex officio. The membership is reviewed periodically.

Quaker Council for European Affairs (QCEA)

9.07 The European yearly meetings support the Quaker Council for European Affairs, which aims to bring Quaker influence to bear on the institutions of Europe and maintains representatives and support staff in Quaker House, Brussels. A British Committee of QCEA works to increase awareness and to raise funds. Local meetings are encouraged to appoint a British Committee correspondent. Britain Yearly Meeting is committed to the support of QCEA.

Meeting for Sufferings, on the recommendation of the Central Nominations Committee, appoints one representative of Britain Yearly Meeting, with an alternate, to serve on QCEA for three years. There will often be value in considering re-appointment for a second three-year term.

Britain Yearly Meeting and the ecumenical movement

The historical background

9.08 Britain Yearly Meeting is not a member of the World Council of Churches (WCC). This is because its Basis of Faith was considered by Yearly Meeting in 1940 to require acceptance of a credal formulation. FWCC, being representative of Friends world-wide, receives invitations and sends observers to the WCC and some of its constituent bodies. It also sends representatives to the annual meetings of secretaries of Christian World Communions, attended by representatives from the world bodies of the Roman Catholic, Orthodox, Lutheran, Anglican, Reformed, Baptist and many other churches.

Having declined membership of the WCC, then in process of formation, London Yearly Meeting took the same position of principle in response to a similar invitation from the nascent British Council of Churches (BCC). In this case, however, it was met by the BCC's decision to extend its Basis of Faith so as to include in its membership those bodies which had previously been associated with the ecumenical movement, thus embracing London Yearly Meeting. Friends continued to play an active part, corporately and individually, in the BCC from 1942 to 1990; London Yearly Meeting was only precluded, as an associate member after 1965, from voting on amendments to the BCC's constitution. Through the BCC it developed an indirect relationship with the Conference of European Churches. Because of the Conference's credal basis, however, the Yearly Meeting was never a member.

Friends enjoyed full membership of the Scottish Churches Council, which had no credal basis. Friends sent observers to the Council of Churches for Wales, which did. Both councils were, like the BCC itself, superseded by 'new ecumenical instruments' in 1990, as set out in the following paragraphs. During the lifetime of the BCC there was no national ecumenical body for England.

Formal relationships and their constitutional foundations

9.09 Britain Yearly Meeting is a member of Churches Together in Britain & Ireland (CTBI) and of three national bodies, namely ACTS: Action of Churches Together in Scotland, CTE: Churches Together in England and Cytûn: *Eglywsi ynghyd yng Nghymru*, Churches Together in Wales. These 'new ecumenical instruments', launched in 1990, have a broader membership than those of 1942–1990. Following Friends' participation in the five-year preparatory process known as 'Not strangers but pilgrims', the Yearly Meeting in 1989 after a difficult exercise decided despite hesitations to apply for full membership of the then Council of Churches for Britain and Ireland (now Churches Together in Britain & Ireland) and the national bodies. Yearly Meeting in 1997 confirmed this decision. Each of the four bodies accepted London (now Britain) Yearly Meeting into membership under a clause (Clause 2b) which appears in each constitution as follows:

> A church, which on principle has no credal statements in its tradition and therefore cannot formally subscribe to the statement of faith in the Basis, may nevertheless apply for and be elected to full membership provided that it satisfies those member churches which subscribe to the Basis that it manifests faith in Christ as witnessed to in the Scriptures and is committed to the aims and purposes* of the new

* The *Objects, aims and purposes* of CCBI provide the context within which the *Basis and commitment* are to be understood. The relevant constitutional texts are available on request from the Recording Clerk and at www.quaker.org.uk/qfp.

> ecumenical body, and that it will work in the spirit of the Basis.

The Basis reads:

> The Council of Churches for Britain and Ireland is a fellowship of churches in the United Kingdom of Great Britain and Northern Ireland and in the Republic of Ireland which confess the Lord Jesus Christ as God and Saviour according to the Scriptures and therefore seek to fulfil their common calling to the glory of the one God, Father, Son and Holy Spirit.

9.10 The underlying principle of CTBI and the national bodies is the commitment of member churches to one another and to taking seriously the principle that the churches should only do separately what they cannot in conscience do together. Working this out in practice is not always easy and will take time, but it should be one of the underlying principles used in deciding on the work carried out in the name of Britain Yearly Meeting.

9.11 CTBI works through an Assembly and a Church Representatives Meeting, and through associated agencies, commissions and networks. The three national bodies have similar patterns of work. Increasingly Britain Yearly Meeting's committees and departments work directly with their ecumenical counterparts and its members serve on ecumenical groups and committees. It is a principle of CTBI that authority remains rooted in the decision-making bodies of the member churches.

9.12 Meeting for Sufferings appoints Britain Yearly Meeting's representatives to CTBI and CTE Forum. The Quaker Committee for Christian & Interfaith Relations (9.13) appoints to CTE Enabling Group and other CTE bodies.

The committee has agreed in principle that Britain Yearly Meeting should be represented at CTBI as follows:

a. at the Senior Representative Forum by the Recording Clerk or a Quaker member of staff delegated by her or him;
b. at the biennial Summit of Church Leaders by one or two Friends appointed on the basis of their relevant experience on the nomination of Central Nominations Committee.

General Meeting for Scotland makes appointments to ACTS; the Meeting of Friends in Wales makes appointments to Cytûn.

Representatives report to the appointing body and the Quaker Committee for Christian & Interfaith Relations maintains contact with any reference group set up to support them.

Quaker Committee for Christian & Interfaith Relations (CIR)

9.13 The Quaker Committee for Christian & Interfaith Relations is responsible for keeping Britain Yearly Meeting informed of the various movements towards co-operation within the Christian church and opportunities for interfaith dialogue, and for responding on behalf of the yearly meeting so that Friends' views on issues of faith and order are represented to other churches and communities of faith.

The Quaker Committee for Christian & Interfaith Relations consists of up to thirty Friends appointed by Meeting for Sufferings, names having been submitted by the Central Nominations Committee. The Committee may co-opt a further ten members. The membership is reviewed periodically. The Yearly Meeting of Friends in Ireland (which is a member of the Irish Council of Churches but decided in 1989 not to seek membership of CTBI) appoints a few Friends to keep in touch with the work of the committee.

Local implications

9.14 Britain Yearly Meeting's membership of CTBI does not commit local meetings or individual Friends to any particular course of action with regard to interchurch relationships. However, in 1989 Yearly Meeting asked monthly meetings and general meetings to review the involvement of meetings in local and regional ecumenical activities, encouraging greater participation where need be. The recognition by CTBI member churches of our yearly meeting's non-credal tradition which is implied by Clause 2b (see 9.09) may make it easier to formalise these local relationships.

Local meetings and ecumenical relationships

9.15 Local meetings are seeking to develop their religious life in relationship with members of other Christian churches, and with adherents of other faiths and of none. Any local meeting may find itself at some point along a wide spectrum of possible relationships designed to offer increasing degrees of commitment between churches. These range from local councils of churches, through Churches Together in a particular locality, to local ecumenical projects which may involve joint church membership (see 9.18), shared buildings, mutual recognition of ministers or all three.

Interchurch activity, especially in England, is often assisted by a sponsoring body – a formal association of appropriate church representatives which encourages, assists and oversees ecumenical activity within the boundaries of a city or county. A sponsoring body is enabling, not directive, in nature. Meetings need periodically to review their participation in sponsoring bodies, noting that all the churches have difficulty in matching up their geographical boundaries denominationally and ecumenically.

9.16 Each meeting will decide in its local context the degree of commitment which is appropriate. Friends who are ecumenically active may need reminding of the need not to rush ahead at a pace beyond that at which their meeting as a whole is comfortable. Those who have earlier experiences of belonging to other churches will need to recognise that such churches may change over time in their beliefs and practices. Like Britain Yearly Meeting other churches include within their membership people of very diverse beliefs.

At interchurch meetings Friends are valued for our willingness to uphold Quaker testimonies and leadings as much as for our tradition of listening and openness. But many aspects of Friends' faith and practice are not widely appreciated; misunderstandings may occur when other churches' lack of familiarity with our discipline and structure of church government, and Friends' imperfect knowledge of theirs, produce mismatched expectations or faulty assumptions.

In defining the relationship between churches, the problem of appropriate wording will sooner or later occur. The wording under which London Yearly Meeting became a member of CCBI (now CTBI) and the three national bodies (9.09) may be helpful in this regard, but other much simpler forms may be preferable. In negotiating acceptable terms of membership, Friends should hold to our testimony that credal statements can fetter the free action of the Spirit.

See also 27.21–27.26 Creeds

9.17 Meetings may find it useful to check the wording of any local Basis of Faith to which they are invited to subscribe with the Recording Clerk, through whom advice may be obtained in case of need from the Quaker Committee for Christian & Interfaith Relations.

9.18 Membership by a meeting of a particular ecumenical body may be impossible, for example because the wording of its Basis is unacceptably exclusive, or because the mutual recognition of ministers which is involved does not extend to the Quaker understanding of ministry, or because joint membership for all participating churches' members is required. (Such automatic joint membership is unacceptable both because of the practical problems encountered upon transfer into an area meeting without the same ecumenical experience, and because, in departing from the principle of the individual application for membership, it is not in accordance with our discipline as set out in chapter 11.) In cases of doubt, reference should be made (as under 9.17) to the Recording Clerk, through whom advice may be obtained. If membership of a particular body proves impossible the meeting will have to consider how its relationships with other churches can be carried forward in different ways. Many practical forms of joint activity, from Christian Aid Week to work on housing and other social issues, are well established and present few if any problems for Friends. Some will wish to go thus far and no farther.

9.19 Our relationships with other churches are likely to involve us in joint religious services of various kinds. Sometimes there will be opportunities to introduce members of other churches to Quaker worship, thereby broadening their ecumenical experience. At other times we may participate in forms of worship which broaden our own. It may be appropriate on some ecumenical occasions for us to arrange meetings for worship that include some programmed elements.

When we find ourselves representing Friends in worship arranged by other churches we may have to make difficult decisions about the extent of our involvement. The difficulty is particularly acute in eucharistic worship, where different forms of eucharistic sharing are now frequently offered and are commonly seen by other

Christians as both the means and the end of unity. Friends' testimony is to a corporate life and experience of God which does not depend on the observance of outward sacraments. Abstaining from the outward sacraments does not inevitably follow from this, but is one way of witnessing to it, particularly when the importance of the outward sacraments in building up the life of the church is being stressed.

See also 27.35–27.36 Priesthood & *27.37–27.44* Sacraments

9.20 To sum up, meetings find themselves engaged in a variety of local ecumenical arrangements. These entail differing responsibilities and degrees of commitment to joint activity. In a time of rapid change and challenging ecumenical encounters, meetings must give careful thought to the implications of any new relationship into which they are invited to enter. They are under no obligation to enter into any formal arrangement, or to move from one kind of relationship to another. The ferment of new initiatives within and among the churches requires Friends to exercise discretion and discernment while seeking to respond to the promptings of the Spirit. We should be wary of prematurely committing our meeting; as representatives on ecumenical bodies we must be ready, on occasion, to say no even if this disappoints the expectations of the other churches. In giving effect to the concept of churches together in pilgrimage, meetings will go as far and as fast along the ecumenical road as each judges, in its local situation, to be consistent with unity in the meeting, with our understanding and practice of church government, and with Quaker testimonies and integrity.

See also 27.12–27.20 Friends and the Christian Church

Friends and interfaith relations

9.21 Relationships beyond the Christian church embrace dialogue with other communities of faith. Individual Friends have long been active in interfaith work. Britain Yearly Meeting has not only pursued this work in the context of community relations, but has also come to appreciate the theological issues implicit in interfaith dialogue, the connections between our work for world peace, our work for understanding between faiths and the potential for mutual enrichment through interfaith sharing. This has come to be reflected in new emphases in the work of its Quaker Committee for Christian & Interfaith Relations, which is a member of the Inter Faith Network. Britain Yearly Meeting is a member of the Churches Inter-Religious Network of Churches Together in Britain & Ireland.

Friends' experience is that interfaith dialogue can profitably be undertaken locally, where local issues set the agenda of work which can most usefully be done together. Other communities of faith often find our meeting houses acceptable venues for their worship, and meetings are encouraged to make contact with other faith groups to find out whether their own premises could be so used. This approach, however, does not mean that Friends should see themselves as theologically neutral. We need to seek to be part of the dialogue, attesting to our own insights and convictions.

Meeting houses may also be used for multifaith worship. The hospitality of worship which Friends can offer through silence may serve as a meeting point for many religious traditions.

See also 27.01–27.11 Friends and other faiths

Chapter 10

Belonging to a Quaker meeting

Our community

10.01 Our life is love, and peace, and tenderness; and bearing one with another, and forgiving one another, and not laying accusations one against another; but praying one for another, and helping one another up with a tender hand.

Isaac Penington, 1667

10.02 We know the power of God's Spirit at work in the lives of people within the community of our meetings. These people may have been drawn into the community by a sudden convincement, a long period of seeking, or have grown up within it from childhood. We also know that we are engaged in a life-long growth into faith, and experience a continuing irruption of grace into our lives which demands and sustains a commitment to a life of discipleship. We recognise this power at work in people of all ages, races and creeds: a transforming power which can issue in lives of joy, humility and service.

London Yearly Meeting, 1986

10.03 The Religious Society of Friends is organised into local meetings, each of which should be a community. It is our search for God's way that has drawn us together. In our meeting we can each hope to find love, support, challenge, practical help and a sense of belonging. We should bring ourselves as we are, whatever our age, our strength, our weakness; and be able to share friendship and warmth.

Some of us now live away from our families; some of us move house quite often. Although surrounded by others we may be leading isolated and lonely lives. It is important that our meetings welcome newcomers warmly and that we include them in invitations to our homes.

Our sense of community does not depend on all professing identical beliefs, for it grows from worshipping together, knowing one another, loving one another, accepting responsibilities, sharing and working together. We will be helped by tried and tested Quaker methods and procedures, but the meeting will only live if we develop a sense of community, which includes children and adults alike. If all those who belong to our meeting are lovingly cared for, the guidance of the spirit will be a reality. The celebration and commemoration of life's great events draw us together as we share the occasion and rejoice or mourn with one another.

Our shared experience of waiting for God's guidance in our meetings for worship and for church affairs, together with careful listening and gentleness of heart, forms the basis on which we can live out a life of love with and for each other and for those outside our community.

1994

10.04 *William Charles Braithwaite (1862–1922), a lawyer and banker, was the author of* The beginnings of Quakerism *and* The second period of Quakerism. *He was active in establishing the Swarthmore lectures and in the transformation of* Christian Doctrine *1883 into the 1921* Christian life, faith and thought.

The life of a religious society consists in something more than the body of principles it professes and the outer garments of organisation which it wears. These things have their own importance: they embody the society to the world, and protect it from the chance and change of circumstance; but the springs of life lie deeper, and often escape recognition. They are to be found in the vital union of the members of the society with God and with one another, a union which allows the free flowing through the society of the spiritual life which is its strength.

William Charles Braithwaite, 1905

10.05 We recognise a variety of ministries. In our worship these include those who speak under the guidance of the Spirit, and those who receive and uphold the work of the Spirit in silence and prayer. We also recognise as ministry service on our many committees, hospitality and childcare, the care of finance and premises, and many other tasks. We value those whose ministry is not in an appointed task but is in teaching, counselling, listening, prayer, enabling the service of others, or other service in the meeting or the world.

The purpose of all our ministry is to lead us and other people into closer communion with God and to enable us to carry out those tasks which the Spirit lays upon us.

London Yearly Meeting, 1986

10.06 The custom of appointing certain named Friends to attend our meetings for church affairs may lead others to the mistaken conclusion that their responsibility for these gatherings is of less importance than that for the meeting for worship. But the privilege of membership implies that every Friend should feel concerned to attend these meetings.

1959

10.07 We must place within the reach of all our adult members advanced religious teaching similar in aim to that which we have seen to be needful for our children. We seek to secure such a general condition of church life that spiritual growth shall be fostered, and a high standard of spiritual intelligence shall be maintained. We are but seeking a rich and well-tilled soil from which every type of ministry shall spring with a robuster growth.

John Wilhelm Rowntree, 1899

See also 2.77–2.78 & 27.33

10.08 After a leisurely and useful preparative meeting, Friends sat at a long table in the children's room to enjoy supper together. We depend on those who till the soil, and tend the produce which forms our daily food, so it was good to remember them in thankfulness and for us to eat in fellowship the food mutually contributed, prepared and served. It was sacramental, in the sense in which Friends so profoundly believe. We spoke of those unable to be present, so that there was a sense of the entire meeting gathering in community.

This feeling of community pervaded the weekend. In preparative meeting the allotment committee reported and outlined plans for an orchard in the upper section of our ground; the fruit may not remain to be gathered by us but the blossoms will gladden everyone. The entire ground is in our care: allotments, burial ground, lawns, and we see it as one unit together with the meeting house which it surrounds. Yet true significance lies not in the grounds and buildings but in the people: those who tend the flowers, the grass and the allotment; members of the poetry group (some of whom gave pleasure by readings after supper); the study groups; the gathering of younger people; those whose activities lie in other places... The gravestones speak of the past, of those who also served the meeting, whose lives are woven into ours, as ours will affect those still to come.

William G Sewell, 1977

10.09 We were meeting in the long sitting-room, and the floor-space was as usual filled by the children. The room was pretty full. Then Sophie's father came and put her in her carry-cot on the floor. She was very young, and we hadn't expected to be greeting her so soon. I looked around the adults, wondering which of us would minister.

At the other end of the room Cathy, aged three, slipped down from her mother's knee. Slowly, carefully, and mostly upright she clambered in and out, past all the other children. She reached the carry-cot and peeped in at the baby. Then she turned and gave everyone a smile of pure delight. Still smiling, without a word, she returned to her mother.

Nobody else spoke either. Sophie had been welcomed into meeting.

William Fraser, 1989

10.10 If we take seriously the nurture of our children in the worshipping group, we must start by re-appraising the whole life of the group. What kind of communication exists between us all? Do we know one another as people sharing joys and sorrows?

Do we have enough confidence in each other to know that our problems as well as our convictions and uncertainties can be shared with understanding? How is the child and the stranger received amongst us? Do we see our young people as individuals we want to know and care for and do we want to provide opportunities when they can get to know and care for us? Are they encouraged to feel that they have much to give us, that we value them and are the poorer without the insights and questioning they provide? Are we across all the ages a community learning together? Do we consciously look for experiences which can be shared by the whole community? Children and young people need their own peer groups but are encouragingly appreciative of the whole group sharing when they feel an integral part of it and can share in situations which deepen relationships and form lasting friendships. Part of that sharing is learning to know of our past as Quakers and of our

Christian roots but even more necessary is the sharing of what we as Quakers believe today and how this should be shaping our lives both individually and corporately. Together we have a task in exploring our faith today with all its implications for action.

Peggy McGeoghegan, 1976

10.11 It was said of the early Christians, 'Behold, how they love one another'. Could this equally be said of us? Or are our meetings places where newcomers may not always be welcomed, where people feel alone? What happens to those who are part of our meetings? Are their lives changed? Do they care more? Love more? What do we know of one another's lives outside of the meeting? Of one another's spiritual journeys? Do we seek to share joys and humour as well as sorrows, or are we perhaps too near the 'sober-sides' images of popular belief? Surely the nurturing of relationships and the response to their breakdown will arise from the willingness of each of us to enter with imagination and love into one another's lives. If we truly know one another then we are likely to be sensitively aware of one another's needs. Often it is just being alongside someone; listening; a gentle touch when words cannot be found. Our extreme busyness, and the pressure and tension of modern life, make it at once more necessary and at the same time more difficult that our meetings should become living and loving communities.

June Ellis, 1986

10.12 It is a good practice and one which has taken place in Friends' meetings I have known, for a small group to hold a meeting for worship in the bedroom of a seriously ill member, who feels that he or she would like others to come to them in this way. Since we have no set form of service for such occasions or for funerals, it is of great importance that elders and concerned Friends should be sensitively aware of the need of a real 'word of life' to be spoken and should be prepared for such needs and for ministry to the bereaved. I have been a member of more than one loving meeting, but I have to admit that the word I longed for was not spoken to me or my family when we suffered great grief, though much sympathy and kindness were shown to us. I am thankful to say that I have both before and since that time heard it spoken to others.

Ruth Fawell, 1967

10.13 Quakerism need not be defined exclusively as white, Christian and middle-class, and such culture need not be adopted as the culture of those who are convinced. When this does happen the inequalities and unequal power dynamics of our society are reflected in our meetings and in this way Black people are discouraged from fully participating in worship.

Our Society is often blind to the gifts and richness of other traditions and this cultural chauvinism impedes its development. Racism within the Society of Friends is perhaps more damaging because it is unconscious and springs from stereotyped assumptions: 'And no harm is meant by it. Harm may be done but it is never meant'.

Epistle of Black, white, Asian and mixed-heritage Friends, 1991

10.14 Er mai Saesneg fu prif gyfrwng y Gymdeithas yn yr ynysoedd hyn trwy'r blynyddoedd, dylid cydnabod fod rhan o'i bywyd wedi ac yn cael ei fynegi trwy ieithoedd eraill, ac yng Nghymru hefyd trwy'r Gymraeg. Darostyngir traddodiad ein Cymdeithas, ein hanes a'n tystiolaeth os anwybyddir hynny. Yn ddiarwybod bu i rai siaradwyr Cymraeg gael y teimlad iddynt gael eu hymylu. Dylid sicrhau fod y Gymraeg yn cael ei phriod le yng ngwaith a gweithgareddau'r Cyfarfod Blynyddol yng Nghymru.

Cyfarfod Dwyfor, 1994

For a translation of this text into English see next page

Translation from Welsh:

10.14 Although English has been the main medium of the Society in these islands through the years, it should be recognised that part of its life has been, and is, expressed through other languages, and in Wales also through the medium of Welsh. Our Society's tradition, our history and our witness are demeaned if that is ignored. Some Welsh speakers have been made, unwittingly, to feel marginalised. The rightful place of the Welsh language in the work and activities of the yearly meeting in Wales should be secured.

Dwyfor Meeting, 1994

10.15 We know that the spiritual growth of the meeting is inextricably linked to the growth of its life as a community, and that spiritual development is a continuous process for both older as well as the younger members of a meeting. Many young people have had and are having bad experiences in their local meetings, especially the smaller ones, where they often feel patronised, smothered or bored, and where they have found little evidence of a spiritual search amongst the older Friends: in places the Society seems fossilised, locked into the past or a mistaken comfortableness.

Young Quaker, 1985

10.16 For many years The Leaveners was my only contact with the Society of Friends and, despite being a birthright Friend, I would probably have drifted away from Quakers completely without the influence of the Quaker Youth Theatre.

The summer residential projects had a sense of purpose which I did not find at my Young Friends gatherings and used skills which appealed to me personally. Living and working together so closely towards a common goal always bonded the company together well, but in the heady mix of exhaustion and adrenalin caused by the long hours and public performance the intensity of friendships formed was extra special. I came home from these gatherings invigorated and uplifted, filled with the joy and wonder of life that now forms a central part of my spiritual outlook.

The necessary noise and activity of The Leaveners emphasised the quiet and peace of meeting for worship which began and ended each day. More than ever before I learned how Quaker worship is something to be treasured, a real act of sharing.

Nick Putz, 1994

10.17 The spiritual welfare of a meeting is greatly helped if its social life is vigorous, and its members take a warm personal interest in one another's welfare. The pastoral work of the Society is specially committed to the overseers, but our members generally should not allow themselves to feel that they are relieved from responsibility. In the greater events of life, such as marriage, the birth of a child, illness or death, it is our duty and privilege to share in one another's joys and sorrows; and sympathy thus shown is a potent means of binding us in closer fellowship. Those who hold public offices, or are engaged in various forms of social service, should be made to realise that they have the sympathetic support and prayers of their friends in their work. Opportunities might well be found for such Friends to tell of their activities, and receive encouragement and counsel; the other members of the meeting would thus acquire a deeper sense that they are called to a real share in the service.

1925

10.18 To make a safe home for small children, to comfort one person in sorrow, to do one's work as efficiently as possible, to listen with understanding, to be gentle with the old and courteous to the young – these are the humble tasks to which most men and women are called. They build the home or the meeting or the community which is the first step towards the Kingdom of Heaven on earth. The second is to be aware of greater tasks and to be ready to be used in solving them – ready, not worried or anxious or envious, but content to wait, exercising a ministry of prayer to sustain the healers and the reconcilers already at work in their thousands.

Olive Tyson, 1966

10.19 In a true community we will not choose our companions, for our choices are so often limited by self-serving motives. Instead, our companions will be given to us by grace. Often they will be persons who will upset our settled view of self and world. In fact, we might define true community as the place where the person you least want to live with always lives!

Parker J Palmer, 1977

10.20 One of the unexpected things I have learnt in my life as a Quaker is that religion is basically about relationships between people. This was an unexpected discovery, because I had been brought up to believe that religion was essentially about our relationship with God.

If we are sensitive, we find that everything that happens to us, good or bad, can help us to build a vision of the meaning of life. We can be helped to be sensitive by reading the Bible and being open to experience of nature, music, books, painting, sport or whatever our particular interest may be. It is in and through all things that we hear God speaking to us. But I do not think I am alone in my certainty that it's in my relationships with people that the deepest religious truths are most vividly disclosed.

George Gorman, 1982

Conflict within the meeting

10.21 There are times of conflict in every meeting when we are required to find and show the love we have for one another and to face our difficulties squarely, for it is only when we work through them, using our meeting for church affairs and other appropriate methods, that we can move forward together. Such conflict may involve a clash of personalities, a difference over the quantity or style of vocal ministry, or issues about the place where meetings for worship are held. Problems may become tangled and one sort of issue may masquerade as another. Care will be required to identify the root cause. Skill, time and great love are needed to overcome these problems, but where they have been openly faced and successfully overcome, meetings have sometimes been much richer for the experience.

The primary responsibility for finding a way to resolve these problems lies with elders and overseers. It may be that the use of a meeting for clearness (see 12.22–12.25) would offer a way forward.

Deep-seated problems are sometimes more easily resolved when an experienced facilitator from outside the situation is called on. Quaker Life or monthly and general meetings may be able to suggest Friends with an understanding of how groups and individuals interact with one another and who are able to spend time with a meeting that has got into seemingly insoluble difficulties.

1994, 2001

10.22 Part of the creative experience of a community is learning how to deal with conflict when it arises, and Friends are not usually good at this. 'Speaking the truth in love' is a Quaker cliché, but 'papering over the cracks' is the principle more commonly acted upon. Conflict met in 'brokenness' of spirit can take a meeting a long way on its spiritual journey, whereas unresolved it deadens the life. We are a small Society. Clashes have always arisen, just as they arise in any family group. In one sense the members of a family know each other too well, in another sense not well enough. It is impossible to impress one's relations, but they can be a great stand-by in time of need, and it is then that they come to know each other better, if the bond is strong enough.

Joan Fitch, 1980

10.23 One of the realities of our meetings these days is that sometimes two people, whom we have come to know as a couple, are unable to sustain their relationship and decide to separate. However much we may regret it, separations are becoming commonplace in society at large. Quakers are not immune to this affliction and when it happens the event often challenges the meeting in all sorts of unexpected ways. The reasons for the break-up may perplex us and we may feel hurt and unsettled, particularly if the estrangement deprives us of the company of a familiar friend. 'If it could happen to them where will it end?' There may even be a sense of guilt as if somehow the meeting allowed this to happen. 'If only our oversight had been better.' 'After all, Friends should endeavour to uphold the sanctity of the marriage relationship.'

Through all of this we must remember that we are often only bystanders who may not be aware of all the circumstances that led to the breakdown. It is important to affirm our love for all those who are directly affected, especially if there are children known to the meeting. The task of supporting an abandoned partner may call for special sensitivity and a willingness to be available during the dark moments. But the need to show our care for the other partner should not be overlooked either. Above all the meeting must try to affirm that of God which is in all of us, whatever our feelings about who is to blame. This is a time for great prayerfulness, unobtrusive caring and gentle support. We must trust that, with grace, we may all find paths to grow, leading us out of the painful experience.

John Miles, 1994

10.24 In our desire to be kind to everybody, to appear united in spirit, to have no majorities and minorities, we minimise our divisions and draw a veil over our doubts. We fail to recognise that tension is not only inescapable, however much hidden, but when brought into the open is a positive good.

Kenneth C Barnes, 1984

See also 4.23 Disputes among Friends, *20.67–20.75* Conflict *& 22.47–22.50* Facing change and difficulty

Individual commitment

10.25 When we consider the criteria for membership, the two greatest factors are community and commitment. Not just a practical commitment, but a spiritual willingness to grow and learn, out of which our practical commitment will evolve ... YFCC [Young Friends Central Committee, which in 1993 became Young Friends General Meeting] has demonstrated that it is possible today for a large Quaker meeting to operate without any formal membership whatsoever. Our membership is more positive: simply our commitment to attend, our willingness to participate as 'Young Friends of the Truth'. In recent years, recognising the importance of oversight has been an essential part in creating the community spirit with which we are now blessed. We feel that the present lack of basic communication in our local meetings can be helped by such work and by the consideration of active Friends... We must be prepared to make ourselves vulnerable and care for each other. We suggest that methods of increasing communication be widely used, so that all active Friends are visited annually by other Friends, to listen to each other and to confirm the spiritual growth in our lives which we so often ignore.

A group of Young Friends, 1986

10.26 One of life's hardest lessons is that there is no justification for expecting that our neighbour is to traverse precisely the same path as that which we ourselves have followed... The difficulty a man has in grasping this truth is increased in proportion as his own experience has been vivid and clearly defined. One who has been lifted out of the horrible pit, has had his feet set upon a rock, and a new song put into his mouth, finds it hard to believe that another who has arrived quietly and without crisis, with no strong consciousness of guilt and no corresponding ecstasy of deliverance, can really be a disciple at all.

William Littleboy, 1916

10.27 Are there not different states, different degrees, different growths, different places? ... Therefore, watch every one to feel and know his own place and service in the body, and to be sensible of the gifts, places, and services of others, that the Lord may be honoured in all, and every one owned and honoured in the Lord, and no otherwise.

Isaac Penington, 1667

10.28 It is often hard to accept that other people have their own valid relationship with God, their own specialness and insights. We are not just disciples – we are disciples together.

Our vision of the truth has to be big enough to include other people's truth as well as our own. We have to learn to love difficult unlovable people. Accepting each other, and each other's relationship with God, let us continue to hold together at our deepest level. We are a forgiven community. Part of the cost of discipleship is living with the other disciples.

Beth Allen, 1984

10.29 *Pierre Ceresole (1879–1945), the Swiss pioneer of work camps and founder of International Voluntary Service, suffered repeatedly as a conscientious objector. He broke with*

Christian orthodoxy, which he felt no longer believed in its own dogmas, and joined Friends in 1936.

I feel very strongly ... that the spiritual life absolutely requires that we should not remain isolated. It is this deep need of getting out of a prolonged and dangerous relative isolation which urges me to ask now to be admitted among the Quakers. It is more and more clear to me that it is only in the bosom of a religious family, freely but very strongly constituted, that the individual can render to the world the services it sorely needs and which no politics, not based on a deep inspiration, can hope to organise.

Pierre Ceresole, 1936

10.30 Even if it were possible to be a member of every church at once, there would still be incompleteness; the infinite fullness of God will always exceed our powers of understanding and obedience, even our powers to receive vision and joy. Dual membership for me is not a formula whereby I may find satisfaction because to be both a Friend and a United Reformed Church minister has all the gaps of one tradition filled by the other, though it is certainly a practice in which there is a great and satisfying measure of complementarity. Membership is rather a commitment, and membership of the People of God is a total commitment. But it is a fact of this earthly life that the total claim of God must be expressed in the actual and limited claim of those people with whom in fact life is shared. It has been my tremendous privilege and joy to find myself so committed in two communities, receiving from each more than I could well express and believing I am called to give in each whatever God enables.

Dorothy Havergal Shaw, 1994

10.31 Friends are not about building walls but about taking them down. For us as rural Friends, living many miles from each other and a Quaker meeting, having dual membership is a way of acknowledging our involvement with where we live: with local activities including Christian ones. Our origins have been in other branches of the church, giving experience which we value. Yet we wish to affirm that, for us, waiting on God in the silence of Quaker worship is at the very centre of our lives and the mainspring of our other activities.

Some members of North Northumberland Meeting, 1994

10.32 Why, I ask myself, did I go to worship with those rather small and not very distinguished groups of people? Surely it was that sitting among these quite ordinary people, to most of whom I remained a stranger and a foreigner for some months, I sensed an experience of belonging – of community. A true Friends' meeting for worship drawing individuals with varieties of temperament, talent and background always manages to engender a climate of belonging, of community which is infectious and creative. This experience of 'belonging' has remained with me over the years and it has grown both in intensity and universality... The 'giving out' of such a sense of community is the natural witness of a Quaker meeting which has in it the seed of life and creative experience.

Ranjit M Chetsingh, 1967

10.33 Why am I a Friend? Because Quakerism takes a whole view of life. Everyday living and religion are all of one piece, and we are including, not excluding, in our approach... Over the years the Society has given me continuing friendship. To be human is to be a separate person and, therefore, to know the fact and the mystery of aloneness. Although I find I can make surface contact with people quite readily, I am often lonely and experience stretches of doubt and dryness. Then especially I need friends who will accept a quality of friendship which involves praying for me. By this I mean that they care enough to think of me, to ask themselves if there is any special need of mine they can meet, to commend what they don't know about me to God's wisdom, and when we meet to make me welcome.

Donald Court, 1965

10.34 I suppose the question to ask is not, why am I applying for membership, but, why not sooner than this? All I can say is that I am not a hasty person. I have been considering applying for at least four years. I have felt myself to be part of Friends for so long that it has shocked me, on occasions, to realise that I am not thought of as 'one of us' but rather 'one of them'. I have come to see that how I perceive myself in terms of commitment and belonging is not necessarily how I am perceived. At times this has made me sad. But I can see that I owe it to Friends to make my position clear. If the Society can be thought of as a ship, I would like to be one of the crew, not a passenger, and to be seen like this.

Jai Penna, 1989

Chapter 11

Membership

The meaning of membership

11.01 'The Kingdom of Heaven did gather us and catch us all, as in a net,' wrote Francis Howgill in 1663, 'and his heavenly power at one time drew many hundreds to land. We came to know a place to stand in and what to wait in.'

Early Friends felt no need for formal membership; they were a community of seekers who recognised in each other a similar hunger, a similar quest. Seeking the 'hidden seed of God' they were prepared to recognise it wherever they found it.

The seventeenth century, however, was not an easy time to be a dissenter; and Friends, like many others, suffered ridicule, arrest, imprisonment, fines, distraint of their goods and death. In this harsh climate it required a degree of personal commitment to avow membership openly. This, combined with the recognition of a 'heavenly power' at work, was all that was required.

Today membership may not involve putting liberty, goods or life at risk but the spiritual understanding of membership is, in essentials, the same as that which guided the 'Children of the Light'. People still become Friends through 'convincement', and like early Friends they wrestle and rejoice with that experience. Membership is still seen as a discipleship, a discipline within a broadly Christian perspective and our Quaker tradition, where the way we live is as important as the beliefs we affirm.

Like all discipleships, membership has its elements of commitment and responsibility but it is also about joy and celebration. Membership is a way of saying to the meeting that you feel at home, and in the right place. Membership is also a way of saying to the meeting, and to the world, that you accept at least the fundamental elements of being a Quaker: the understanding of divine guidance, the manner of corporate worship and the ordering of the meeting's business, the practical expression of inward convictions and the equality of all before God. In asking to be admitted into the community of the meeting you are affirming what the meeting stands for and declaring your willingness to contribute to its life.

When early Friends affirmed the priesthood of all believers it was seen as an abolition of the clergy; in fact it is an abolition of the laity. All members are part of the clergy and have the clergy's responsibility for the maintenance of the meeting as a community. This means helping to contribute, in whatever ways are most suitable, to the maintenance of an atmosphere in which spiritual growth and exploration are possible for all. It means contributing to the meeting by giving time and energy to events and necessary tasks, and also being willing to serve on various regional or yearly meeting committees and other groups. There is a special expectation that Friends attending meetings for church affairs will benefit from working together under Quaker discipline on the decisions that need to be made. Membership also entails a financial commitment appropriate to a member's means, for without money neither the local meeting nor the wider structure can function.

Membership does not require great moral or spiritual achievement, but it does require a sincerity of purpose and a commitment to Quaker values and practices. Membership is a spiritual discipline, a commitment to the well-being of one's spiritual home and not simply appearance on a membership roll. The simple process of becoming a member is part of the spiritual journey: part of the seeking that is so integral to our religious heritage.

The membership application process is not only about seeking but also about finding.

The process is an important part of the life of the area meeting, too; accepting a new member means not only welcoming the 'hidden seed of God' but also affirming what it is as a community that we value and cherish. Quakers once called themselves 'Friends in the Truth' and it is the finding of this truth that we affirm when we accept others who value it into membership.

11.02 Our membership ... is never based upon worthiness... We none of us are members because we have attained a certain standard of goodness, but rather because, in this matter, we still are all humble learners in the school of Christ. Our membership is of no importance whatever unless it signifies that we are committed to something of far greater and more lasting significance than can adequately be conveyed by the closest association with any movement or organisation.

Edgar G Dunstan, 1956

11.03 *Richard Claridge (1649–1723) of Peel Monthly Meeting had been rector of the parish of Peopleton in Worcestershire for nineteen years when in 1691 he resigned and joined the Baptists. In 1697 he became convinced of the truth as understood by Friends. He recalled his experiences in these words:*

This was the way that Friends used with me, when I was convinced of truth; they came oftentimes to visit me, and sat and waited upon the Lord in silence with me; and as the Lord opened our understanding and mouths, so we had very sweet and comfortable seasons together. They did not ask me questions about this or the other creed, or about this or the other controversy in religion; but they waited to feel that living Power to quicken me, which raised up Jesus from the dead. And it pleased God so in his wisdom to direct, that all the great truths of the Christian religion were occasionally spoken to. Now this was Friends' way with me, a way far beyond all rules or methods established by the wisdom of this world, which is foolishness with God: and this is their way with others that are convinced of the truth.

Becoming a member

11.04 An individual becomes a member of their area meeting, and through it of Britain Yearly Meeting, by a simple process agreed and adopted by the area meeting. Variety and flexibility in procedures are needed to reflect individual and local circumstances. Each area meeting will develop one or more of such procedures.

Guidance on current procedures used by various area meetings can be obtained from the Recording Clerk.

Principles

11.05 Coming into membership is a two-sided process involving the individual on their spiritual journey and a whole community of faith. It is a process of discernment that involves both the applicant and the wider Quaker community: local Friends, the area meeting and possible contacts with other Quakers in other contexts such as a listed informal group or a university chaplain. It is the outward acknowledgement of an inward growth of commitment or a sense of belonging to the Religious Society of Friends.

11.06 The area meeting will be mindful of the need for simple, open and inclusive processes, involving the potential member throughout. The applicant should be party to any written report prepared as part of the process, which must be compliant with legal requirements such as for data protection (see 4.45). The Quaker community should be sure that the individual has an appropriate understanding of the meaning and responsibilities of membership. Potential members should be supported and nurtured before, during and after the process.

11.07 Although aspects of the process may be devolved to smaller groups, the area meeting has the responsibility to:

a. establish and explain what local procedures are;
b. maintain records as appropriate;
c. take the decision on whether to admit the individual into membership and minute it.

Stages of the process

Nurture and support

11.08 Meetings have a responsibility to nurture and support individuals so that they can develop a sense of belonging and an understanding of our shared beliefs, testimonies and spiritual discipline.

Nurture is a continuing process for all who come to our meetings whether or not they decide to consider membership. Each area meeting will have its own ways of approaching this. For example they may provide attenders' packs for information and literature about membership, there may be special nurturing or supporting Friends or there may be an attenders' group.

Some area meetings have adopted alternative arrangements and procedures by which they carry out the responsibilities of overseers. In such cases, the following paragraphs should, where applicable, be interpreted according to whatever procedures the area or local meeting has in place: 11.09, 11.22, 11.23, 11.26, 11.30, 11.32, 11.39, 11.41

11.09 Overseers should be sensitive to the needs of attenders and, when the time is right, encourage a consideration of membership (see 12.13.h). Part of this encouragement, which need not necessarily result in an application, could include the provision of formal or informal discussion groups and suggestions about relevant reading. Many meetings have found it helpful to present applicants with a copy of our book of discipline or other relevant book, either during the application process or when the application has been accepted by the area meeting. Whatever the method or moment selected, it is important for the applicant to become familiar with our discipline: for example, meetings for church affairs are a part of the life of the meeting and applicants should be alive to the reasons we conduct our affairs the way we do and the importance of playing an active role in them.

Initiating the process

11.10 If and when the time seems right, the process of discernment which can lead to membership may be initiated by the applicant or someone else. For example, others may approach an attender to encourage her or him to consider membership and may begin the process on their behalf. Attenders themselves may take the first step. The decision to apply may, perhaps, emerge from being part of a discussion or pastoral care or nurture group.

For the individual this process is likely to reflect a wish to make a public statement to show their commitment to the discipline of Friends and their recognition that this is their spiritual home.

Discerning the rightness of the application

11.11 The process of discernment that membership is right for both the applicant and the meeting is at the heart of the acquisition of membership. Once it has been discerned that it is right for the application process to be taken forward, area meetings may offer a number of options. For example, it may be that the traditional process is followed, with a letter from the applicant to the area meeting clerk and the appointment of two Friends, one from the applicant's meeting and the other from a different local meeting within the area meeting, to visit the applicant and report back to the area meeting. In other cases supporting Friends may hold discussions with the attender and together they may write an application letter or a minute which is taken to area meeting. For some a meeting for clearness (12.23) may be right.

Some applicants will have found a wider Quaker community beyond the local geographical area, and those involved in the discernment process may find it helpful to contact individuals from this wider Quaker community (such as members of a listed informal group, a young person's link group, or a university chaplain).

The final part of the process of discernment is consideration by the area meeting. As area meetings are responsible for holding membership they are responsible for the final decision about an application. The decision may be informed, for example, by a minute from the local meeting, a report written by visitors with the applicant, or by the outcome of a meeting for clearness. All of these are the product of discernment.

Recognition and continuing nurture

11.12 Membership can be seen as an outward expression of what is already there. The acceptance of a new member should be a joyful occasion and may be marked by some kind of celebration. For all meetings the responsibility to nurture and guide the new member is a continuing one. Area meetings will find their own ways of providing this, for example by supporting Friends (11.08) or pastoral groups. Pastoral care, which in many other churches is given in part by a separated ministry, is in our yearly meeting a responsibility shared by all members.

Membership of children

Application on behalf of a child

11.13 There are three main ways of looking at children's membership, each with solid historical roots in Quaker tradition.

a. You are not a Friend until you make a profession of faith, which you can do only at a mature age and after careful consideration; you must consciously and deliberately decide, declare and commit yourself: something you are unable to do as a child.
b. A child who is brought up within the community of a Friends' meeting is a full member in every sense; children were used by Jesus as patterns of the Kingdom and a child as well as an adult may have deep insights; your religious pilgrimage begins at, or before, birth and at any moment you are at a particular point on the journey.
c. A child may be a full member, but growing up demands confirmation; every one, at a given point of their physical and spiritual growth, should take up their membership for themselves and express it in some of the many forms of service.

11.14 These three approaches have usually been seen as mutually contradictory – if one is right the other two must be wrong. But in reality all three can be right: they express different aspects of membership. Each emphasises something of what it means to be persons shaped by the family and community we are born into, but having to choose our own position in relation to our family and community. Parents should try to recognise that their child may quite properly choose, in the light of the child's own temperament and experience, a way different from the one chosen on her or his behalf, even if that way lies outside the Society. Children, for their part, may recognise that any choice made for them will reflect the temperament and experience of their parents. (See 11.17.)

11.15 Parents or those with parental responsibility or guardians who intend to bring up a child in accordance with the religious principles of the Society may apply for acceptance of that child into membership, while he or she is under the age of sixteen. The application, stating this intention, should be in writing and give the full name and date of birth of the child and be signed by both parents or by those with parental responsibility or guardians. Area meetings may, in special circumstances, dispense with the signature of one of the parents.

11.16 On receipt of the application the area meeting may appoint Friends to visit the parents or those with parental responsibility or guardians before reaching a decision as to admission into membership. The decision of the area meeting is to be conveyed to the parents or those with parental responsibility or guardians in writing. The names of the children so admitted are to be entered on the official register of members with the date of admission and the date of birth, and the appropriate local meeting is also to be informed.

Options available to those admitted on parental application

11.17 Membership acquired on parental application constitutes full membership and the member is under no obligation to confirm it on reaching a certain age. It is entirely valid, however, for a member to wish to indicate a personal acceptance of membership acquired in this way, or to wish to resign and seek re-admission as a 'convinced' Friend. Such requests may be made after much serious thought and area meetings should respond carefully, being guided by the spiritual needs of their members rather than by the desire to establish or follow a uniform practice.

11.18 A member whose admission was secured under section 11.15–11.16 may at any time take one of the following courses of action:

a. continue in membership acquired on the application of parents without making any formal statement;
b. indicate personal acceptance of membership acquired on application of parents and have this personal acceptance formally recognised by the area meeting (the member may in addition desire the appointment of one or two Friends as visitors);
c. resign from membership and, at the same or some later time, seek admission 'by convincement' under the normal procedure;
d. resign from membership without further formality since he or she does not consider himself or herself a member.

A member wishing to follow course b, c or d shall so indicate in writing to the area meeting clerk, whereupon the area meeting shall take such action as it thinks appropriate. It should record in its minutes the action taken.

11.19 Overseers should bring these options to the attention of younger Friends on reaching maturity but should be sensitive enough not to press them to make any decision when they might not be ready for it (see 12.13.g).

See also 11.30 Resignation by the individual

Nothing in this section precludes young people under the age of sixteen from applying under the procedure described in 11.04–11.12

Transferring membership

Principles

11.20 It is necessary for the accuracy of the Society's records and the effectiveness of its two-way communications, as well as for the convenience of the individual, that up-to-date records are kept. Therefore it is important for each area meeting to know its members' current addresses, phone numbers and email addresses (where used), particularly when members are moving geographically from one part of the Quaker community to another. After a move has taken place, it is desirable for membership to be held with the area meeting that covers the area in which the Friend is living.

The reciprocal nature of the relationship between members and their meetings means that, when changing address to the area covered by another area meeting, and when transferring membership to another area meeting, action is required both by the individual member and by the area meetings concerned.

Any part of the process may be conducted via electronic media. It is advisable that hard copies are made of such communication for the record.

Change of address

Responsibilities of the member or attender

11.21 On change of address, whether temporary or permanent, to an area covered by another area meeting with which the member or attender is likely to become associated, it is necessary as soon as possible to inform the clerk of their 'old' area meeting of the new address, postcode, and telephone number and email address if appropriate.

Responsibilities of clerks

11.22 On receiving notice of a change of address, either incoming or outgoing, the clerk should immediately forward the details to overseers.

Responsibilities of overseers

11.23 On receiving details from their clerk, overseers of the 'old' area meeting should immediately forward them to the clerk of the 'new' area meeting. Printed forms for these notices can be obtained from the Recording Clerk and at www.quaker.org.uk/qfp. Overseers of the 'new' area meeting will want to make timely contact with their new member or attender.

A notice should be sent even when a member or attender is moving some distance from any meeting or abroad. If the move is to a country where there is no known group of Friends, Friends World Committee for Consultation (FWCC) should be consulted as to where the nearest Friends live so that contact may be made. If it is to an area where several yearly meetings overlap, FWCC may be able to advise on the most useful point of contact.

Transfer of membership: procedure

Responsibilities of the member

11.24 It has been found in general that it can take up to three months for a member to familiarise themselves with their 'new' area meeting. When within this time it seems right, the member should ask the clerk of either area meeting to arrange for a transfer of their membership. This can be done by letter, email or phone.

Responsibilities of clerks

11.25 On receiving such a request from its member, their current meeting should issue a certificate of transfer, or the receiving meeting should apply for one. If a request for transfer of membership is not received after three months of leaving an area meeting's area, that meeting may issue a certificate of transfer, or the receiving area meeting may apply for one. Printed forms for these certificates may be obtained from the Recording Clerk and at www.quaker.org.uk/qfp.

On receiving such a certificate, the clerk should immediately inform the local overseers and request their advice as to the acceptability of the transfer of membership.

The membership is not transferred until the certificate of transfer is accepted by the receiving area meeting and a confirmation of that acceptance has been received by the issuing area meeting. Printed forms for certificates of acceptance are available from the Recording Clerk and at www.quaker.org.uk/qfp.

In cases of doubt regarding the address in another yearly meeting to which a certificate should be sent, the Recording Clerk would be able to help and may also be able to give general information concerning meetings and Friends resident abroad (and see 11.23).

Responsibilities of overseers

11.26 Contact should be made with the Friend concerned as soon as a certificate of transfer has been received. Overseers are responsible for advising the area meeting with regard to the transfer.

In some rare cases, a receiving area meeting may object to the transfer. It is expected that this will be done only in exceptional circumstances. Area meetings are reminded that, though a Friend may have taken little or no part in the life of the meeting, even for many years, their move may prove an occasion for renewed participation in the life of the Society.

Nevertheless, a meeting may properly return a certificate of transfer:

a. where it seems clear that the Friend will not become part of the receiving area meeting;
b. where in the view of the receiving area meeting the Friend is likely to remain, or to become, more closely associated with the issuing meeting or another;
c. where in the view of the receiving area meeting the issuing area meeting should consider whether termination of membership may prove to be more appropriate.

It may be desirable that the overseers of the issuing meeting write to the clerk to the overseers of the receiving meeting giving such information as may seem useful.

Overseers are reminded that where information is supplied in confidence the Friend concerned has the right under data protection legislation to see any correspondence (4.45).

11.27 If because of special circumstances a Friend's membership is not transferred to the area meeting in the area in which the Friend lives, he or she should nevertheless be encouraged to give such service as seems appropriate within that meeting (see also 4.08 & 4.32).

Sojourning membership

11.28 An area meeting may at its discretion accept as a sojourning member a Friend maintaining membership outside Britain Yearly Meeting who wishes to be associated with the area meeting while residing temporarily within its compass. Sojourning members are expected to share as fully as they are able in the life of the area meeting, and to live under the discipline of Britain Yearly Meeting. Sojourning membership is not a category of membership for those who move permanently into the geographical area of Britain Yearly Meeting.

The request shall be supported by a minute or certificate requesting the association from the home meeting of the Friend concerned (or Friends World Committee for Consultation if the Friend is on the international membership list).

Decisions on sojourning membership shall be recorded by the area meeting in its minutes and the number of sojourning members entered on the annual tabular statement (see 4.10.h & 6.07). The area meeting is advised to review the status of its sojourning members regularly to ensure it does not become permanent.

The area meeting shall inform the home area meeting (or Friends World Committee for Consultation if the Friend is on the international membership list) when a sojourning Friend has left the compass of the meeting or has become inactive, and shall record this termination by minute. Sojourning membership will also be terminated if the Friend's membership is later transferred into the area meeting (see 11.23–11.24) as remains the normal recommended practice. (See also 4.32 & 6.14.)

Termination of membership

11.29 The membership of any Friend shall cease when a record to this effect is made in the minutes of the area meeting to which he or she belongs. Either the Friend or the area meeting may initiate steps leading to the termination of membership. The termination recorded in the minutes of the area meeting shall be understood as no more than a record that meaningful spiritual membership has ceased to exist (but see also 11.30).

Resignation by the individual

11.30 Any Friend who has attained the age of sixteen may address a letter of resignation to the clerk of the area meeting. Area meetings should arrange for such letters to be referred to the local or area meeting overseers for advice. Normally a resignation should not be accepted until after a visit on behalf of the area meeting. On the acceptance of a resignation the area meeting clerk shall immediately inform the Friend concerned.

Termination by the area meeting

11.31 Area meetings may take the initiative in terminating membership in cases where:

a. over a prolonged period a Friend has ceased to show any interest in the life of the Society and there seems no reasonable likelihood of renewed participation;
b. a Friend's address has been unknown for a period of at least three years and cannot, after a careful search, be ascertained;
c. the conduct or publicly expressed opinions of the member are so much at variance with the principles of the Society that the spiritual bond has been broken.

11.32 In the relationship between Friends and their local meetings there may be periods of misunderstanding or strain. Though the main responsibility of pastoral care properly rests, in most area meetings, with local overseers, they may not necessarily have the sense of perspective or required skills to reach right judgments in all cases. A proper desire for confidentiality may make local overseers reluctant to bring such matters to area meeting overseers, and area meetings are therefore urged to see that clear and workable arrangements exist whereby local overseers can bring a few judicious Friends from elsewhere in the area meeting into consultation at an early stage in any membership matter that is likely to prove difficult.

11.33 If any Friend, by conduct or publicly expressed views, appears to be denying the Society's beliefs and principles or bringing it into disrepute, and private counsel has proved of no avail, the area meeting shall appoint well-qualified Friends to attempt to restore unity. If it appears that advice and counsel are, and are likely to continue to be, without their desired effect, the area meeting may record a minute of disunity with the action of that Friend and, in exceptional circumstances, terminate membership.

11.34 Area meetings should not normally terminate membership under 11.31 a or c until after a visit. An official letter inviting the Friend to reply should be issued by direction of the area meeting, signed by the clerk and sent to the Friend concerned before a decision to terminate membership under a or c is reached. On the actual termination of membership the area meeting clerk should immediately inform the Friend or Friends concerned, drawing their attention to the right of appeal should they feel aggrieved by the decision of the area meeting (see 4.25).

11.35 Pleas for the continuance of formal membership on sentimental grounds should have no place in a religious society, but area meetings are reminded that many Friends go through periods, sometimes prolonged, when their association with the life of the meeting is tenuous. Area meetings are urged to be very tender in all such cases and to beware of undue haste or unwarranted assumptions in proposals for the termination of membership.

Children

11.36 Letters of resignation on behalf of children who have not attained the age of sixteen should normally be signed by the parents or those with parental responsibility or guardians. Area meetings are at liberty in special circumstances to dispense with the signature of one of the parents. Such a resignation should be accepted by the area meeting unless in its judgment this is contrary to the best interests of the child. Area meetings may also initiate the termination of membership of the children of any Friends whose membership has ceased under 11.29 or 11.30. If it seems likely that any child whose membership has been terminated will continue in association with the meeting, the area meeting should transfer the name to the list of children connected with the meeting but not in membership.

Classification for returns

11.37 For tabular statement purposes (see 4.10.h, 6.07) returns shall be classified under:

a. resignations on the initiative of the member;
b. terminations of membership on the initiative of the area meeting;
c. resignations on behalf of children.

Area meeting clerks shall complete a footnote stating how many terminations under b are in each of the categories in 11.31 and how many under c are on the initiative of the area meeting. It is therefore important that minutes recording the termination of membership be specific.

Records of membership

Official register of members

11.38 Each area meeting shall maintain an official register of members and shall appoint a suitable Friend to have care of it. (See 4.45 about data protection.) No alteration shall be made to the register save in accordance with decisions minuted by the area meeting. The official register of members shall be examined annually and checked with the area meeting minutes by the Friends appointed to prepare or check the tabular statement. The official register may be maintained in loose-leaf form provided that proper precautions are taken. Superseded official registers of members shall be preserved by area meetings among their records (4.40).

Lists of attenders and children not in membership

11.39 Each area meeting shall maintain a list of attenders and of children not in membership associated with its several meetings for worship or shall arrange that such lists shall be kept by overseers. An attender is one who, not being a member, frequently attends a specific meeting for worship.

Printed lists of members, attenders and children not in membership

11.40 It is recommended that in the printed lists of members, attenders and children not in membership the date of birth should be printed and continued until the age of eighteen.

Respecting the essentially private nature of such lists, meetings should exercise care to limit their availability and guard against the risk that they might be put to undesirable use (see 4.45).

Recording of marriages and deaths

11.41 Area meetings shall record in their minutes marriages of their members according to our usage. Area meetings shall likewise record in their minutes the deaths of their members. It is recognised that some area meetings will wish to receive information on deaths in a standard form of their own devising while others may be satisfied with a letter from a close relative or local overseer or be content, in certain circumstances, with an oral report.

On records see also 4.40 & 4.45

Conclusion

11.42 Friends have often had difficulty with the concept of membership and the definition of its basis. However, in practice, there is rarely any difficulty over particular applications.

In 1966 London Yearly Meeting accepted a new statement on membership after a difficult exercise in which problems of disunity were faced. This statement introduced the membership chapter in *Church government* from 1967 to 1995 and it remains an inspiration to many Friends:

> 'George Fox and his early followers', wrote Rufus Jones, 'went forth with unbounded faith and enthusiasm to discover in all lands those who were true fellow-members with them in this great household of God, and who were the hidden seed of God.' Our Society thus arose from a series of mutual discoveries of men and women who found that they were making the same spiritual pilgrimage. This is still our experience today. Even at times of great difference of opinion, we have known a sense of living unity, because we have recognised one another as followers of Jesus. We are at different stages along the way. We use different language to speak of him and to express our discipleship. The insistent questioning of the seeker, the fire of the rebel, the reflective contribution of the more cautious thinker – all have a place amongst us. This does not always make life easy. But we have found that we have learned to listen to one another, to respect the sincerity of one another's opinions, to love and to care for one another. We are enabled to do this because God first loved us. The gospels tell us of the life and teaching of Jesus. The light of Christ, a universal light and known inwardly, is our guide. It is the grace of God which gives us the strength to follow. It is his forgiveness which restores us when we are oppressed by the sense of falling

short. These things we know, not as glib phrases, but out of the depths of sometimes agonising experience.

Membership, therefore, we see primarily in terms of discipleship, and so impose no clear-cut tests of doctrine or outward observance. Nevertheless those wishing to join the Society should recognise its Christian basis. Words often seem inadequate to convey our deepest experiences, yet words – however imperfect – are necessary if we are to share with one another what we have learned. In Christian faith and practice and in the Advices and queries we have tried to express those broad principles of belief and conduct on which unity is essential. These find expression in our testimonies, which reflect the Society's corporate insights, and a loyal recognition of this is to be expected, even though precise agreement on every point is not required. We are aware of continual failures in our discipleship, and no one should hesitate, from a sense of unworthiness, to apply for membership.

Membership implies acceptance of responsibility and a sense of commitment. It implies a willingness to be used by God, however imperfect we may feel ourselves to be as his messengers. He will not miraculously deliver us from the trials of temper and temptation, pettiness and pride, which are a part of human nature. In our worship together, and as we learn together in a Christian community, he will help us to overcome the limitations of our nature, to become more fully the people he intends us to be. 'Not as though we had already attained, either were already perfect, but we follow after ... forgetting those things which are behind, and reaching forth unto those things which are before, we press toward the mark for the prize of the high calling of God in Christ Jesus.'

See also chapter 10 Belonging to a Quaker meeting

Chapter 12

Caring for one another

Introduction

12.01 All of us in the meeting have needs. Sometimes the need will be for patient understanding, sometimes for practical help, sometimes for challenge and encouragement; but we cannot be aware of each other's needs unless we know each other. Although we may be busy we must take time to hear about the absent daughter, the examination result, the worries over a lease renewal, the revelation of an uplifting holiday, the joy of a new love. Every conversation with another Friend, every business meeting, every discussion group, and every meeting for worship can increase our loving and caring and our knowledge of each other.

Loving care is not something that those sound in mind and body 'do' for others but a process that binds us together. God has made us loving and the imparting of love to another satisfies something deep within us. It would be a mistake to assume that those with outwardly well-organised lives do not need assistance. Many apparently secure carers live close to despair within themselves. We all have our needs.

Careful listening is fundamental to helping each other; it goes beyond finding out about needs and becomes part of meeting them. Some would say that it is the single most useful thing that we can do. Those churches that have formal confession understand its value, but confession does not have to be formal to bring benefits. Speaking the unspeakable, admitting the shameful, to someone who can be trusted and who will accept you in love as you are, is enormously helpful.

Plain speaking is a longstanding Quaker testimony. It is not only that we hold a witness to the value of truth but also that straightforwardness saves us from many mistakes and much time wasted. On first acquaintance some Quakers can seem rather brusque; without the conventions of flattery and half-truths, we particularly need to make clear the steadfast love we have for one another.

Caring can take many forms. Some help will be beyond the resources of the local meeting, but it should not be beyond our resources to see when it is needed and to see that it is provided. Often it is what we are rather than anything we do which is of help to others. We should be wary of giving advice: a sympathetic ear, whilst a person finds their own way forward, will usually do more lasting good. Some people may not want to be helped, seeing our concern as an intrusion. Great sensitivity is called for.

The adults in a meeting have a shared responsibility for making a reality of our claim that the presence of children and young people is valued and that everybody's needs and feelings matter. People vary in how comfortable they feel with silent worship; some children, like some adults, take naturally to its disciplines and joys; others have to work at it. Some meetings offer other forms of worship from time to time. In any case it is important that the needs of all age groups are considered when we plan our activities.

12.02 To be without an ordained clergy is not to be without either leadership or ministry. The gifts of the Spirit to us include both. For us, calls to particular ministries are usually for a limited period of time, and those gifts pertain to the task rather than the person. In one lifetime a person may be called to a number of ministries.

London Yearly Meeting, 1986

12.03 With our structure, we risk failures in understanding and transmitting our tradition, and failures in pastoral care.

We do not always adequately support one another. When we appoint people to carry out tasks for us, there is a danger of approaching this in too secular a way... We can and must pray for them to receive the necessary gifts and strength from the Spirit.

London Yearly Meeting, 1986

12.04 The great aim of a Christian community is to enable its members to know what their gift is and then to enable them to exercise it to the glory of God. This may sometimes involve a prolonged and perhaps painful exercise before some members come to accept that the gift they have to offer is not the one they thought.

New life from old roots, 1965

Eldership and oversight

12.05 Some Friends, whether called elders or not, have been looked to for spiritual counsel from the beginning. So in 1653 William Dewsbury proposed that each meeting should appoint 'one or two most grown in the Power and the Life, in the pure discerning of the Truth' to take responsibility for the spiritual welfare of the meeting and its members.

While the nurture of the spiritual life and responsibility for the right holding of meeting for worship continued to rest with 'elders', the more practical aspects of pastoral care were, towards the end of the eighteenth century, assigned to appointed 'overseers'.

Most area meetings continue the practice of appointing elders and overseers from their membership to ensure that the needs of the worshipping groups within their compass are met.

Area meetings' responsibility for pastoral care

12.06 The responsibility for providing each local meeting with the necessary resources for eldership and oversight rests with the area meeting, while much of the ongoing work is carried out in its constituent meetings. Good communication between these meetings and the area meeting should be maintained at all times so that items referred by one body to another are attended to and, where necessary, action is taken.

Elders and overseers (where appointed) will only be able to serve well if they are known and accessible to Friends and attenders. Care should be taken that members of a meeting know which of their number are serving for the time being in each capacity.

Meetings of those responsible for eldership and oversight should be called at least once a year by the area meeting. Here they can consider the needs of other meetings besides their own as well as the fundamentals of their faith and practice. Here too, newly appointed elders and overseers can learn about the tasks laid upon them and about how these responsibilities are carried out in other meetings. The area meeting should ensure that opportunities for consultation and inspiration are made known and appoint representatives to conferences on pastoral care matters, which might also be arranged by general meetings. Meetings are urged to learn about, and make use of, the wide variety of experience and resources available. Guidance on many aspects of pastoral care is available from Quaker Life and at www.quaker.org.uk/qfp.

Area meetings shall keep under regular review the provision of pastoral care in their constituent meetings (see 4.13.d & 12.16). Area meetings should seek the forms of eldership and oversight in each constituent meeting that best meet needs (12.15).

Appointment of elders and overseers

12.07 Appointment as elder or overseer does not imply that the Friends concerned are elevated to a higher position but that the meeting recognises that they may have the capacity to serve it in a particular way. Appointments are for a three-year period and may be renewed for a further three years; sometimes it may be necessary or desirable for a Friend to serve as elder or overseer for more than six consecutive years but this should not happen routinely (see 3.23). There is need for adequate continuity but there should be no expectation of continuous uninterrupted service. Care should be taken that newly appointed elders and overseers understand the duties involved. Those who are not to be re-nominated should be informed before new names are submitted to the area meeting.

Nominations to these offices are made either by the area meeting standing nominations committee or by a special area meeting nominating committee, consisting of a group of Friends drawn from the constituent meetings for this purpose. Members should bear in mind that they are not bringing forward names from their local meetings for ratification but nominating elders and overseers from the area meeting as a whole.

12.08 Beatrice Saxon Snell relates a story from her own experience, which reminds us that we are all potentially the instruments of God:

> I had a salutary lesson in sober thinking when I was first asked to become an elder. The invitation appalled me; I felt I was not old enough, had not been in the Society long enough; I suspected strongly that my monthly meeting had asked me on the inadequate grounds of vocal ministry; I read up the appropriate passages in *Church government* and felt still more appalled. Nevertheless I had been in the Society just long enough to know that the group often has

a wisdom which can seldom be justified on logical grounds but which is, nevertheless, superior to the wisdom of the individual. I therefore went to consult a much respected elder of my acquaintance. She and her house were late Victorian; she sat on her ugly sofa with the poker up her spine, her feet set neatly together and her hands folded in her lap; and she let me talk myself out. When I had quite finished she inclined herself slightly towards me and said: 'My dear, we have to take what we can get.' I have since been convinced that this is a text which ought to be framed and hung up over the bed of every elder in the Society: it ought to be hung over the bed of every Friend who is tempted to refer to the elders as 'they'.

1982

12.09 When asked to consider nomination for this service to the meeting, Friends should do so prayerfully and in the knowledge that the task will be entrusted to them for a period only. No one should be reluctant to pass on the responsibility to others when one triennial appointment comes to an end.

Once the area meeting has made the appointments, the area meeting clerk shall immediately notify every Friend appointed and shall convene the first meetings of elders and of overseers respectively unless the area meeting has adopted other procedures for so doing. At the first meeting of each group a clerk or convener shall be appointed, unless the area meeting has already appointed one.

The area meeting clerk shall transmit to each constituent meeting and to the Recording Clerk the names of elders and overseers appointed for the next triennial period, and of their respective clerks or conveners, as soon as possible after their appointment.

An area meeting may release individual elders or overseers from service, and may make interim appointments, at any time during the triennial period.

All such changes are to be notified to each constituent meeting and to the Recording Clerk. It is important that the area meeting make known to its members the method by which it wishes to receive nominations for such interim appointments. It may, for example, wish them to be brought forward by its standing nominations committee, or it may prefer to receive nominations from the existing area meeting elders and overseers or from the local meeting most directly concerned.

A Friend whose membership is transferred from the area meeting that made the appointment shall cease upon transfer to be an elder or overseer.

Caring for one another in the local meeting

12.10 The work of eldership and oversight is mainly carried out locally. Those responsible for pastoral care will need wisdom and sensitivity. Their ability to inform, advise and counsel will often be called on. Those invited to serve in either capacity may feel that the challenges sound daunting and that they will not match up to expectations. The meeting will be a source of support to those asked to be elders or overseers. The responsibility of eldership and oversight will bring its own rewards.

Understanding of human personality and motivation gained from a variety of disciplines will be of help in effective pastoral caring. Additionally, it may be necessary to be informed about ways of acquiring skills and, where necessary, to seek information from those qualified to give it. Members of our meetings or those associated with us will often have the required knowledge and experience.

It is important to distinguish between everyone's need to be listened to with sympathetic acceptance, especially when faced with bereavement or other painful situations, and those whose need goes beyond the competence of members of the meeting. It should not be thought of as failure to enlist specialist help from outside the meeting when what is needed cannot otherwise be provided. In all advisory work it is important to recognise that much of it is confidential. If in doubt as to what is confidential and what is not, it is good practice always to check with those involved before passing on any information.

In situations where a meeting for clearness may be appropriate, the individual(s) wishing to call it should consult those responsible for pastoral care in their meeting. An appropriate handbook may be available.

See also 12.22–12.25 on meetings for clearness in general and 16.19–16.21 on meetings for clearness concerning intentions of marriage

12.11 Traditionally the first concern of elders is for the nurture of the spiritual life of the group as a whole and of its individual members so that all may be brought closer to God and therefore to one another, thus enabling them to be more sensitive and obedient to the will of God. So the right holding of our meetings for worship will be their particular care. The chief concern of overseers is with the more outward aspects of pastoral care, with building a community in which all members find acceptance, loving care and opportunities for service.

Though there is a difference of function, much of the work of elders and overseers is of the same nature. It is important that the two groups should at all times work in close collaboration and should, wherever possible, share their common commitment to the service of their meetings. Whether they meet in separate groups or not, they should, from time to time, arrange joint meetings locally as well as in the area meeting area.

Responsibilities of eldership

12.12 Some of the responsibilities listed here may be carried out by overseers, or by specially appointed groups or committees, but it is important that elders should see that they are fulfilled. It is laid upon elders:

a. to meet regularly to uphold the meeting and its members in prayer; to guide those who share in our meetings towards a deeper experience of worship; to encourage preparation of mind and spirit, and study of the Bible and other writings that are spiritually helpful; to encourage individual and united prayer in the meeting;
b. to promote the right holding of meetings for worship, remembering that responsibility for the meeting, including the fitness of the ministry, is shared among all the members of the worshipping group;
c. to foster helpful vocal ministry, seeking to discern the needs and gifts both of individual contributors to the vocal ministry and of the meeting as a whole: some Friends may hesitate to risk speaking in meeting because they lack confidence in their own call to speak – they will need encouragement; others may too easily rise to their feet without being clear as to the helpfulness of the message; sometimes it may be necessary to restrain unsuitable ministry;
d. to be responsible for the quiet gathering of the meeting for worship in order, reverence and harmony, for the arrangement of seating and for encouraging punctuality; elders will arrange for the closing of the meeting, normally by shaking hands;
e. to ensure that the basis and method of conducting meetings for church affairs are understood; to accept responsibility for their right ordering (see chapter 3);
f. to take responsibility for the right holding of meetings for worship on special occasions such

as marriages (16.31) and funerals (17.08–17.09), and, if memorial meetings are asked for, to make sure that their purpose is clear to those who attend (17.10) – some meetings like to make special arrangements for welcoming new babies or celebrating other events (see also 10.12, 10.17 & 22.44–22.46);

g. to care for individual Friends and attenders, entering with sympathy into their needs; to remember those who are unable to attend our meetings through age, illness or for other reasons; to visit them or where helpful to make special arrangements for meetings for worship in their homes; to take special responsibility for ministry to the dying and comforting the bereaved;

h. to encourage opportunities for all in the meeting to broaden and deepen their knowledge and understanding – this might include learning about the roots and foundations of our faith, becoming aware of the insights of other faiths and being challenged by new ideas, exploring with one another how to deepen our ministry, making opportunities for quiet reflection, increasing our understanding of ourselves and others and acknowledging our share of responsibility where there is conflict and loss;

i. together with overseers, to care for the children and young people associated with our meetings; to listen to what they have to say and to enable them to take as full a part as possible in our life and worship; to ensure there are regular opportunities for their spiritual nurture (see also 12.13.f);

j. together with overseers, to take care of the needs of enquirers and attenders, encouraging them to join in the life of the meeting;

k. to encourage Friends to take responsibility for their rightful part in the life of the community in which the meeting is situated; to welcome to our meetings those who belong to other Christian bodies, to other faiths and to none;

l. to consider the question of vocal ministry in the constituent meetings of the whole area meeting area and to give support where there is need for intervisitation.

It is advised that elders keep minutes of their meetings.

For responsibilities of elders in relation to non-members wishing to attend Yearly Meeting see 6.15. On the participation of elders in meetings for clearness see 12.22–12.25 and in meetings for clearness concerning intentions of marriage see 16.19–16.21. See also 12.10.

Responsibilities of oversight

12.13 Some of the responsibilities listed here may be carried out by elders, or by specially appointed groups or committees, but it is important that overseers should see that they are fulfilled. It is laid upon overseers:

a. to encourage attendance at meeting for worship and to make sure that newcomers to the meeting are welcomed and introduced to other members of the worshipping group;
b. to encourage members to attend meetings for church affairs whenever possible and to take their rightful part in them;
c. to make opportunities for Friends and attenders to get to know one another so that their diverse needs can be discovered and so that all will become aware of their gifts and experience, which may be of service to the meeting and to the Society – to be valued and needed is an enrichment for all concerned;
d. together with elders, to take particular care of the needs of enquirers and attenders;
e. to meet regularly to ensure that the pastoral needs of everyone associated with the meeting are being noticed; to check the membership list frequently, not only for accuracy but also in order to cover unmet needs – each child and young person should

be considered as an individual and not solely as a member of a family group;

f. together with elders, to exercise care over the children and young people associated with the meeting, whether in membership or not, and to see that suitable activities are arranged (see also 12.12.i); to encourage them, where appropriate, to take part in gatherings arranged for young people at local or national level, consulting with parents when appropriate;

g. to make opportunities to talk with young people whose parents have brought them into membership about whether they wish to confirm it; at this stage they, and young attenders, may like to address a personal application to the area meeting and to be visited in the usual way; some may, at this point, wish to resign from the membership acquired for them by their parents (see also 11.17–11.19);

h. to give advice and information about how to apply for membership both to attenders and to parents who may wish to apply on behalf of their children; some attenders, either through shyness or because of a feeling of unworthiness, may be holding back from seeking membership – they may need encouragement to apply to the area meeting; it will be helpful to remind them that the letter of application to the area meeting clerk need not necessarily be more than a statement of the wish for membership, and that when they meet with the Friends appointed as visitors there is opportunity for asking questions and exploring matters of faith rather than examining fitness for membership (see also 11.10);

i. to visit members and attenders who have recently joined the meeting or moved into the area and to visit new-born babies; to see that the regulations on notices of change of address (11.23) and certificates of transfer of membership

(11.26, 16.52) are promptly attended to and that certificates are applied for when not duly received; to advise the area meeting on the acceptance or non-acceptance of certificates of transfer;

j. to encourage caring friendship within the Quaker community: should difficulties between Friends arise, overseers may be able to offer help at an early stage so that misunderstandings may be resolved; overseers are encouraged to make opportunities to talk privately with a Friend whose behaviour and manner of life is inconsistent with a Quaker witness, to explore underlying causes and endeavour to restore harmony (see also 11.32–11.35);

k. to send recommendations to the area meeting for the termination of membership in accordance with 11.31–11.35, once every effort has been made to follow up those who have drifted away from the meeting or have not been heard from for several years;

l. to ensure that young members and attenders living away from home are cared for and made welcome; to maintain contact with Friends residing abroad or in other parts of the country;

m. to advise local treasurers, collectors or finance committees, as appropriate, which members and attenders should and which should not receive contribution schedules;

n. to advise Friends who are in financial difficulty or who need help with education or training of their children about ways of obtaining assistance; to ensure that financial help is available, where this is needed, to enable Friends to attend meetings for church affairs and to accept appointments connected therewith;

o. to make sure that those intending to marry understand the principles on which the Society's usage is based and to refer them to the registering officer (see 16.05);

p. to see that sick people and elderly people, whether in their own homes, in hospital or in sheltered housing, are visited and cared for; to seek means of alleviating financial hardship; where overseers become aware that an elderly person is no longer able to look after herself or himself, it may be appropriate to offer help in consultation with the person concerned and any relatives or others involved: overseers should try to be aware of the statutory and voluntary provision of residential and other care in their locality, including Quaker homes;

q. together with elders, to respond to the needs of the bereaved at time of loss; to provide comfort and sympathetic listening, however grief may be expressed.

It is advised that overseers keep minutes of their meetings.

On the participation of overseers in meetings for clearness concerning intentions of marriage see 16.21.b, and in other meetings for clearness see 12.22–12.25. See also 12.10.

Sharing responsibility for pastoral care

12.14 However pastoral care is organised, it is essential that the responsibilities for spiritual, intellectual, emotional, material and physical care for each member of the Quaker community, as listed above, should be given prayerful consideration. As the responsibilities of eldership and oversight overlap in many instances, there should be close co-operation between elders and overseers at all times.

12.15 Some of our meetings are undertaking to care for one another without specially appointed elders and overseers. These meetings need to give careful consideration to the best way of attending to pastoral care without neglecting any of the responsibilities of eldership or oversight outlined above. Thought must be given, for example, to those who attend the meeting only rarely or are housebound.

If a local meeting wishes to adopt an alternative method of providing pastoral care, it should take time to work out how the responsibilities would be shared and who would represent the group in meetings for eldership and oversight within the area meeting. It should undertake a periodic review of the effectiveness of any procedure adopted.

In some cases Friends may decide that shared oversight works well for them but that they still see advantages in appointing elders to attend to the spiritual nurture of the group. Traditional practices are tried and tested. For some meetings, however, there will be advantages in exploring newer and possibly more appropriate ways of meeting their particular needs.

Any proposals for changes in the way pastoral care is exercised in a meeting or meetings should be taken to the area meeting for guidance, support and decision. Area meetings should have a particular care for those meetings involved in novel ways of exercising eldership and oversight, both to offer guidance if difficulties or deficiencies arise and to ensure that the benefits of new practices can be shared with other meetings. (See also 4.34.)

12.16 Whether elders and overseers are appointed or not, local meetings should regularly review their spiritual life and its expression in caring. A meeting might like to compile and use a series of queries for this purpose. Such a review could take place every two or three years and might in itself be a form of pastoral care. The process might start in small groups, in which unmet needs could be revealed and confidentiality respected, then move on to an occasion drawing all together. Special attention might need to be given to involving those associated with the meeting who take little part in its regular life because of youth, age, disability or disaffection. (See 4.10.d & 12.06.)

12.17 And all such as behold their brother or sister in a transgression, go not in rough, light or upbraiding spirit to reprove or admonish him or her, but in the power of the Lord, and the spirit of the Lamb, and in the wisdom and love of the Truth, which suffers thereby, to admonish such an offender. So may the soul of such a brother or sister be seasonably and effectually reached unto and overcome, and they may have cause to bless the name of the Lord on their behalf, and so a blessing may be rewarded into the bosom of that faithful and tender brother or sister that so admonished them.

George Fox, 1669

12.18 Nor would we limit the performance of these duties to those who occupy such stations; we are all to watch over one another for good and to be mutually interested one for another, being united together as lively stones in the spiritual building of which the Lord Jesus Christ is the chief corner-stone.

Yearly Meeting in London, 1851

12.19 [Let not] Friends in the station of overseer ... take a limited view of their duties... To them is committed the oversight of the flock, in the love of Christ. [Let them] give themselves to this ... duty in faith and prayer, seeking, in the wisdom of God, to encourage all in the right way of the Lord; to bind up that which is broken; to bring home the wanderers; to visit the sick and the afflicted; and to extend loving care over the young and inexperienced. Desirable as it is that some should be specially entrusted with these duties, an earnest concern has prevailed that all may take their right share in the privilege of watching over one another for good.

Yearly Meeting in London, 1871

Small groups

Meeting together in small groups

12.20 As Friends, we know that the quality of our unprogrammed worship is enhanced, and our care of one another is more effective, the better we come to know and understand one another.

We grow closer to one another as a worshipping community develops through regular attendance at meeting for worship, through working together physically or mentally, and in meeting with one another informally. Meeting together in small groups may have its part to play in this process, and may be valuable in helping us to explore and share our spiritual experience. Study and discussion groups provide well-tried opportunities, as do more informal social gatherings.

From time to time it may be helpful for a meeting to look at itself and try to identify specific areas that need attention, such as how to improve pastoral care, how to include attenders and newcomers, or how to improve communication and outreach. While these matters may well be raised in a local or area meeting, valuable suggestions and solutions may come from individuals who do not always find it easy to voice them in a more formal business meeting. The time given to preparation of heart and mind may also contribute very usefully to the right ordering of our meetings for church affairs. (See also 3.26.)

Elders and overseers may consider it part of their role to review the needs and workings of small groups in their meetings.

Worship sharing and creative listening groups

12.21 Some Quaker meetings have discovered the value of small groups in developing the art of listening to God, to others, and to oneself. Such 'worship sharing' or 'creative listening' groups can provide a setting where all who take part are involved in the process of learning about themselves as well as about others. Here silence, too, can heal and restore. For Quakers this approach fits in naturally with our experience of worship.

The terms 'creative listening' and 'worship sharing' are often used interchangeably, the difference between them being perhaps that the latter comes closer to a meeting for worship with a more pronounced emphasis on the worshipping atmosphere.

Careful preparation is needed to establish the basis of such groups, and there are several publications and sources which may give help. Advice may also be had from Quaker Life.

Good practice would normally include: the limitation of the size of the group to a maximum of twelve; beginning and ending the meeting in silence; the requirement of absolute confidentiality; allowing space between contributions; speaking from personal experience; not commenting directly on what another has said; listening with attention; not lapsing into discussion.

It may be that some do not contribute in spoken words. There is a need to respect the possibility that members of the group may not wish to discuss further what they have begun to share in the group. These groups can be particularly useful in allowing us to explore deep and personal thoughts and experiences in a supportive and safe environment.

Meetings for clearness

12.22 In earlier times Friends saw the need for 'clearness' as part of the necessary preparation for marriage. Only after a group of Friends, appointed by the area meeting, had established that there was clearness from other conflicting obligations could they recommend the solemnisation of a marriage. In some North American yearly meetings this practice has been maintained and the concept has broadened. It has become a loving and caring exercise on behalf of the meeting. The couple are helped to explore their commitment to God, to one another and to the meeting, to look in depth at the outcome of previous relationships or marriages, to consider their attitudes towards the care of existing or future children and at how the couple can make decisions about their life together. (See also 16.19–16.21 & 12.10.)

12.23 A number of meetings within Britain Yearly Meeting are making use of clearness groups for a variety of purposes. They may be called to prepare a couple for marriage, to test a concern, to make decisions about membership, to consider new forms of service or to seek guidance at times of change or difficulty. Such meetings may sometimes be of help and comfort to the dying.

Sometimes individuals or a family will need help when confronted by difficult choices at turning points in their lives. There may be interpersonal differences that sour relationships, or a meeting may have identified a particularly fraught area of divergence of opinion or belief in its membership. Any of these and similar situations, if they are faced openly and with love, may be tested in an atmosphere of worship. So those concerned may find a way forward.

12.24 By focusing on a particular issue, a meeting for clearness enables everyone present to become 'clear' about possible options and ways forward. Such a meeting may be a matter of private arrangement but if a local meeting is to be involved, elders or overseers will normally be consulted. The suggestion for a meeting may come from them or from those seeking clearness. In the case of clearness for marriage the registering officer will in most cases be a member of the clearness group, so that he or she will be in a position to give guidance to the meeting on whether a Quaker marriage should be allowed (see 16.19–16.21).

An elder or an overseer may need to explain the nature and conduct of the meeting to those asking for one. Four or five trusted Friends, not necessarily those closely involved with the matter under consideration, should be invited to participate. Their main qualification will be that they are likely to be able to contribute constructively in the process of discernment.

12.25 Meetings for clearness should be held in a relaxed atmosphere of trust yet a certain degree of formality is helpful. A facilitator should be chosen to assist in clarifying the question or questions being asked. Some groups may decide that notes should be taken. It will have to be made explicit that confidentiality is to be maintained within the group. There is need for listening with undivided attention, for tact, affirmation and love for those seeking clearness.

Each member of the group should have opportunities to question and explore the background to the matter that is to be clarified. It is important not to be diverted by side-issues but to concentrate on exploring options and understanding underlying difficulties. It will take time to reach clearness and periods of gathered worship will be helpful.

The meeting should have an unambiguous ending and should not continue once tiredness sets in. A further meeting or meetings may be needed if the original issue, or practical details, would benefit from further thought. When clearness is reached the group should be laid down.

Threshing meetings

12.26 This term currently denotes a meeting at which a variety of different, and sometimes controversial, opinions can be openly, and sometimes forcefully, expressed, often in order to defuse a situation before a later meeting for worship for business. Originally the term was used to describe large and noisy meetings for convincement of 'the world's people' in order to 'thresh' them away from the world.

Support groups

12.27 Friends sometimes undertake, or are asked to undertake, tasks which they find challenging, either on a single occasion or as a continuing commitment. Under these circumstances they may value the support of a small group of Friends. This could be offered by the body requesting the service or it may be requested by the Friend concerned. Membership of the group should reflect the preferences of the Friend to be supported. The group may need to remind itself that its job is not so much to judge the task as to support the Friend carrying it out.

Chapter 13

Varieties of religious service

Introduction

13.01 It is part of our commitment as members of the Religious Society of Friends that we try to live our lives under the guidance of the Spirit. Whatever the service to which we are called, whether it be great or small, our meeting can uphold us in prayer and other ways.

Our service may be in the home, an unpaid job, a vocation or a lifetime's career. For some there will be service in the local meeting, in one of the many roles that help to make our meetings true Christian communities. Some of these are explained later in this chapter. Britain Yearly Meeting itself offers people opportunities for service both as members of staff and on our various Quaker committees.

Personal leadings can be tested in a variety of ways. Other Friends and those with special responsibilities in the meeting will be ready to listen and to encourage. Where important and difficult decisions have to be made it may be appropriate to ask for a meeting for clearness (12.22–12.25).

Quakers have long been involved in a wide range of action rooted in our faith: in the cause of peace and reconciliation, local, national or international; on behalf of oppressed or deprived people; in furtherance of our testimonies to honesty and integrity. The diversity of Quaker activity has been remarkable. In all these areas, however, there have been particular Friends who have felt themselves at certain times to be singled out to act in response to a spiritual compulsion. This we call concern and we distinguish it from those things that we are concerned about.

Matters which we are 'concerned about' are often very important. They might include changing the way that Britain Yearly Meeting does something or hoping that it will undertake a particular service. These matters are best brought to our meetings for church affairs and dealt with under our well-tested business method, as outlined in chapter 3.

Concern: faith in action

The Quaker understanding of concern

13.02 Throughout the history of the Religious Society of Friends we have recognised that to anyone may come, at any time, a special inward calling to carry out a particular service. It is characterised by a feeling of having been directly called by God and by an imperative to act.

The ministry which has been carried out 'under concern' is a remarkable record of strength and perseverance in adversity. Many speak of the peace that came to them with the certainty that they were working with God. Recognising concern has also placed an obligation on the meeting which tests and supports it. Friends have on occasion been released from financial considerations and in some cases their families have been cared for whilst they carried out the service required of them.

A concern may arise unexpectedly out of an interest or may creep up on one out of worshipful search for the way forward. It may be in line with current desires and projects or it may cut across them; it may lead to action which is similar to that undertaken by others or it may require a brave striking out into the unknown.

13.03 There is a feeling of being right or fitting associated with the experience of concern:

> There was from the early stages of our discussion a strong sense of the 'rightness' of what we were talking about. The ideas flowed freely, and although we were not conscious of it at the time, we would say now that we were clearly working under guidance.
>
> Barry and Jill Wilsher, writing about the origins in 1978 of the Quaker Peace Action Caravan.

13.04 Others have spoken of a moment of calling, of an overwhelming sense of love and light, leading to a certainty that they must act:

> If you ask me for the important dates they are as follows: meeting for worship several Sundays at Morley, Wilmslow early 1967; Cambridge 22–23 September 1967, at the village of Grantchester where the message came opposite to the war memorial: '*You* shall do it and *I* shall help'. This message was the driving force. Friends were hesitant; some thought it very emotional, others thought it very moving. Only, I knew that that Power would never allow a failure.
>
> George Murphy writing about the concern which led to the founding of the Bradford University School of Peace Studies in 1973.

Discernment in concern

13.05 Achieving clarity about a concern is a particular exercise in discernment. It is a process that begins with considerable private reflection and the asking of some tough questions. Is this a desire that someone else do something or is it really a call to act oneself? Is this concern in keeping with the testimonies of the Society? Is it genuinely from God?

The discernment process is not confined to solitary reflection. As a Religious Society we are more than a collection of people who meet together – we meet as we do because we believe that gathered together we are capable of greater clarity of vision. It is therefore the practice in our Society for a Friend who, after due consideration, believes that he or she has a concern, to bring it before the gathered community of Friends. This is both a further part of the testing process and an expression of our membership in a spiritual community. It is a recognition of mutual obligations: that of a Friend to test the concern against the counsel of the group and that of the group to exercise its judgment and to seek the guidance of God.

13.06 As a general rule concerns should be brought before a local or, where appropriate, area meeting for church affairs. The concern may, if recognised by that meeting as a true leading, then be forwarded to other meetings for consideration by a wider or more specialised group of Friends. It is not appropriate, however, for concerns to be sent forward automatically to another meeting. One part of the discernment process is judging at what point a concern has been considered by all appropriate bodies. Meetings should beware of the risk of using the process of forwarding concerns to avoid their responsibilities (see 4.19–4.20).

Throughout the discernment process there should be one overriding principle before the hearts and minds of all: is this individual or group right to believe that this action or service has been 'laid upon' them by God?

13.07 'Concern' is a word which has tended to become debased by excessively common usage among Friends, so that too often it is used to cover merely a strong desire. The true 'concern' [emerges as] a gift from God, a leading of his spirit which may not be denied. Its sanction is not that on investigation it proves to be the intelligent thing to do – though it usually is; it is that the individual ... knows, as a matter of inward experience, that there is something that the Lord would have done, however obscure the way, however uncertain the means to human observation. Often proposals for action are made which have every appearance of good sense, but as the meeting waits before God it becomes clear that the proposition falls short of 'concern'.

Roger Wilson, 1949

Responsibilities of individuals and meetings

To Friends with concerns

13.08 Friends with a concern should take counsel from experienced members of the meeting, particularly those who may have a different approach to the problem. Consider setting up, or asking for, a support group of trusted Friends (12.27). A meeting for clearness may also be part of the process of discernment (12.22–12.25). Allow the process to take time and do not rush yourself.

At each stage Friends will try to bring their insights to bear. Be prepared for their comments to cause some soul-searching and possible revisions. Be very clear what you are asking of each meeting (see 13.12–13.14).

Occasionally the process of discernment and adoption does not operate as it should, for we are not perfect and sometimes lose the spirit in the letter. We may lose sight of genuine inspiration in the press of daily events and overcrowded agendas. This may happen at any stage in the process and may necessitate re-presentation or presentation in a new format. It is useful to have a support group (12.27) at moments like this.

The role of the meeting

13.09 The importance of the local worshipping group in fostering active concerns cannot be over-emphasised. Where Friends know and trust one another the gifts we all have can be used more fully in obedience to the Inward Light. This is the source from which concerns spring.

The atmosphere of mutual confidence and understanding that fosters concerns also leads naturally to sharing concerns with the meeting. A concern that is brought before a meeting should be considered with the greatest love, kindness and discipline. Much as we like to support our Friends in the things for which they have an unbounded enthusiasm, it is no kindness to recognise as a concern something which has not received the fullest attention possible.

13.10 When a Friend has laid a concern before an area or local meeting, there should be a chance for questioning and elucidation, after which it is normally the practice for the Friend to withdraw while the matter is being considered. If the concern is recognised the Friend may be given a minute with which to go forward.

It may be determined that the concern is not in harmony with the testimonies of our Society. It should be remembered, however, that:

> It is with individuals rather than with communities that new truth originates… While corporate guidance is of great value in controlling individual extravagance, it is a source of great danger to the church if it is opposed to a genuine individual concern.
>
> William Charles Braithwaite, 1909

Both individual and meeting should pay heed to the advice: 'Think it possible that you may be mistaken'.

13.11 It may not always be possible to give adequate consideration to a concern in the course of a normal area or local meeting for church affairs, or in the course of a regular committee meeting. The option of a special area meeting and/or a meeting for clearness to help work through the issues should be considered (see 12.22–12.25).

13.12 The meeting which has considered a concern needs to be absolutely clear whether it is:

a. recognising a concern seen as religiously valid;
b. supporting the concern and accepting responsibility for its furtherance, including financial support where necessary (13.18);
c. adopting the concern as one it shares, whereupon the concern becomes a concern of the whole meeting;
d. recognising the concern and forwarding it with its support to a more widely representative meeting;
e. forwarding it because the meeting is unable to reach a decision on the validity of the calling – in this case however it is likely that further preparation and consideration is preferable to forwarding it to another meeting at this stage;
f. deciding that the matter before it is not a religiously valid concern.

13.13 Where they are clear that they have recognised a concern, Friends in the meeting will turn their attention to the practical details of its implementation and consequences. It may happen that a meeting recognises a Friend's concern but can see no way in which it can be taken forward or given practical effect at this time. It is then appropriate to hold it over for further consideration when the circumstances are more favourable.

If a concern relates to the corporate life of Britain Yearly Meeting it should be sent forward by the area meeting, either to Meeting for Sufferings or to Yearly Meeting (see 4.19).

When service abroad in any capacity is proposed, early consultation with the relevant committees of Britain Yearly Meeting is imperative. Consultation with the Friends World Committee for Consultation and appropriate yearly meetings may also be necessary.

It has already been noted that meetings that support a Friend's concern will sometimes assume the financial responsibility for the concern. Whether or not this is so, they may also consider offering other forms of help such as the use of a car, offers of childcare or the setting up of a support group of people close to the Friend or concern (see 12.27).

When a concern has run its course, consideration should be given to how this may be recognised and acknowledged. A meeting that has supported a concern should be informed when it is seen to be right to lay that concern down. Celebration for the right ending of what was rightly begun may be appropriate.

See also 4.09 & 4.19–4.20

Minutes and finances

13.14 When a Friend applies to a meeting with the object of taking a concern to a more widely representative meeting, any minute agreed should be addressed to that meeting and a copy forwarded without delay to its clerk. A copy should also be given to the Friend or Friends presenting the concern.

When such a concern has been supported or adopted by an appropriate body other than the area meeting, it is the duty of the clerk of the supporting or adopting body to send notice at once to the clerk of the area meeting of which the Friend is a member. Giving such information promptly enables the area meeting to enter with understanding into the Friend's concern, and to offer whatever support seems appropriate (see 12.27).

13.15 When an area meeting has encouraged any Friend to apply to Meeting for Sufferings for support in service, it is the duty of the clerk to give notice to the Recording Clerk without delay to enable, where possible, advance notice to be given to members of Meeting for Sufferings.

13.16 Minutes should, when appropriate, make clear the nature and probable duration of the intended service. If long-term service is intended suitable arrangements should be made, by means of a corresponding committee or in other ways, for interim reports to the meeting issuing the minute.

13.17 When a concern is fulfilled the Friend should return the minute to the meeting which has supported the service and the meeting should record the return of the minute.

13.18 If financial help is needed when a Friend travels in the service of the Society, it shall normally be given by the meeting supporting the service. If the service is by invitation the inviting meeting shall normally give it.

The listed informal groups

13.19 The listed informal groups are independent groups through which Friends may share common interest, seek affirmation or carry out witness. The groups are seen by their members as arising from their Quaker faith and provide a way in which conviction and witness can be explored and developed outside our formal structures – but perhaps returning to them when the concern has been tested by action or reflection.

> The informal groups at present in action within and around the Society are all concerned, in one way or another, with the renewal of Quaker tradition and insight or with the application of these to contemporary issues in a way that is inspired and guided by our perception of God's leadings. If this is so, then their credentials are established, and whilst the activities of individual groups may seem to some odd or eccentric – in some cases even inappropriate – their intent must be accepted as striving to seek new light. We need to remember that spiritual development for many of us entails trips along cul-de-sacs, and

> that these sometimes, surprisingly, turn out to be highways. Whatever the outcome in any one instance, the courage to explore them with an open but not uncritical heart is a hallmark of both spiritual and intellectual integrity.
>
> Hugh Valentine, 1982

The recognised listed informal groups are listed annually in the *Book of meetings*, and the criteria for recognition may be obtained on application to the Recording Clerk. Being independent bodies outside the structures of Britain Yearly Meeting, the listed informal groups have no right of communication by minute with them.

Groups using the name 'Quaker' or 'Friends' in their title are reminded of the responsibility to uphold our testimonies, and that care is needed in case the work and witness of the group is understood to be part of the yearly meeting's corporate activity when it is not.

Other forms of service

13.20 Within our meetings there are many tasks which need to be performed and many responsibilities to be taken. This volume has details of many of these. For instance clerkship is dealt with in chapter 3 and eldership and oversight in chapter 12. What follows is a fuller description of some of the more specialised forms of service.

Travelling in the ministry and intervisitation

13.21 Travelling to visit and worship with Friends, both within our yearly meeting and beyond, is greatly to be valued. It helps to bind together the family of Friends. London Yearly Meeting endorsed its value in 1925:

> We should take an interest not only in our own particular meetings, but also in other adjacent meetings, especially if they are few in numbers or otherwise in need. The visitation of another meeting in the spirit of Christian fellowship is an act of service, even if unaccompanied by any words of spoken ministry. When carried out under right concern it may bring encouragement and refreshment both to those who visit and those who are visited.

13.22 It should be remembered by all who visit Friends in other yearly meetings that great sensitivity is required. Each yearly meeting is autonomous and each has its own tradition and practice. Do not think yourself a fount of all knowledge just because you are from Britain Yearly Meeting. Our understanding of Quakerism grew out of the experiences of Friends in the history of these islands. Our assumptions are bound up with our culture, heritage and history. All yearly meetings have changed their practice over time and now have a variety of traditions to draw upon. It is necessary to know the local Quaker tradition as well as the history of the country in order to communicate fully with the Friends you are visiting. Quaker committees concerned with work overseas may be able to give advice and guidance to Friends visiting meetings abroad that will increase the usefulness of their visits.

Travelling in the ministry

13.23 This will usually be preceded by the testing of a concern and its recognition by the area meeting to which the Friend belongs. Everything in the previous sections 13.05–13.18 will apply. The Friend concerned may have been given financial support by the sponsoring meeting. Pastoral support has in the past been provided by Friends travelling in pairs, sometimes a younger Friend with an older. There may be circumstances where this practice is still helpful. The minute recognising the Friend's concern should be short enough to be read out after a meeting for worship.

13.24 Friends hoping to travel abroad in this service will be well advised to consult with the relevant committees of Britain Yearly Meeting and with the Friends World Committee for Consultation. After the concern has been recognised, the Friend should contact the yearly meeting(s) within which they intend to travel and be guided by their advice. As noted above it is important to remember that all yearly meetings are autonomous and that traditions and practice vary widely.

13.25 It is vital that Friends hoping to travel in the ministry test their concern thoroughly; we may be reminded of the practice of John Woolman, who travelled in the ministry extensively:

> Having been some time under a religious concern to prepare for crossing the seas in order to visit Friends in the northern parts of England, and more particularly in Yorkshire, after weighty consideration I thought it expedient to inform Friends at our monthly meeting at Burlington of it, who, having unity with me therein, gave me a certificate. And I afterwards communicated the same to our quarterly meeting, and they likewise certified their concurrence. Some time after, at the General Spring Meeting of Ministers and Elders, I thought it my duty to acquaint them with the religious exercise which attended my mind, with which they likewise signified their unity by a certificate, dated the 24th of third month, 1772, directed to Friends in Great Britain.

13.26 That Quakers could be called to the ministry other than in meeting for worship on Sundays was a new thought to us when, in 1967, a dear American Friend asked us whether we felt we had such a call. Its full significance did not strike us until later; the itinerant or travelling ministry had been the lifeblood of the Society of Friends in its earlier days and had continued into the beginning of the twentieth century. We served our apprenticeship with Lewis and Sarah Benson, travelling mainly in North America. We tried to catch some of their eagerness to bring to everyone the freshness of the message, their humility, their spirituality and their concern to gather all people to Christ, their Teacher. We soon found ourselves travelling with others or alone in Ireland, Scotland, France, Germany and Denmark as well as nearer home, while others ventured as far as Kenya and Australia. What drove all of us was a Christian message that needed to be shared wherever the door opened within or outside the Society of Friends.

Arthur and Ursula Windsor, 1994

13.27 We should be prepared to receive someone sent by another Quaker meeting with as much care as we send someone to travel in the ministry.

> It is not enough to send foreign Friends into small groups of Friends who will listen politely to their visitors: they should first know their visitors' culture and tradition in order to receive them with open minds and hearts. Friends in London Yearly Meeting need to discover where they stand individually. As we often do not know the personal theologies of members of our own meetings, how can we prepare our own Friends to listen to others? Yet we must. If Friends world wide are to be a world family of Friends we have to learn to hear and to understand each other.
>
> Quaker World Relations Committee, 1992

Types of minutes

13.28 A Friend released for service, under concern, by her or his meeting is provided with a minute of liberation. This will normally be written by Meeting for Sufferings (see 13.15).

A Friend travelling on Friends' business, or to perform a particular, limited service is provided with a travelling minute. This may be provided either by Meeting for Sufferings or by the area meeting. Such a minute may be endorsed by the welcoming meeting.

Letter of greeting

13.29 This is a letter issued by a meeting to one of its members or long-term attenders who is going to travel amongst Friends in other parts of the world for reasons not immediately connected with the service of the Society. In this case the local, area or general meeting may give the Friend a letter of introduction, signed by the clerk, to take with them. Such a letter is not a minute of authorisation for a particular service and care should be taken to avoid suggesting that it is.

Intervisitation

13.30

> We urge Friends, when staying away from home during holiday or on business, to attend a meeting for worship if there is one within reach. Such attendance may well have the effect of strengthening the meeting, and of helping Friends who were hitherto strangers to know one another.
>
> 1925, 1994

When visiting meetings in another yearly meeting be careful not to be a burden. Remember the caution in 13.22.

13.31 For over 35 years I have been visiting meetings other than my own. For the last 15 years monthly meeting has given me a travelling minute which is returned annually with its endorsements. I have visited the smaller meetings in my own monthly meeting; I have visited nearby meetings in other monthly meetings and thus kept contact with neighbours who might easily be strangers; when further from home I have sought out smaller meetings which might be encouraged by a visitor, and I am sure that the two or three present have been so encouraged. I have attended special occasions such as the reopening of a refurbished meeting house and rejoiced with those who rejoiced.

The words of John Woolman are in the travelling minute: 'A concern arose ... that I might feel and understand their life and the Spirit they live in, if haply I might receive some instruction from them, or they be in any degree helped forward by my following the leadings of Truth amongst them'. John Woolman's hopes have been abundantly fulfilled for me.

Richard Schardt, 1994

13.32 At the very small recognised meeting where I am a member – we have been as few as two at meeting for worship – we welcome visitors from other meetings, whether casual or regular, and look upon them as a source of enrichment. We understand that we in turn can give from our quietly gathered meeting.

Ingrid Williams, 1994

Wardens

13.33 As Friends, we cannot separate our religious calling from our practical work for the kingdom of God. As Friends concerned for wardenship, we make our contributions in the local community to those who come to our meeting house. We appear to offer our facilities, but in fact we offer our love.

Quaker Home Service conference on wardenship, 1981

13.34 The aim of wardenship is to provide a warm and welcoming atmosphere within the meeting house, to create conditions conducive to worship and to offer a service to the community. Wardenship should be seen as an integrated part of Quaker life and worship, and a responsibility which is shared by the whole meeting. There are unique opportunities for outreach. Many demands are made of wardens who are regularly available; these range from requests for financial and practical support to appeals from those with deep emotional, social or spiritual needs. Wardens acquire a fund of knowledge about the meeting and its place in the neighbourhood and can often help the meeting with initiatives in outreach.

Wardens and meeting houses

13.35 Wardens are appointed to look after some of our meeting houses. In many cases they also live on the premises. The appointment is normally made by the area meeting, as the primary meeting for church government, but for practical purposes this responsibility is sometimes delegated to a local meeting or to trustees. Wardenship in its present form is a recent development among Friends and arises not for its own sake but from our desire that our meeting houses be more widely used for the benefit of the communities in which they stand.

Just as our meeting houses vary from those in a busy city centre or new town location to historic Brigflatts or Jordans, so their use varies from those which are open throughout the week to a wide range of community groups and commercial lettings, to others where there is little use except for meetings for worship. Consequently the work and conditions of employment of wardens vary enormously.

Employment of wardens

13.36 The employing area meeting and the local meeting concerned should be quite clear about the terms of employment. Wardens are usually provided with accommodation in or adjacent to the meeting house, but a few are non-resident. Some see wardenship as a service they wish to give, perhaps on early retirement; others regard it as a very worthwhile form of employment. Some wardens are paid as full-time employees, others on a very part-time basis; some receive free accommodation only, whilst others (usually where there is little work involved) make a contribution towards the rent, heating, and other costs. Wardens may also have other employment.

Employing meetings and wardens are reminded that there are laws detailing the formal rights and responsibilities of both employers and employees. Quaker Life can provide up-to-date information.

There must be a clear job description which is reviewed regularly. Advertisements should be comprehensive and interviews thorough. A policy of equal opportunities is appropriate. It is essential that the warden or wardens have written terms and conditions of employment linked with a suitable written agreement covering the accommodation provided. Time off and adequate holidays should be agreed and consideration given to pension needs. Rehousing on completion of service requires careful consideration before appointment.

13.37 Work which is rightly the responsibility of office holders and members of the meeting should not be left to wardens, and wardens should not be appointed to those offices which could give rise to a conflict of interest: clerk, assistant clerk, treasurer or managing trustee. There should be clear guidance as to who is responsible for lettings. Ex-officio attendance at premises and wardenship committees is a frequent and helpful practice. Care must be taken to respect the privacy of wardens during their leisure time and not to make unreasonable demands upon their services. Their private accommodation should not be considered as an extension of the meeting house.

13.38 Wardens should not be asked to accept conditions of accommodation and work which most Friends would not tolerate personally. Casually made appointments can lead to misunderstandings and unintended exploitation. Meetings employing a warden are urged to consult with Quaker Life, to ensure that good practice is observed in their meeting.

Support for wardens

13.39 Wardens and meetings benefit from the provision of good support. This may be provided by premises committees, wardenship committees or a link Friend or Friends. The needs of the warden should be considered by the employing meeting and reviewed on a regular basis. Wardens may obtain help from Quaker Life, which organises regular national and regional conferences and specialist training courses, and provides a consultancy and information service. (See also 12.27 *Support groups.*)

Resident Friends and caretakers

13.40 Much of the above applies also to resident Friends who give general oversight to meeting houses with few outside users, and to caretakers, whose work is often confined to cleaning and preparing rooms for meetings, opening and closing the building and caring for the garden.

Librarians and libraries

13.41 Area meetings are required to keep under regular review the maintenance and use of libraries in local meetings (see 4.10.r); they should encourage any meetings which do not have their own library to establish one. The running of the library, however, remains the responsibility of the local meeting. Most local meetings appoint a librarian, who will need the support of the meeting and a budget for the purchase of books. In some meetings this task is shared by a number of Friends. Some area meetings draw their librarians together from time to time to share their experience. Help and advice are also available from the Library Committee of Quaker Life.

13.42 A well-stocked and organised library is a powerful aid to the life of the meeting and its outreach. The books can represent a resource for learning about the Religious Society of Friends, about Christianity, the Bible, other world faiths and the social issues of our day. New books can stimulate and challenge as we continue our religious education.

Librarians will find many ways of making the books within their library accessible to Friends and attenders. Some meetings publish reading lists and reviews of recently acquired books in their newsletters. Others will introduce new acquisitions at a local meeting for church affairs or in the notices after meeting for worship. The librarian should be familiar with the contents of the library and be prepared to offer recommendations to those wanting to use it. Book boxes can be obtained from the Quaker Bookshop at Friends House and are a good way of encouraging Friends to enlarge their reading. Other resources than books are available and useful, and librarians may wish to consider including these.

Where there are physical limitations, such as when meeting for worship is held in rented accommodation, imagination and a determination to share our discoveries of helpful books will suggest ways in which the problems may be alleviated.

Treasurers

13.43 People who perform this task for meetings do a great service. Their work often receives scant attention from other Friends, but without them we could quite simply not operate. They will need to be familiar with numbers but neither accounting skills nor a computer are necessary. More important is sensitivity in helping each member and attender to give what is appropriate, allaying feelings of guilt whilst informing them of the need for money both at a local level and for our central work.

The treasurer is a servant of the meeting, advising and helping but leaving decisions to the meeting itself.

13.44 Every meeting which holds funds or handles money should appoint a treasurer, who should be in membership (3.24.i). Some meetings find it helpful to appoint an assistant treasurer or 'collector' to encourage and assist Friends in their giving. More details can be found in chapter 14 *Finance*.

Whilst continuity and experience are important in financial matters, the appointment of a treasurer should be reviewed triennially and the length of service should not be unduly extended. It is good practice for a meeting to plan ahead for the timely release of its treasurer, possibly appointing an assistant who will prepare to take over the task.

A handbook is available (see www.quaker.org.uk/qfp) and advice can be sought from Quaker Finance & Property at Friends House. Area meeting treasurers are entitled to attend the Annual Conference of Treasurers (14.16–14.17).

Prison ministers, visitors and chaplains

13.45 In the early days of the Quaker movement many Friends were imprisoned for their beliefs. Many Friends were imprisoned in the twentieth century too, as conscientious objectors to military service. Perhaps because of this there has been a continuing concern for prisoners and the conditions in prisons, exemplified in the work of Elizabeth Fry (see 23.98–23.100), which is continued by others to the present day. The section that follows explains the terms used and the procedures to be followed. It also offers advice to all Friends about supporting those who do this work.

13.46 A *prison minister* (formerly termed a 'visiting minister') is a priest or minister of a recognised religious denomination appointed by the Home Office to a specific institution under the Prison Act 1952 to perform duties of a religious nature inside that particular institution. Quaker prison ministers are included in this definition.

Prison visitors are appointed by the Home Office on the recommendation of the prison governor to befriend a prisoner who has requested visits. Prison visitors have no duties of a specifically religious character. It is important that they are not confused with the Board of Visitors, who have a quite different function.

'Quaker prison chaplain' is the term used in Scotland in place of 'Quaker prison minister'. In Scotland, following notification from an area meeting of the name of a Friend appointed as a Quaker prison chaplain, General Meeting for Scotland is responsible for providing this name to the governors of all prison establishments in the area meeting area. These Friends then volunteer to serve on a prison chaplaincy team by directly contacting the prison chaplain. To exercise their pastoral responsibility, Quaker prison chaplains in Scotland have to operate in liaison with the official prison chaplaincy team members.

In Scotland 13.49 and 13.50 do not apply.

Quaker prison ministers

13.47 A Quaker prison minister has four tasks: to visit and minister to those in prison who have registered themselves as Quakers; to assist the work of the prison chaplaincy; to be a Quaker presence in the prison, particularly in relation to staff; and to be a channel between the prison service and the area meeting, keeping Friends aware of prison issues.

Where it is possible for the Quaker prison minister to arrange an occasional or regular meeting for worship, these can be of great value.

13.48 When prisoners are under restraint or punishment, in segregation or in the hospital wing, they will be in particular need of spiritual comfort and reassurance. The Quaker prison minister has a right and duty in these circumstances to visit a prisoner registered as a Quaker, whether in membership or not, whilst a visit from a prison visitor may not be allowed.

Appointment

13.49 A Friend is recommended for this service by the area meeting (4.10.s), which then applies to the particular institution for the nomination to be approved and the appointment made.

13.50 If the nomination is approved, the particular institution informs the Quaker prison minister that a formal appointment has been made. The area meeting should then ensure that Quaker Peace & Social Witness is informed of the appointment. This process may take some weeks. Potential prison ministers should be aware that they will be investigated by the Criminal Records Office.

Preparation and support

13.51 Quaker Peace & Social Witness can offer a newly appointed Quaker prison minister the benefit of knowledge and experience. In the first instance they will send the handbook for Quaker prison ministers published by Quaker Peace & Social Witness (and see www.quaker.org.uk/qfp). Conferences are held each year which provide information on aspects of penal affairs, but also offer those attending good opportunity to discuss particular problems and to gain the informed support of Friends working in other penal establishments.

13.52 The Quaker prison minister undertakes to bear the area meeting's responsibility for ministering to the spiritual needs of prisoners who are registered as Quakers. Prison ministers have their needs too, and it is very important that the area meeting should support the Friend doing this demanding work on their behalf. The Quaker prison minister and area meeting will probably want to decide amongst themselves how support can best be given (see 12.27) and whether or not it should come from a formally appointed group.

Area meetings will find it helpful to encourage Quaker prison ministers to report on their work once a year.

Prison visitors

13.53 Prison visitors are appointed by the Home Office, or the Scottish Office Home and Health Department, on the recommendation of the prison governor to visit certain prisoners who have asked for visits to be arranged. Their duty is to befriend those they visit. They have no duties of a specifically religious nature and are sometimes required to avoid religious topics. Friends wishing to offer this service should approach the governor of the prison where they wish to serve.

Some Quakers are both prison ministers and visitors. The roles overlap and Quaker prison ministers find themselves moving naturally from one to the other.

13.54 Going into a prison can be intimidating and it may be difficult to find the right way of communicating with those you meet there. It is often hard to know what to say particularly to those serving long sentences or far from home, but if the preparation of the heart is taken seriously the right words will come. Ministry is giving of oneself and allowing others to give to us; our common humanity enables us to minister. Laughter, too, is part of the healing ministry.

College chaplains

13.55 The role and the title of the Friends responsible for the pastoral care of students can vary according to the institution; they may also be called student welcomers, student overseers or student chaplains. These Friends may be appointed either by the area meeting or by one of its local meetings according to local circumstances. Their role can be the oversight of Quaker students, linking them to the local meeting. If there are Friends on the staff they will usually help. Sometimes the college chaplains may be part of an ecumenical team and their role will extend to all students and staff. The work may need support, both financial and spiritual, from the appointing meeting (see 12.27).

13.56 Work in colleges and universities is an opportunity for outreach. Friends' non-credal approach and openness to new light, from whatever quarter, may be particularly appealing to the enquiring minds of students. Friends should be ready to make Quaker views known as well as providing pastoral care.

There may be opportunities for holding a meeting for worship in a college. In this case local elders should share in responsibility for such a meeting.

Some areas may have several educational institutions and several Friends responsible for pastoral care; local meetings should have an overall responsibility to support all these Friends both practically and spiritually.

Where there is a local Young Friends group this may offer a welcome to younger students who are close to them in age.

13.57 Quaker Life offers information and advice to college chaplains and links them together.

Indexes can be found in Volume 3
on pages 792–836